UNIVERSITY OF NORTH CAROLINA AT CHAPEL HILL

DEPARTMENT OF ROMANCE LANGUAGES


# NORTH CAROLINA STUDIES
# IN THE ROMANCE LANGUAGES AND LITERATURES

*Founder:* URBAN TIGNER HOLMES

*Editor:* FRANK A. DOMÍNGUEZ

*Distributed by:*

UNIVERSITY OF NORTH CAROLINA PRESS

CHAPEL HILL
North Carolina 27515-2288
U.S.A.

NORTH CAROLINA STUDIES IN THE
ROMANCE LANGUAGES AND LITERATURES
Number 303

# GENDERED GEOGRAPHIES IN PUERTO RICAN CULTURE

## SPACES, SEXUALITIES, SOLIDARITIES

# GENDERED GEOGRAPHIES IN PUERTO RICAN CULTURE

## SPACES, SEXUALITIES, SOLIDARITIES

BY

RADOST RANGELOVA

CHAPEL HILL

NORTH CAROLINA STUDIES IN THE ROMANCE
LANGUAGES AND LITERATURES
U.N.C. DEPARTMENT OF ROMANCE LANGUAGES

2015

**Library of Congress Cataloging-in-Publication Data**

Names: Rangelova, Radost, 1979-
Title: Gendered geographies in Puerto Rican culture : spaces, sexualities,
    solidarities / by Radost Rangelova.
Description: Chapel Hill : University of North Carolina Press, [2016] |
    Series: North Carolina Studies in the Romance Languages and Literatures ;
    303 | Includes bibliographical references and index.
Identifiers: LCCN 2015031704 | ISBN 9781469626161 (hardcover)
Subjects: LCSH: Puerto Rican literature–History and criticism. | Sex role in
    literature. | Place (Philosophy) in literature.
Classification: LCC PQ7421 .R36 2016 | DDC 860.9/97295–dc23
    LC record available at http://lccn.loc.gov/2015031704

Cover: Delana, Jack. *San Juan (vicinity), Puerto Rico. In a needlework Factory*, 1942.
Safety Film Negative. Library of Congress, Washington, D.C. *Prints &*
*Photographs*. Web. 02/20/2015



ISBN 978-1-4696-2616-1

IMPRESO EN ESPAÑA

PRINTED IN SPAIN

ARTES GRÁFICAS SOLER, S. L. - LA OLIVERETA, 28 - 46018 VALENCIA (SPAIN)
www.graficas-soler.com

# TABLE OF CONTENTS

ACKNOWLEDGEMENTS

THERE are many people whose guidance, support, and friendship have been instrumental for the completion of this book. First among them is Larry La Fountain-Stokes, a generous mentor, thoughtful teacher, and enthusiastic interlocutor during my graduate work at the University of Michigan, Ann Arbor, and ever since. His dedication to the project has been instrumental at all stages of the writing process, from the conceptualization of what was first a doctoral dissertation, to the revisions of the book manuscript. Similarly, Jossianna Arroyo has been an unwavering source of advice and encouragement, and I thank her for remaining part of the project from The University of Texas at Austin. To both, I am deeply grateful.

Gettysburg College has provided generous, sustained institutional support that made possible the completion of this project through a Pre-Tenure Leave, two Research and Professional Development Grants, and multiple Provost's Professional Papers Grants that enabled me to finalize the research, complete the writing and get valuable feedback on different sections of the book. I thank Provost Christopher Zappe and Associate Provost for Faculty Development Robert Bohrer for their support.

The Spanish Department at Gettysburg College has allowed me to combine my love of teaching and my dedication to the field of Caribbean literary and cultural studies. For their collegiality and professionalism, my sincere thanks to Currie Thompson, Ron Burgess, Paula Olinger, Kent Yager, Alicia Rolón, Alvaro Kaempfer, Beatriz Trigo, Rebeca Bataller, Cristina Martínez, Verónica Calvillo, and Jennifer Dumont.

My colleagues in the Latin American, Caribbean, and Latino Studies Program have built a space of rigorous interdisciplinary exchanges for people with a common purpose. The work of the core LACLS committee and of other colleagues who engage with Latin America and the Caribbean continues to motivate me. My profound thanks to Emelio Betances, Nathalie Lebon, Florence Jurney, Paul Austerlitz, and Barbara Sommer. The intellectual curiosity and the hard work of my current and former students in the Spanish Department and in the Latin American, Caribbean, and Latino Studies Program are a constant source of inspiration and joy.

At Gettysburg, I am thankful to friends and colleagues who have welcomed me in their homes, and with whom I have shared meals and conversations across disciplines–Alvaro and Malinda Kaempfer, Verónica Calvillo and Joe Downing, Tsu-ting Tim Lin, Kerr and Susan Thompson, Lola Pérez and Adeyemi Oshunrinade, Kerry Wallach and Jess Firshein, Hakim Williams, McKinley Melton, Rimvydas Baltaduonis, thank you for the camaraderie.

The University of Michigan offered the resources to complete the dissertation project on which this book is based, including awarding me a Humanities Research Fellowship and a Graduate Student Research Grant that allowed me to dedicate time to research and writing. At UM, I thank Jarrod Hayes and Maria Cotera, who embraced the project and took it in directions that have enriched it immensely. Other members of the Departments of Romance Languages and Literatures, Screen Arts and Cultures, Latina/o Studies and History have helped me develop my intellectual trajectory and shape this book: in particular, Cristina Moreiras, Gareth Williams, Juli Highfill, Gustavo Verdesio, Yeidy Rivero, and Jesse Hoffnung-Garskof. Raquel Vega-Durán, Danny Méndez, Beatriz Ramírez Betances, Mariam Colón, Megan Saltzman, Alana Reid, Andrea Dewees, Pedro Porbén, and Jesal Parekh, among many other former graduate students, have been the source of a continuous exchange of ideas, of friendships within and outside our academic fields.

My work has also benefited from conversations with Roberto Márquez, Maritza Stanchich, Arnaldo Cruz-Malavé, Jorge Duany, Carmelo Esterrich, Catherine Benamou, Lucía Suárez, Gabriel Martínez-Serna, Arturo Márquez Gómez, and other scholars of Latin American cultural studies, history and film that I have met through the Puerto Rican Studies Association and LASA conferences. Anne Lambright and Guillermo Irizarry have demonstrated consistent interest in my work, and have offered generous advice and warm friendship. Gustavo Remedi has been a thoughtful and challenging mentor and interlocutor for years. Pablo Delano, Luis Figueroa, Darío Euraque, Angel Rivera, and Odette Casamayor have inspired me to think about the Caribbean in creative and critical ways.

In Puerto Rico, I am grateful to the Archivo General de Puerto Rico, El Archivo Nacional de Teatro y Cine, El Centro de Estudios Avanzados de Puerto Rico y el Caribe, and the librarians at the Colección Puertorriqueña of the University of Puerto Rico.

Sections of Chapter IV of this book have been published, in significantly different form, in the journal *Letras Femeninas* ("La ciudad de la mujer: Solidaridad y resistencia en el salón de belleza." *Letras Femeninas* XXXIX. 1 Verano 2013), and in the edited collection *Lección errante: Mayra Santos Febres y el Caribe contemporáneo* ("Espacios femeninos y sexualidades insubordinadas en los cuentos de Mayra Santos Febres." *Lección errante: Mayra Santos Febres y el Caribe contemporáneo*. Ed. Nadia Celís and Juan Pablo Rivera. Puerto Rico: Editorial Isla Negra, 2011).

Finally, I thank my parents and my brother Zoran, whose support I have always felt, in spite of the distance. Abou Bamba, I am grateful for so many reasons. Your solidarity, your constructive commentary, your ethical commitment to intellectual pursuit, and your care and compassion have made this process infinitely more stimulating and enjoyable. *I barika.*

CHAPTER I

INTRODUCTION

> Marina esbozó una sonrisa victoriosa. A paso fir-
> me, entró en el aposento de doña Georgina. Fu-
> migó el cuarto con una aroma a melancolía deses-
> perada (lo había recogido del cuerpo de su padre)
> que revolcó por sábanas y armarios. [. . .] El apo-
> sento de la patrona olía a recuerdo de sueños
> muertos que aceleraban las palpitaciones del cora-
> zón. La casa entera despedía aromas inconexos,
> desligados, lo que obligó a que nadie en el pueblo
> quisiera visitar a los Velázquez nunca más.
>
> "Marina y su olor," Mayra Santos-Febres

AT first sight, Mayra Santos-Febres's story "Marina y su olor" is a fantastic narrative about a young woman who transforms emotions into scents, and emits them as a physical response to situations in her everyday life. On a metaphorical level, Marina's talent gives her the ability to alter spaces (shops, family houses, city streets), to mark them, and to claim them as her own. It is through this fantastic gift that she attains the power to resist, subvert, and ultimately avenge racial, class and gender hierarchies that devalue her self and that deny her social agency. The image of a nation composed of the spaces appropriated and transformed by Marina's body–the body of a working-class, Afro-Puerto Rican, independent woman in control of her own sexuality–no longer responds to the "modernist representations of the nation as a territorially grounded, linguistically uniform, racially exclusive, androcentric, and heterosexual project" (Duany, "Rough Edges" 187), and instead inspires a powerful critique of that model.

Santos-Febres's story exemplifies one way in which Puerto Rican feminist writers strategically transform the spaces of the nation and set literary works in places not normally associated with the traditional cultural nationalist model of the nation, in order to question the cohesion and the uniformity of Puerto Rican national discourse. Among the spaces that have figured prominently in Puerto Rican literary production since the 1970s have been the house, the factory, the beauty salon, and the brothel, all acting as sites of negotiation of gender and sexuality in the island's modern urban environment.

Gender, sexuality and space have had a complex and often contradictory relationship with Puerto Rican cultural nationalist discourse and with the Estado Libre Asociado (ELA), Puerto Rico's Commonwealth status in relation to the United States. In the 1950s, ELA called upon women to support its community modernization and industrialization projects like Operation Bootstrap, and to conform to the patriarchal gender norms of the *gran familia puertorriqueña*, while systematically discouraging them from seeking leadership roles in the emerging national imaginary. In ELA's early decades women were mothers and workers, building the nation through productive and reproductive labor while suffering the effects of the "feminization of poverty."[1] The sexuality of black and working-class women was controlled through mass sterilizations and contraceptive experiments,[2] and they were expected to support the social project of their male counterparts through their labor and their sexuality.[3] Their role had a prominent spatial dimension, as the domestic space

---

[1] For a theoretical discussion of the feminization of poverty in Puerto Rico and the diaspora, see Alice Colón Warren's articles in *The Commuter Nation: Perspectives on Puerto Rican Migration* (1994) and *Puerto Rican Women and Work: Bridges in Transnational Labor* (1996). Also, Colón Warren and Alegría Ortega on "Shattering the Illusion of Development: The Changing Status of Women and Challenges for the Feminist movement in Puerto Rico" (1998).

[2] For more on the forced sterilizations and the contraceptive experiments conducted on Puerto Rican women, see Margarita Ostolaza Bey's *Política Sexual en Puerto Rico* (1989), as well as Linda Gordon's *The Moral Property of Women: A History of Birth Control Politics* (2002). Ana María García's documentary film *La operación* also offers a timeline, in addition to numerous testimonials by women affected by these policies.

[3] Most notably, DIVEDCO's films *Modesta, Doña Julia* and *El de los cabos blancos*, among others, praise women's support of the modernization project and condemn their occasional failure to understand and to uphold its principles.

remained the women's domain (hence the abundance of literary and cinematic texts set in rural and urban family homes).

The failure of Operation Bootstrap, and of some of ELA's founding concepts, resulted in a crisis that inspired feminist intellectuals and artists to rethink the principles of cultural nationalism and of its model of *puertorriqueñidad*. The feminism of the 1970s enabled more women to enter the salaried workforce, and to gain visibility in the public sphere.[4] Together with this ongoing process of empowerment and participation, however, reports of femicides and domestic violence continue to appear daily in the island's main newspapers, depicting male privilege as a defining characteristic of the gendered experience of the nation.

In the realm of culture, the feminism of the 1970s used space as one of its main, albeit rarely analyzed, technologies of resistance. Influenced by the feminist and the civil rights movements, the Vietnam War protests, the Cuban Revolution and the Latin American Boom, the authors of the Generation of the 70s, to which many of the writers and film directors analyzed here belong, began to critique the roles imposed on women by patriarchy, colonialism and white privilege. Writers and film directors like Rosario Ferré, Magali García Ramis, Carmen Lugo Filippi, Sonia Fritz and Ana María García, among others, were among the first to strategically "misplace" their female characters from the domestic to a series of other spaces, and, from these spaces, to question the cohesion of the patriarchal national discourse.

This book is a critical study of the ways gendered spaces are constructed through feminine labor and capital in Puerto Rican literature and film (1950-2010). It analyzes gendered geographies and forms of emotional labor, and the spaces of possibility that they generate within the material and the symbolic spaces of the factory, the family house, the beauty salon and the brothel. My central argument is that, in the process of challenging traditional images of femininity, the protagonists of the texts that I analyze gender and queer the spaces that they inhabit, contesting the official Puerto Rican cultural

---

[4] See, for example, the work of María del Carmen Baerga on women's work in the needlework industry in Puerto Rico, Carmen Teresa Whalen's work on Puerto Rican female workers in the years after World War II, as well as Mary Frances Gallart's work on the political empowerment of Puerto Rican women since the 1950s, the last two published in *Puerto Rican Women's History: New Perspectives*, eds. Félix Matos Rodríguez and Linda Delgado.

nationalist discourse on gender and nation, and proposing alternatives to its spatial tropes through feminine labor and solidarities.

By examining spatial tropes, the book reassesses women's attempts to reconfigure the relationship between nation, gender and sexuality in Puerto Rican literary and cinematic discourse. It engages the historiography on women's labor since the 19th century, and reflects on the critical work on the creative and political changes in contemporary women's literature. It analyzes the construction of the female body in a variety of contexts, from its negotiation of urban settings to its possibility as an instrument of resistance to patriarchy and colonialism, and as a technology of independence.

The book's main goal is to analyze how the gendered and sexual geographies produced by contemporary Puerto Rican authors critique the official cultural nationalist model that equates the nation with a great family, whose space par excellence is the family house. In my definition, gendered geographies are those gendered and sexual experiences that, through their intersection with hierarchies of race, class and capital, question the limits of official discourses on gender, space and nation, and deconstruct traditionally patriarchal spaces as spaces of feminine agency. By critically applying the work of feminist geographers like Doreen Massey, Nancy Duncan, Katherine McKittrick and Melissa M. Wright, I show how writers like Magali García Ramis, Rosario Ferré, Mayra Santos-Febres and Carmen Lugo Filippi, and film directors like Sonia Fritz and Ana María García, have been particularly effective in dismantling the discourse of gender and nation, and in proposing alternative tropes through the politics of space and labor. In the context of the limited critical literature on space in Puerto Rican cultural studies, I build on José Luis González's and on Juan Gelpí's work on the house as a symbol of the nation, and on Gelpí's analysis of the crisis of patriarchy and colonialism on the island.

The second main goal of the book is to engage the fields of Feminist Geography, Caribbean and Puerto Rican Studies in a productive conversation, and to show how feminine geographies and the cultural construction of space are indispensable for understanding gender and sexuality in the Caribbean. Until recent years, the discussion of space in Puerto Rico had focused primarily on the island and on its relationship to the United States, whether regarding Puerto Rico's political status, the economic and cultural interactions between the island and the mainland, or the politics of language and identity, exemplified in the work of Jorge Duany and Juan Flores, among others. This book makes an original contribution to these debates, and opens a discussion on the intersections between material everyday spaces, gender, sexuality and national discourses.


## HISTORICAL CONTEXT: GENDER, SEXUALITY, SPACE AND NATION

The gendered geographies that emerge from the literary and cinematic texts analyzed here are foregrounded by a specific historical, geographical and social setting, which they help construct, critique and rethink. Their context is framed by the establishment of the Estado Libre Asociado (Free Associated State, also known as the Commonwealth), Puerto Rico's political status in its colonial relation to the United States, and its assertion of cultural nationalism and the myth of the *gran familia puertorriqueña* (the Great Puerto Rican Family) as its dominant discourse.

Over the course of the 20th century, Puerto Rican national discourse has portrayed gender and sexuality in spatial terms. The writers of the generation of the 1930s did that by rearticulating earlier discussions of the origins and the constitution of the Puerto Rican nation that, in some instances, went back to the turn of the 19th century.[5] In doing so, they engaged gender and sexuality for the purpose of reaffirming a masculine, heterosexual vision of the national imaginary. For most of them, the woman's role was domestic, a wife and a mother, whereas professional women were perceived as a threat to virility, the quality that these intellectuals saw as intrinsic to *la puertorriqueñidad*. Antonio S. Pedreira, the figure that best exemplified the masculine discourse on nation and gender in the 1930s, claimed that the most a woman could do for her nation was to be "la perfecta dueña de casa" (Pedreira 95), determining social and gender roles, and delimiting the space that a woman was to occupy.

The two decades following Pedreira's 1934 book were a time of profound political changes that set the stage for the redefinition of Puerto Rico's national identity in relation to the United States.

---

     [5] See Scarano, Francisco. "The Jíbaro Masquerade and the Subaltern Politics of Creole Identity Formation in Puerto Rico, 1745-1823." *The American Historical Review* 101.5 (Dec. 1996): 1398-1431.

The dilemma of independence vs. statehood, which had preoccupied intellectuals and politicians since the U.S. invasion of the island in 1898, was seemingly resolved with a third alternative that tried to accommodate the concerns of both sides of the political debate. Puerto Rico's status as Estado Libre Asociado was formalized on July 25, 1952 by Luis Muñoz Marín, the leader of the Popular Democratic Party (PPD, or Partido Popular Democrático) and the first elected governor of the island. The conditions that redefined Puerto Rico's relationship to the United States were an attempt to find a middle ground between independence and statehood, in a situation in which Puerto Rico had no independent government, while at the same time continued to identify as a nation separate from the metropolis. This accommodating arrangement was characterized by a series of contradictions:

> Although Puerto Ricans elect a resident commissioner to Congress, they don't have their voting representatives or senators in Washington. Even though Puerto Ricans cannot vote for the president of the United States, they are bound to serve in the U.S. armed forces like any other citizens. While island residents do not pay federal taxes, they qualify for most federally funded programs, including nutritional assistance and welfare benefits. Such contradictory elements may well warrant the term 'postcolonial colony' to describe Puerto Rico's problematic relationship with the United States (Duany *The Puerto Rican Nation* 123).

The status of the Estado Libre Asociado was rationalized through discourses and practices of cultural, rather than constitutional nationalism, which the PPD proposed in order to reconcile Puerto Rico's national identity with its lack of political sovereignty. Supporters of cultural nationalism rely on a discourse of a common history, culture and language that make sovereignty unnecessary for the existence of the Puerto Rican nation, and reinforce "the spiritual autonomy of their nation by commemorating their heritage, celebrating their rituals, rescuing their traditions, and educating the people" (Duany *The Puerto Rican Nation* 123-4). Muñoz's cultural nationalism reconciled national identity with political dependence, and in so doing became a populist project that generated "mitos integradores para unas generaciones empeñadas en asumir de una vez por todas la modernidad [. . .] el desarrollo, la industrialización, la auto-determinación política respecto a los centros mundiales, la armonía social y racial y la identidad nacional" (Álvarez-Curbelo, "El discurso" 16). These ideals were part of a populist discourse wherein "La mediación del líder carismático, la ilusión de participación y los mitos de una identidad colectiva compartida aseguraban, así, la paz y el orden nacional" (Rodríguez Castro 101), overlooking the fact that many of the conditions that enabled the construction of that national identity would only be possible by means of the legal power to pass laws, a power part of which Puerto Rico had to give up under the new colonial arrangement.

One of the central social pillars of cultural nationalism was the concept of *la gran familia puertorriqueña*, or the Great Puerto Rican Family. The concept was not a novelty in the social and political discourse of the middle decades of the 20th century. In fact, it dates back to the late 19th century, when it was first used as a resource in the discourse of liberal professionals and a significant faction of large landowners (*hacendados*) seeking political autonomy within the context of Spanish colonialism (Cubano-Iguina; Scarano, "Liberal Pacts"). Later, the trope was "activated as a strategic response to the economic and social displacement suffered by them after 1898, precisely as U.S. absentee capitalism began to buy and merchandize the sugar production process previously controlled by this sector" (Aparicio 5). The hacendados "summoned up the image of the patriarchal dynamics that structured the hacienda in the past [thus constructing] a homogenized discourse of unity, harmony, and most important, convivencia" (Aparicio 6). By proposing a schematic model of Puerto Rican society dominated by "Creole landowners as benevolent father figures and subsistence farmers as their grateful peons, [the concept] obscures important conflicts and tensions within nineteenth-century coffee and sugar plantations" (Duany, *The Puerto Rican Nation* 20). Following this trend, during the 1940s and 1950s the PPD appropriated the concept and transformed it into the founding myth of Puerto Rican cultural nationalism. With the help of The Institute for Puerto Rican Culture, *la gran familia puertorriqueña* became a model of national unity and cohesion that conveniently neglected to recognize and address racial, gender, class and other hierarchies in Puerto Rican society. As one example, following similar trends in much of Latin America (Miller 1-26), the Institute of Puerto Rican Culture "defined the essence of contemporary Puerto Rican culture as the harmonious integration of aboriginal, Spanish, and African traditions, prior to the U.S. invasion of the island"

(Duany, *The Puerto Rican Nation* 130), a model that excluded elements like the United States or the early Puerto Rican migration to the mainland. It is the spatial aspect of this notion of unity and cohesion, and its effort to maintain and disguise social hierarchies, that the authors and the film directors analyzed here rethink and challenge in their literary and cinematic texts.

In addition to the model of *la gran familia puertorriqueña*, another pillar of the Estado Libre Asociado was Operación Manos a la Obra, reframed as Operation Bootstrap for its audience of U.S. businessmen. An economic program instituted in the late 1940s, Operation Bootstrap,

> relied on U.S. capital and markets. U.S. corporations borrowed money from the Commonwealth (which in turn sold bonds in the U.S. municipal funds markets) and invested in labor-intensive manufacturing. These factories bought raw materials from abroad, processed or assembled the products in Puerto Rico, and then sold their products in continental markets. Operations tended to be labor-intensive, paid significantly lower wages than those earned by U.S. workers, and enjoyed almost full tax exemptions (Meléndez 7).

An additional element of Operation Bootstrap was the silent, yet widespread facilitation of the emigration of Puerto Rico's "excess population" to the United States–workers unable to find employment on the island were encouraged to look for one in factories or farms on the mainland. This policy set the stage for the mass migration of Puerto Ricans to New York and later to other parts of the U.S. While at first Operation Bootstrap was highly successful in creating better-paying, more stable jobs than in seasonal agriculture, its success only lasted a few decades, until owners chose to make bigger profits by transferring their factories to locations in Latin America and Asia, where their production costs would be even lower. As a consequence, in the 1970s Puerto Rico's gross national product "declined sharply, the unemployment rate almost doubled, and income levels stagnated. Many factories closed their operations in Puerto Rico and moved to other low-wage countries" (Meléndez 7). The failure of Operation Bootstrap, and, many would argue, of some of the founding concepts of the Estado Libre Asociado, resulted in a crisis that inspired intellectuals, artists and social critics to rethink the core principles of cultural nationalism and of its model of Puerto Rican national identity.

The context of Operation Bootstrap, the decades of the establishment of the Estado Libre Asociado, and, more broadly, the period that extends from the 1900s to the 1960s were marked by policies and regulations that subjected working-class, black and mixed-race women to forms of labor characterized by different modalities of disciplinary order and violence. Much of this labor exploitation was racialized and gendered, and occurred in the cigar-making and the needlework industries, along with the spaces that correspond to them: the factory, the garment shop, and the home as a work place.

The tobacco industry subjected women to forms of labor violence that was facilitated by the space of the cigar-making factory. There, women usually occupied "los escaños inferiores. [. . .] Los peores salarios y las más sórdidas condiciones de trabajo se daban en estas industrias" (Rivera Quintero 52). The large U.S.- and Puerto Rican-owned tobacco companies established wages and working conditions that were often detrimental to the women's health and economic wellbeing, and exploitation continued in the smaller *chinchales*, where women were consistently paid less than the leaf-strippers employed by foreign companies (Quintero-Rivera, "Socialist" 24). Similarly, in the needlework industry women had male supervisors (Dietz *Historia* 136), worked long hours and with little light (Boris 35). In the 1930s, protests like those organized in María Luisa Arcelay's garment shop in Mayagüez were quickly thwarted by police. In response to such exploitative practices and instances of violence, women used a variety of personal, labor and spatial strategies that involved union organization, structural subversion, and, importantly, intellectual and artistic criticism, to challenge labor violence that sought to incorporate them in the national discourse of productivity without recognizing the value of their labor.

The literary and intellectual context during the years marked by the institutionalization of cultural nationalism and the Estado Libre Asociado in Puerto Rico was also a time of transitions between what cultural critics have more recently identified as two distinct generations of artists and authors–that of the 1950s and that of the 1970s, to which most of the writers analyzed in this book belong.

Among the most prominent writers of the Generación del 50 were José Luis González, Pedro Juan Soto, Abelardo Díaz Alfaro,

Emilio Díaz Valcárcel and René Marqués–a group of storytellers and playwrights still dominated by male voices and by patriarchal approaches. Their work emerged out of multiple social transitions, "cambios provocados por el reformismo político y social del Partido Popular, la creación del Estado Libre Asociado, la industrialización de la isla, la ruina del sector agrícola, y la creciente anexión económica y agresión cultural norteamericana" (Acosta-Belén, "En torno" 220). While many of these authors were welcomed and incorporated in the institutionalization of the cultural nationalist model through their participation in initiatives like DIVEDCO,[6] they also felt a profound concern for the society that, in their view, left behind the old values and principles. Among their main themes were "la ruralía desplazada y agonizante, el mundo enajenante que surge con la industrialización y urbanización de la isla, la emigración masiva de los puertorriqueños a los Estados Unidos y el creciente poder asimilista de los Estados Unidos" (Acosta-Belén, "En torno" 221).

During the 1950s, the traditional image of women in the Puerto Rican literary canon continued to be the result of patriarchal views of social relations,[7] which sought to make women a productive instrument in the developing cultural nationalist project. In literary and cinematic discourse, the dominant cultural nationalist politics of gender often translated into situations in which a female character, often a young single woman or a wife, either assumes her reproductive role in the Puerto Rican nation, or betrays it, and is conse-

---

[6] The purpose of La División de Educación de la Comunidad (The Division for Community Development), one of the most ambitious and successful projects of cultural nationalism, was to educate and integrate Puerto Ricans, especially those living in rural zones, into the national project. Starting in 1949 and into the 1970s, DIVEDCO, whose members included Jack Delano, Amílcar Tirado, Pedro Juan Soto, and René Marqués, among many others, produced over 112 short and feature films, most of them with unprofessional actors, addressing issues of community development and modernization. ("Retrospectiva," *Fundación nacional para la cultural popular*). Together with films, the organization helped develop many other arts, like silk-screens, posters, music, and others. DIVEDCO is undoubtedly the project that has made the most important contribution to the development of Puerto Rican cinema in the 20th century, as it not only resulted in the production of a large body of cinematic work, but was also responsible for professional training of future filmmakers and for popularizing cinema on the island.

[7] It is significant to point out that this occurred not only at the level of the text, but also of the author's voice, as René Marqués's 1959 anthology *Cuentos puertorriqueños de hoy*, for example, includes short stories by eight male writers (including the editor himself) and no female writers.

quently condemned and punished for it. It is during this period that René Marqués, one of the proclaimed patriarchs of Puerto Rican national literature, lamented women's increased social participation, expressing a preoccupation with "la docilidad del hombre–triste figura del ex-pater familias–ante el avance progresivo de la mujer en todas las esferas en que él era una vez–¡nostálgico pasado!–dueño y señor" (Marqués, *Puertorriqueño dócil*, 171). The women in Marqués's plays *La carreta* and *Los soles truncos* respond to this concern, personifying the loss of traditional patriarchal values. Juanita's prostitution and her claim that "no hay dinero sucio ni dinero limpio. Hay dinero" (Marqués *La carreta* 124) marks the loss not only of her honor, but also that of her family, and, by extension, of *la gran familia puertorriqueña*. Conversely, Inés, the protagonist of *Los soles truncos*, burns down the family house in an effort to preserve its spirit in time, projecting a desperation that reproduces the sentiments of her author's generation–a nostalgia for a lost colonial past and for its paternal figure.

Other literary and cinematic examples of this patriarchal approach can be found in "La cautiva" by Pedro Juan Soto and in Orzábal Quintana's film *Maruja*.[8] Both texts have melodramatic elements and didactic purposes, depicting "unacceptable" female gender and sexual behaviors and locations in space, for which the protagonists are unequivocally punished. The young woman in Soto's short story is forced into exile because of her relationship with a married man, while Maruja's death is a symbolic reminder that transgression of gender norms, especially when accompanied by sexual liberation, has no place in the national imaginary.

The transition from this patriarchal depiction of gender and sexuality to the feminist standpoint of the writers and artists of the Generación del 70 was gradual and conditioned by a series of social and political processes that occurred in the 1950s and the 1960s, and to which Puerto Rican artists and authors responded:

> Durante los años del 60 tuvieron lugar una serie de eventos históricos a nivel mundial que, junto a la realidad sociopolítica e histórica de Puerto Rico, contribuyeron a moldear la conciencia litera-

---

[8] Orzábal Quintana is an Argentine director whose depiction of Puerto Rican female sexuality could raise questions about the perception of Caribbean women in the rest of Latin America and, in a sense, about Latin American "tropicalism."

> ria de los jóvenes literatos de la Generación del 70, tales como la
> Revolución Cubana y su ideología socialista, las protestas en con-
> tra del reclutamiento militar obligatorio, la guerra de Vietnam, la
> denuncia de los hippies en contra de la injusticia social y de ideas
> arcaicas que dividen al género humano en jerarquías sociales, el
> resurgimiento del movimiento feminista y, en la literatura, la nue-
> va revolución literaria hispanoamericana bautizada como el "Bo-
> om." Todos esos factores históricos, sociales y culturales contri-
> buyeron [. . .] en moldear la conciencia intelectual y literaria de
> los escritores de la nueva literatura puertorriqueña (Palmer-Ló-
> pez, "Rosario Ferré").

These factors inspired Puerto Rican authors and intellectuals to rethink cultural nationalism and to explore the hierarchies and axes
of identity that affected their everyday life as women, Afro-Puerto
Ricans, queer citizens, and members of the working class. As a consequence, topics like "la falsa moralidad burguesa [y] la crisis
política y económica del Estado Libre Asociado," (Acosta-Belén,
"En torno" 224) and "[el] feminismo, la negritud, y la homosexua-
lidad" (226) started to dominate the literary, cinematic and artistic
production. In contrast to the 1950s, women predominated in the
Generación del 70, as now "Puerto Rican feminists, like feminists
throughout the world, faced the critical challenge of articulating
feminist concerns alongside issues of national liberation" (Meléndez 11)–a situation that was even more complex in Puerto Rico due
to its relationship to the United States. Authors like Rosario Ferré,
Carmen Lugo Filippi, and Manuel Ramos Otero, among others, belong to the group of artists of this generation that deemed it imper-
ative to rethink the way in which the Puerto Rican official political
discourse addressed the issues of gender and sexuality in relation to
space and nation.

In more recent years, scholars of gender and sexuality like
Lawrence La Fountain-Stokes, Arnaldo Cruz-Malavé, Jossianna Arroyo and Alberto Sandoval-Sánchez have problematized the patriarchal foundations of the Puerto Rican national model from the
standpoint of sexuality and space, including spaces like the city and
the plaza, and the spaces of film, theater, dance and performance.
By looking at authors and texts that privilege queer issues, these authors emphasize the exclusions of the cultural nationalist canon,
and bring forth some of the literary and cinematic voices that had
previously been silenced.

## Feminist Geographies, Space and Gender

My analysis of gendered geographies in Puerto Rican cultural production departs from traditional depictions of space as objective and immutable, and instead looks at it as contested, transformed by multiple axes of identity and impacted by both patriarchal structures of oppression and gender and sexual solidarities. I begin by asking, how do the female characters in literary and cinematic works negotiate patriarchal relations of power associated with the Puerto Rican nation in the gendered spaces of the factory, the house, the beauty salon and the brothel? How do women construct alternative national imaginaries in spaces that simultaneously resist and perpetuate patriarchy? How does gender intersect with race, sexuality and labor in these spaces to critique historically constructed notions of femininity associated with symbolic models of the nation? How does the relationship between gender and space in Puerto Rican cultural production enrich the literature on feminist geography and on the construction of space?

The relationship between space and gender is marked by a multiplicity of forces, which propel a constant negotiation of gendered constructions, associations and assumptions of space. Issues like knowledge, power, patriarchy, and rationality impact the ways in which people perceive their position in, interactions with, and relationship to space. To a great extent, that is due to the historical relationship between gender and the traditionally patriarchal field of geography, where "feminism has been consistently marginalized by mainstream geography. Feminism's concerns are never fully acknowledged by the geographical arguments with which it engages, and geography continues to virtually disregard feminist theory" (Rose 3). One of the main objectives of mapping literary and cinematic gendered geographies in this book is precisely to reconfigure the study of space and gender in Puerto Rican cultural production through a feminist critique, and to uncover the role that masculinity and patriarchal hegemony play in the intersection of knowledge, power and gender.

Much of the struggle over the construction of meaning occurs in everyday spaces previously neglected in traditional geography's urge to describe, document and map territories through a masculine gaze and claimed rationality. In contrast, the everyday spaces that women inhabit in the context of the social limitations and the patriarchal pressures to which they are subject construct alternative, gendered geographies. On the one hand, these everyday geographies are "bound into the power structures which limit and confine women, [becoming] the arena through which patriarchy is (re)created–and contested" (Rose 17). On the other, they are the spaces of possibility, of subversion and of solidarity along gender, sexual, racial and class lines. In this sense, the urge to study "everyday spaces" is not only feminist geographers' call to critique patriarchy, but can also be understood as a call to uncover the ways in which women use certain spaces to turn patriarchy upon itself, and to exercise agency in the creation of different relations of power in spaces that they make inaccessible to patriarchal order. In numerous ways, the house, the factory, the beauty salon and the brothel, as represented by Puerto Rican writers and film directors, become such spaces of resistance and creative feminist agency.

The gendered geographies that emerge from the texts that I study consist of everyday spaces but also of bodies–bodies both feminine and masculine, bodies that blur and question fixed definitions of gender, bodies that emerge "as a site of struggle" (Rose 29) and which, "far from being natural, [. . .] are 'maps of power and identity'; or, rather, maps of the relation between power and identity" (Rose 32). Since it is bodies that occupy spaces and since it is bodies that experience spaces, the body becomes a fundamental analytical concept for the study of space. Again, the body, embodiment and corporeal experiences are among the most frequent and important issues for Puerto Rican feminist authors, and their representations of the experience of the factory, the house, the beauty salon and the brothel benefit from an understanding of the experience of space as material and gendered.

This line of analysis of gender and space in Puerto Rican cultural production allows me to read "space" and "place" not as static or isolated concepts, but as traversed and negotiated by forces that operate in the society of which the particular space is part. Any space–landscapes, homes, workplaces–is subject to transformation:

> The identities of place are always unfixed, contested and multiple. And the particularity of any place is, in these terms, constructed not by placing boundaries around it and defining its identity through counterposition to the other which lies beyond,

but precisely (in part) through the specificity of the mix of links and interconnections to that 'beyond'. Places viewed this way are open and porous. (Massey 5).

The idea that no space can be analyzed independently of the spaces that surround it and with which it interacts through both social forces and material players (people, goods, money) is fundamental in the analysis of gendered geographies in this study. Even though they are seemingly contained, clearly defined and isolated on multiple levels, in reality, they are subject to relations of power that come from the outside and that permeate them.

Looking at space as contested and transformable makes it possible to reconsider the traditionally perceived stability of some of the dichotomies associated with the spatial analysis of gender. Perhaps the most commonly accepted one is the notion that public space belonged to men and that women occupied domestic, private places, the epitome of which was the home. This dichotomy had the effect of defining acceptable and unacceptable spaces for women, and intentionally limited their ability to step out of the home: "The attempt to confine women to the domestic sphere was both a specifically spatial control and, through that, a social control on identity" (Massey 179). In the case of Latin America, since the period of post-independence, "Women were especially crucial to the imagined community as mothers of the new men and as guardians of private life, which from Independence onward was increasingly seen as shelter from political turmoil" (Franco 81). Motherhood was seen as women's "natural" role, and a "justification for women's confinement to the home; it explains why they cannot be admitted to serious study of abstract questions, to university or Church careers, and why their intellectual development must remain strictly limited" (Massey 86). This analysis goes beyond just rethinking the meaning of public and private, and suggests the larger implications of the binary understanding of gendered space–implications in terms of mobility, knowledge and power, and the construction of national models. Along these lines, the gendered geographies mapped in this study uncover multiple struggles over public and private spaces, from some female characters' need to justify their presence in the street, in the cinema of the 1950s, to others' reconfiguration of the space of the beauty salon as a site of female solidarity (and not simply the reproduction of feminine beauty standards) through salaried and emotional labor.

Seeing space as unfixed disrupts another dichotomy of gender, that of men's vs. women's work, or what is considered labor, with all the implications that this notion carries for women's social and economic independence. Feminist geography has uncovered multiple ways in which social structures of oppression like patriarchy and capital have made it so that going to work outside the home contributes less to women's liberation than is to be expected in some cases. Among the employers' tactics to keep women's wages low are "establish[ing] the men's job as skilled and the women's as less so" (Massey 203), even when the tasks performed by both genders are similar. Such gendered devaluation of women's labor occurs in the cases of women working in agriculture or factories, and inevitably has economic implications for the reproduction of patriarchy. In the case of the Caribbean, even though since the 1930s women have played a progressively larger role in the economic sustenance of the family, patriarchy and capital continue to reproduce the image of the male authority figure. Since women perform both productive and reproductive labor, their "salaries are deemed supplementary to the primary male breadwinner" (Safa *The Myth* 37), an attitude that maintains patriarchal relations of power even as women gain advances in both the private and the public spheres. Even when women have gained more equal rights and status in the domestic sphere (demanding that boyfriends and husbands share domestic tasks, for example), "they have made much less progress at the level of the state or the political process" (Safa *The Myth* 88). In the workplace, "gender subordination is reinforced by the paternalistic treatment of women by male managers and male union leaders, who tend to dismiss women workers who complain" (Safa *The Myth* 95), while, in the wider social sphere, women's "optimism is giving way to pessimism as they see progress becoming more difficult and fear that the future may not hold the same promises for their children that they once envisaged" (Safa *The Myth* 95). This analysis extends beyond the space of the house, to encompass that of the workplace and the nation, demonstrating that, in the Caribbean case (and in Puerto Rico in particular), as in Massey's analysis in the UK, employment outside the home has not always resulted in the expected recognition of the value of women's work or of their contributions to multiple levels and spheres of society.

Such analyses suggest the need to examine critically the extent to which Puerto Rican cultural production offers a vision of the house, the beauty salon, the factory and the brothel, as well as of the labor performed in these spaces, as sites of female agency and liberation, on the one hand, or of the reproduction of patriarchal order and gender norms, on the other. They call for the implementation of strategies to challenge the continued attempts to marginalize feminist geographic knowledge. Among these strategies, proposed by feminist geographers, are Chela Sandoval's "oppositional consciousness" (Rose 12) and the capacity for a "strategic mobility" through which one can adapt, resist and challenge "the shifting structures of capitalism, masculinism, racism, and so on" (Rose 13). The emphasis here is not only on the need to resist patriarchal structures of oppression, but also to recognize that these structures have multiple sources, which cannot be fought in isolation. One always needs to be ready to shift positions in order to confront a repressive practice that might come from different directions and through different social processes.

Oppositional consciousness and strategic mobility can also be used as technologies for confronting the structures of gender oppression from which this discourse of binaries emerges, such as the connections between patriarchy and capitalism, and their discourse of gender and space that reproduces a system of gender oppression: "over time, women in big cities were less and less easy to contain in heterosexuality and in the domestic sphere (and here of course capitalism and patriarchy have had an uneasy relationship), as metropolitan life itself seemed to throw up [. . .] a threat to patriarchal control" (Massey 180). This represents an uneasiness with women's newly-found capacity to overtly cross spatial borders ("going out," often to work) that had previously been rigid and inviolable limits (which, in the case of Puerto Rico, might help to explain why some of the earliest salaried employment of women in the early 20th century was piece work that they could do at home and which subcontractors even came to collect). While in this case capital and patriarchy are allied, sometimes they act in opposition to each other, not necessarily for the benefit of women's liberation or agency, but as two different, yet complementary structures of oppression. It is important to note that, even though capitalism was one of the factors that foregrounded women's ability to cross spatial borders, and thus challenged a basic patriarchal mechanism of control, it constructed yet another structure of oppression in that it refused to recognize the value of women's work inside and outside the home as equal to that of men.

My analysis of Puerto Rican cultural production takes a materialist feminist approach that has proven useful in analyzing the relationship between gender, sexuality and space. The concept of materialist feminism emerged in the 1980s as a response to Marxist feminism's rigid adherence to categories of class as analytical and political frameworks for feminist liberation. In contrast to Marxist feminism, which urged women to devote their political efforts to class struggle as the only medium of feminist liberation, materialist feminism acknowledges the significance of women's material conditions, but only as they relate to multiple other axes of identity and structures of oppression. Thus, women are not only defined by their productive and reproductive roles, but also by their race, ethnicity, sexuality, and by the variety of social structures that oppress and control their multiple identities–from capital to patriarchy, racism and homophobia.

One of the principal concerns of materialist feminism is who it speaks for. Who creates the knowledge, from what standpoint and in what historical context? How are relations of power, associated with multiple feminist identities, implicated in the creation of knowledge and in its feminist and political potential? And, for the purposes of this study, how does materiality–one's material, contextual, historical conditions, beyond the singular issue of social class–affect the cultural construction of space and its feminist liberational potential, as well as its capacity to reproduce structures of oppression?

The question of space is essential to materialist feminism, since material conditions are associated with spaces that provide the matrix for the production of historical and ideological discourses. Materialist feminism "allows us to see workplace and home, suburb and ghetto, colony and metropolis as specific and interrelated sites of exploitation" (Hennessy 31). Seen from a materialist feminist point of view, a place like the island of Puerto Rico, conceptualized through the multiple spaces that comprise it, emphasizes the interrelation of spaces with structures of oppression like patriarchy (in the home, the workplace and the suburbs, for instance), capital (in the intersection of colony, metropolis and capitalist production and reproduction that occurs in the home and in the workplace), or racism (the construction of images of suburbs vs. caseríos, with the corresponding socially sanctioned class and racial images of the people that live in each space). The spaces analyzed in this book can be seen not only as workplaces, and consequently as sites of production, but also as located in a city or a suburb, and always on an island that remains under neocolonial control.

For many of the characters in the texts that I study, the experience of gender and space goes beyond the creation of an alternative, oppositional discourse. They call for the active, palpable transformation of their material conditions, taking "the feminist standpoint not as an experiential ground of knowledge but as a critical practice" (Hennessy xvii), and insisting on a "commitment to the possibility of transformative social change" (Hennessy 35). This change has to emerge as a reaction to the multiple structures of oppression, out of the multiple axes of identity that define women in contemporary Puerto Rican society, and through alliances across perceived borders of identity and politics.

What is appealing in this conceptualization of feminist agency in relation to the analysis of the spaces of the factory, the house, the beauty salon and the brothel in Puerto Rican literature and film is the possibility of constructing gendered geographies at the intersection of multiple axes of identity and structures of oppression. What seems restrictive is the limited engagement with race. Race, especially as it relates to gender, sexuality and national identity, is a fundamental issue in the texts analyzed here, and its significance calls for a need to expand the theoretical conception of materialist feminism to include a broader understanding of the significance of race in women's material conditions and political agency.

Even more importantly, the call for transformative political agency grounded in women's material conditions provides a template for understanding the power of the solidarity and the alliances created among women in the four spaces studied here, spaces that in some ways are still permeated by patriarchal structures of oppression, by racism and homophobia, but which in other ways provide a spatial opening for the production of liberating feminist discourses.


SPACE, SEXUALITY AND CITIZENSHIP

As race, class and gender are fundamental for understanding the social tensions and the constant negotiations of power in different spaces, so is sexuality, specifically as it relates to questions of desire and consumption. The intersection of sexuality and space poses important questions like: How does space define and delimit sexual citizenship, and how does sexuality redefine different spaces? In what ways does consumption enable or delimit sexual citizenship? How does sexuality interact with class, race and gender to transform spaces often identified as heterosexual and heterosexist? What does the study of desire contribute to the understanding of the relationship between sexuality and space? How do the issues of sexuality and desire redefine the gendered spaces of the house, the factory, the beauty salon and the brothel?

The gendered geographies that I map out in this book are sites of the intersection of sexuality and space, power and resistance. Many of texts that I study recognize that "the lesbian body configures a particular spatiality" (Binnie, et.al. xiii) and pay particular attention to the "issue of the visibility of lesbian bodies, and the exclusions, inclusions, and politics of lesbian identities in the city" (Peace 30). While sexuality continues to be mostly absent from the study of space in Puerto Rico, some of the texts that I discuss do address the relationship between material and symbolic spaces (the street, the beauty salon) and homosexuality, especially in relation to issues of sexual citizenship and homosexual desire.

The preoccupation with sexual citizenship in Puerto Rico and beyond stems from the assumed normative heterosexuality of most urban (public and private) spaces, and from the calls, sometimes subtle, sometimes prominent, to examine critically that heteronormativity. The assumed heteronormativity is profoundly enmeshed with the "control over the way that space is produced [which] is fundamental to the heterosexuals' ability to reproduce their hegemony" (Valentine 154). This control might be exercised and imposed overtly, through legislature prohibiting "public displays of intimacy between gay men" (Binnie 196) or covertly, through a conscious silencing of the issue of sex and sexuality, a case documented in beauty salons in the UK: "Heterosexuality operates as a default position, presumed and uncommented upon. Only when discussing male clients in the salon, or the treatments accessed by male-to-female transsexuals, was the all-encompassing heterosexuality of the salon ever breached" (Black 98). The normativity of heterosexuality impacts the social construction of spaces, including those of beauty salons, even when these spaces might be perceived as having (and might indeed have) liberating potential in terms of gender, race and other axes of identity.

One of the responses to the dominant heteronormativity of urban and national spaces is consumption, as an instrument of resistance, as a claim to inclusion, and often as a call for a transformation of the relationship between space and sexuality. While conscious of the larger context of capital and commodification, critics have noted the ways in which consumption still acts as an instrument of power for those who are marginalized because their sexuality does not conform to the commonly accepted heterosexuality of the modern city: "Could one reason why so many queers enjoy going shopping so much (if and when we can afford to do so) is because shopping offers us the opportunity to assert at least some kind of power? Is it an effect of our not having power in other arenas, specifically in the realm of social rights?" (Binnie 187). Spaces of inclusion like Old Compton Street in London are evidence of how consumer power not only enables, but also limits visibility and sexual citizenship: "among those excluded from Soho (and therefore less visible) are people who cannot afford the prices of food and drink or are unwilling to pay the pink premium" (Binnie 198). Consequently, sexual citizenship is made possible, but also limited by consumer power and the capacity to participate in the reproduction of capital-enabled spaces.

Similarly, consumption can provide lesbian women access, even if only to a limited and specifically designated and identified number of spaces: "The 'ready-made' understandings are that lesbians (and others) can buy their way into designated places in which their identity either may be or is proclaimed: lesbian discos, clubs, saunas, restaurants, cafés, bed and breakfast houses, motels, sports clubs. By 'being there,' they can 'be'" (Peace 47). By guaranteeing herself access in this way, "S/he who appears to have the capacity to consume can equally take on the appearance of the citizen. The consumer is the citizen-subject of the city par excellence" (Peace 51), in those settings in which these spaces do exist. This argument critiques not only the assumed heterosexuality of social space and its "performative nature" (Valentine 154), but also the traditional model of the ideal citizen: white, male and heterosexual. This critique is indeed fundamental to the analysis of the space of the beauty salon, for example, in which the rigidity of the heterosexual order is challenged on a daily basis by the intimate nature of the interactions between female stylists and clients. While some of the stories represent that intimacy as a basis of female alliances and solidarity, others suggest that factors like desire and the need to find ways of transgressing socio-sexual norms might be behind some of the exchanges that occur between the female protagonists.

## SPACE AND GENDER: PUERTO RICO AND BEYOND

At times implicitly, and at times explicitly and directly, Puerto Rican gendered geographies dialogue with the broader work of Caribbean and African American thinkers of race, gender, labor, citizenship, agency and the erotic. The relationships that develop in the spaces that I study point to the interrelatedness of issues like third world women's work, erotic agency and citizenship; solidarity, family and community; and sexuality and the national imaginary, as experienced by women in different "Third World" locations.

The gendered geographies that Puerto Rican women and queer authors reveal in the texts that I analyze redefine the relationship between family, community, and the spatial imaginary of the nation. In Puerto Rican literary criticism that redefinition was inspired by Juan Gelpí's critique of the family as a national metaphor and of the family house as its symbolic space. Gelpí's criticism, however, has broader implications for questions like: Are there tropes, spatial or otherwise, that can represent more faithfully the differences, the conflicts and the negotiations of race, class and gender in the problematic Puerto Rican "national family"? What are the alternatives to the national family that emerge from the Puerto Rican literary and cinematic texts of recent decades, and how do they redefine the notion of community? How do gender, sexuality and community intersect to redraw the gendered geographies of power, domination, resistance and agency in Puerto Rican literature and film?

The gendered maps of power and agency that emerge from these Puerto Rican texts respond to the need, voiced by both Caribbean and African American critics, to "broaden and redefine what we mean by family" (Lorde 21) and to think creatively about how to "organize around [. . .] differences, neither denying them not blowing them up out of proportion" (Lorde 25). Along with their differences (occupational, in "Pilar, tus rizos;" racial and class-based, in "Cuando las mujeres quieren a los hombres;" generational, in "Hebra rota"), the female characters of these texts also recognize their "common context of struggles within specific exploitative structures and systems" (Mohanty 7), a recognition that inspires them to seek new alliances and solidarities. Through such alliances, "third world women are making connections between the forces of domination which affect their lives daily and are actively participating in the creation of a movement committed to radical social and political transformation at all levels" (Torres 275). The alliances develop in different spaces–national, diasporic, transnational, material and symbolic–responding to contexts in which the "workplace" has "migrated in search of cheap labor, and the nation-state is no longer an appropriate socioeconomic unit of analysis (Mohanty 2)–or, at the very least, not the only one. This realization requires a cross-national and a cross-cultural analysis of gender, labor and solidarity. While most of the authors that I study here situate their characters in spaces "contained" in the Puerto Rican nation–from the home to the workplace and to the city street–others, like Mayra Santos-Febres and Luisa Capetillo, position them in the diaspora or in a constant state of transit. What they all have in common is that all of them work towards the creation of female solidarities in the face of patriarchal, heterosexist and oppressive contexts, transforming the spaces that they inhabit from sites of marginalization and voicelessness to places of potential, of feminine agency and of transformative power.

The Puerto Rican gendered geographies that I map out also imply a reformulation of the relationship between women's work, agency and citizenship. Instead of using traditionally understood political agency to carve out for themselves a space in the national imaginary, the protagonists of some of these texts employ "the erotic [which] offers a well of replenishing and provocative force to the woman who does not fear its revelation, not succumb to the belief that sensation is enough" (Lorde 2). What Mimi Sheller, following Audre Lorde's ideas has termed "erotic agency" (Sheller 6) often emerges through women's labor–productive, reproductive, but most of all emotional labor, usually unpaid and often devalued work that women are expected to do by virtue of being women. The importance of understanding "how enslaved women and their descendants used sex with each other to effect a different kind of autonomy, [and] how same-sex eroticism enters into the history of sexual labor in the Caribbean as a practice by which women take control of their sexuality as a resource they share with each other" (Tinsley 20) lies in the need to see spaces of coercion also as spaces of resistance, agency and alliance. Because in the Caribbean these spaces of violence, control and coercion have often been spaces of (feminine) labor, it is important to uncover strategies like the implementation of emotional labor and of erotic agency as ways in which women resisted domination and transformed the spaces that they inhabit.

In their attempts to break out of the restraints of gender norms and expectations, some of protagonists of the Puerto Rican texts that I study use their emotional labor to offer and to receive support and advice, or to strategize and to effectuate change "in the face of a racist, patriarchal and anti-erotic society" (Lorde 8). By gendering and queering spaces like the beauty salon, the family house or the brothel–spaces of female relationships and of women's work–Santos-Febres's, Luisa Capetillo's and Rosaio Ferré's characters invest them with new political meanings, redrawing the maps of their nation and of their communities by claiming more equal and more just spaces for themselves and for other women.

The gendered geographies of Puerto Rican cultural production respond, on the one hand, to these agencies and solidarities, and on the other, to the urgency to fight the conspicuous absence of queer subjects and the "invisibility of Caribbean lesbians in scholarship and art" (King 191) that Rosamond King and others have critiqued. They also respond to the need to recover representations of different sexualities in relation to national discourses and imaginings. All too frequently this intersection between sexuality and the nation has been a violent one, particularly in the case of Caribbean and diasporic subjects who "have a history of being misrecognized and maligned" (King 193). In the case of Puerto Rico and its diaspora, "Homosexuality, and especially gay liberation, has at times been seen as imported or inflated by virtue of the island's colonial relationship with the United States" (La Fountain-Stokes xviii), and national discourse has construed "nonnormative sexual orientation as a form of deviant behavior against which the national population needs protection" (La Fountain-Stokes *Queer Ricans* xvii). Similarly, for a long time the official discourse of the Cuban Revolution maintained a patriarchal and heterosexist image that marginalized "other" sexualities. Instead of erasing nonnormative sexualities from the Cuban national imaginary, this discourse inscribed them "by negation, in the prescriptive models of the national Cuban narrative" (Bejel xiv), carving for homosexuality a space from which it "continually threatens to destabilize those [national] romances" (Bejel xvi).

The exclusion of "other" sexualities from Caribbean national discourses has resulted in subversive and creative strategies, not only of inclusion, but also, and more importantly, of a reformulation of the idea of national belonging. In Trinidadian cultural production, erotic geographies and "new queer cartographies" (Tinsley 25) enable authors to redeploy oppressive tropes and to "imagine a landscape belonging to Caribbean women and Caribbean women belonging to each other" (Tinsley 2), ultimately effectuating a "poetics and politics of decolonization" (2). In the face of official exclusion and invisibility, women employ eroticism and desire to redefine their relationship to each other, to the nation and to the colonial context that subjects them to multiple levels of oppression, physical and sexual violence, heterosexist norms, social limitations and expectations. While the spaces that they occupy are different from the spaces inhabited by the female and queer Puerto Rican characters in my study–Tinsley looks at rivers, trees, open natural landscapes, while this book focuses on what are understood to be more urban places like factories, beauty salons and brothels–both Puerto Rican and Trinidadian women use space, and the queering of space, as a strategy to resist marginalization and oppression imposed by limited definitions of the nation in their specific contexts. Through their emotional labor, characters like Lidia, the protagonist of *Felices días, tío Sergio* or Milagros and Marina, in "Milagros, calle Mercurio," reveal how sexuality, desire and eroticism become the driving forces behind their coming to consciousness and strategies for liberation.

## The Symbolic Spaces of Puerto Rican Cultural Production

Recent studies on the relationship between space and race, class and gender in Puerto Rico demonstrate that over the course of the 20th century, everyday spaces on the island have become progressively more fragmented, controlled and alienated from each other, as a result of structures of power and of social hierarchies that segregate people, locating them in places that they deem "appropriate" for their perceived racial, class and gender identities. While for a long time "The city [was] considered to be a place where heterogeneous individuals come naturally into contact, in neighborhoods, parks, workplaces, transportation systems, shops, libraries, and streets" (Dinzey-Flores 146), in recent decades urban centers like San Juan and Ponce have, in the words of sociologist Zaire Dinzey-Flores, become "gated cities" (147). In them, public areas have been traversed by walls and sectioned off by gates that keep people in or out:

> In private communities, gating arranged by insiders keeps others out; in public housing, gates are controlled by outsiders to gain protection for themselves from those inside. In locking them-selves in, the privileged lock undesirables out. Gates for the poor reverse this order; they shut undesirables in. In both, the gates are erected in the interest of an upper class and, in modern cities, of the primarily white (Dinzey-Flores 10).

In these controlled-access communities, yet again space becomes political, as it begins to denote in ever more obvious ways differences of race, class, and gender relations and expectations.

This fragmentation of the city impacts the social construction of the space of the house, as well as the construction of gender in relation to domestic and to public spaces in the city: "The gates of Puerto Rico have re-created and reinforced a gendered geography; in the city, there is a spatial sorting of men by degree of privilege. The elite gated communities along with sanctioned city spaces like the social clubs, like suburbs within a city, have become the site of a cloistered womanhood" that look for "a refuge from the open spaces of the dangerous city" within the gated communities (Dinzey-Flores 130). This segmentation constructs and reinforces two basic types of femininity–on the one hand, it defines a white, middle-class femininity defined by honor and propriety, which re-produces the patriarchal system of gendered public and private spaces, and is kept behind the gates. On the other hand, in opposi-tion to this model, it constructs a transgressive femininity that is associated with blackness and with a "disobedient" or "undisci-plined" sexuality that stands outside the walls of the model commu-nities, or within those of the public housing projects. In this way, Dinzey-Flores demonstrates how "The house, not the city, becomes the locus of social life and the family, the central unit" (27), as cities become segmented and communities become more exclusive and exclusionary.

The geographies that emerge out of contemporary Puerto Rican literary and cinematic texts are multifaceted and respond to these complex social, political and cultural realities of the island. In contrast to early 20th century work that identified the nation with *el campo*, or the rural areas,[9] recently authors have shifted their gaze to modern, urban settings and to the multiplicity of conflicts that they reveal. In their work, ELA is a "paradoxically entrenched and ambiguous political status [that] has produced a uniquely experienced sense of space and place" (Dowdy 41). In texts like "Letra para salsa y tres soneos por encargo" and *Felices días, tío Sergio* authors of the Generation of the 70s like Ana Lydia Vega and Magali García Ramis, have explored the relationship between gender, sexuality and the city, while their contemporaries like Wilfredo Mattos Cintrón have critiqued hierarchies of race, class, masculinity and the law in detective novels that situate an Afro-Puerto Rican working class detective[10] at the center of the narrative and of the city of San Juan. These urban geographies of gender, race and class often intersect with questions of migration, which became even more relevant in the aftermath of Operation Bootstrap.

Mapping the new geographies of migration in what Duany has called "the Puerto Rican nation on the move" has required that authors situate their texts between the proverbial "acá" and "allá," the island and the metropolis, and in spaces of transit like the airport and the airplane. Set on an airplane headed to New York, Luis Rafael Sánchez's "La guagua aérea," one of the iconic representations of the Puerto Rican migratory experience, problematizes the question of space, by exploring "the tensions and negotiation of cultural space that springs forth from the comings and goings of Puerto Rican migrants to New York City. Through the metaphor of the "flying bus," Sánchez captures the duality, hybridity, and fluidity of US-Puerto Rican identity in the microcosm of an airline flight between New York and Puerto Rico" (Barreneche 15). While Sánchez's text offers a comical, yet compassionate look at the variety of migrants, *El beso que me diste* (both the novel and Sonia

---

[9] One of the iconic representations of *el campo* as the quintessential *puertorriqueñidad* is Ramón Frade's 1905 painting "El pan nuestro," which depicts a jíbaro carrying a bunch of plantains.

[10] Wilfredo Mattos Cintrón's detective Isabelo Andújar has protagonized several novels, among which are *Desamores*, *La puerta de San Juan* and *Las dos muertes de Catalino Ríos*.

Fritz's cinematic adaptation) uses the space of the airport to explore the implications of Puerto Rico's political status, and depicts the trope of the crumbling family to critique the hypocrisy of cultural nationalism. Another, more recent representation of the space of the airport and the airplane explores a different kind of migration, the trans-Caribbean movement of people and capital in Mayra Santos-Febres's novel *Sirena Selena vestida de pena*. In that book, protagonized by two transvestite characters, the transgression of spaces is intertwined with the transgression of bodies (Haesendonck 79), and "el cuerpo del travesti [se convierte en] una máquina de transgresiones del espacio" (88), bridging the space between Caribbean islands. These representations suggest the multiple recent uses of the airport and the airplane as spaces of transit that destabilize the traditional depiction of the Puerto Rican nation.

A space that complements these geographies of transit is the motel, in which both people and relationships become elusive. As the setting of *Cualquier miércoles soy tuya*, another novel by Santos-Febres, the motel becomes the site of elicit deals, spying and suspicions, while at the same time, as Guillermo Irizarry has noted, the underground capital and the unsanctioned exchange of capital "mark[s] the limits of state institutional administration" (Lambright and Guerrero xxiii), proposing a critique of the state's inefficiency in fulfilling its own promise of modernization and development.

In addition to being a space of transit, the motel belongs to another category of spaces that can be seen as marginal in the city, like housing projects, decrepit apartments and the back rooms of restaurants. These spaces compose an often invisible urban geography that comprises a multitude of identities, conflicts and negotiations of class, race, gender and sexuality. Like Mattos Cintrón's novels, Marta Aponte Alsina's novella *Fúgate* and stories like "Tu flor te delata" rely on Gabriel Marte, a detective that does not conform to the traditional model of masculinity and power, to uncover both the humanity and the violence that plagues spaces like San Juan's housing projects. Gabriel Marte's detours into fantasy are another technology of critique of the "real" society in which he lives, of the space of the nation along with the inefficiency of its government.

This invisible geography of marginalized subjects is also composed of the back rooms of restaurants inhabited by undocumented, smuggled and abused immigrants in Manolo Núñez Negrón's *Barrachina*. At first sight, the underground world that the novel reveals is comparable to Santos-Febres's *Cualquier miércoles soy tuya*, but it gradually emerges as more ruthless and fatal than her character Dama Solitaria. The only way for Núñez Negrón's protagonist to emerge from the shadows of the service rooms is to embrace the violence that keeps him a modern-day slave of his captors, and to turn it into an instrument of liberation. The concluding scene of *Barrachina* thus becomes a critique of the law and of the omnipresence of corruption, human trafficking and labor exploitation, along with the invisibility of its victims.

The spaces that I study in this book–the factory, the house, the beauty salon and the brothel–are not necessarily marginal spaces, and at first sight, they may appear rather unrelated. However, a closer look reveals a number of parallelisms between them. First, the four spaces are connected through women's labor, whether salaried or unpaid, skilled or unskilled, productive or reproductive, domestic or in the workplace. The gendered geographies that emerge from this set of texts are defined by women's emotional labor, which politicizes and transforms them. In areas in which global capital tends to create what Melissa M. Wright has called "disposable women," and in certain cases expects them to perform unpaid, emotional labor by virtue of their gender, the female protagonists create solidarities and alliances to resist the patriarchal norms that exploit their work. Early texts, like the 1959 film *Maruja*, use female labor and idleness to condemn models of gender and sexuality that do not conform to ELA's traditional norms. In some texts, women's work is used to reproduce cultural nationalism, as in José Artemio Torres's documentary *Luchando por la vida: las despalilladoras de tabaco y su mundo*, in Efraín López Neris's *Life of Sin*, or in Jacobo Morales's *Dios los cría*. In others, women's labor is subversive, constitutive of a different set of social and gender relations. This is the case of Luisa Capetillo's writings, of Rosario Ferré's depiction of Isabel la Negra, and of the intersection between emotional and physical beauty services in Carmen Lugo Filippi's "Milagros, calle Mercurio."

Second, along with the theme of women's labor, these spaces enable different connections between gender, sexuality and the Puerto Rican cultural nationalist discourse. Some of these connections are established through patriarchal relations of power (the family house), others through consumption and services (the beauty salon and the brothel), or through a discourse of rights, whether explicit, as in the factory, or implicit, as in that of citizenship and female emancipation in the house or in the salon.

Finally, these spaces represent a series of configurations of alternative families and relationships between women, centered on different possibilities for alliances. Some of these relationships are based on power and domination, as those between Isabel and her servants in *The House on the Lagoon*, or between Isabel la Negra and the women that work in her brothel in Manuel Ramos Otero's short story "La última plena que bailó Luberza." Others enable the construction of solidarity and resistance, even as they remain mediated through the exchange of services, as in "Milagros, calle Mercurio," or they are only tentative, like the relationship between Doña Kety and Yetsaida in "Hebra rota." Simultaneously, some of them are effectuated through maternal figures or through a broader political dedication to a combination of causes, as in Luisa Capetillo's and Dominga de la Cruz's struggle for women's and workers' rights.

What these geographies reveal are the complex ways in which gender and sexuality are constructed in everyday spaces, through the negotiations between patriarchy and space. The construction of feminist agency in these four spaces is only possible if, as feminist geographers have argued, spaces are understood not as static, but as flexible, malleable, and always in transformation. The agency that the female characters claim enables the analysis of space in these terms, and consequently, the understanding of national discourse and identity as a dynamic process redefined by feminine geographies.


## Puerto Rican Cinema and National Discourse: Industry and Criticism

Part of my purpose is this book is to examine the representation of gender and space in Puerto Rican film in order to call critical attention to the Puerto Rican film industry and to the still limited scholarship produced about the island's cinema. I analyze film not in addition to a literary corpus, but as a vibrant, integral part of Puerto Rican cultural production. As such, it has contributed in unique ways to the discursive constructions of gendered labor, female sexuality, everyday spaces, and national belonging on the island.

Puerto Rican film criticism gained momentum in the 1990s, thanks to a small number of film critics and historians like Kino

García, Luis Trelles Plazaola, and María Cristina Rodríguez, inspired by a revival of the Puerto Rican film industry made possible in part by governmental policies that expanded the possibilities of funding for domestic projects in the second half of the 1980s.[11] These critics' exploration of the Puerto Rican film history, of the representation of the island in foreign cinematic productions, as well as their copious reviews of foreign and domestic films, festival events and retrospectives, form the foundations of a body of literature for the study of Puerto Rican cinema. Similarly, the publication of book-length historical overviews, journal articles, catalogues and festival booklets during the same period offers an important contribution to the study of the Puerto Rican film industry.

The first comprehensive history of Puerto Rican cinema was written by Joaquín "Kino" García in 1989. Even though the overview it offers is quite brief, it remains the only history of the Puerto Rican film industry. Kino García's other valuable book, *Cine puertorriqueño: Filmografía, fuentes y referencias* (1997) is a national filmography of sorts, providing production, distribution and exhibition information, and offering stills and brief summaries of hundreds of Puerto Rican films from different genres and periods. The filmography begins with Rafael Colorado's long-lost 1912 documentary pieces (García 1-6), and ends in the 1990s, when films like *La guagua aérea* and *Linda Sara* signified a hope for a revival of Puerto Rican film (García 88-89).

García's work has benefited from that of film scholars like Luis Trelles Plazaola, arguably the most prolific of the film historians concerned with the development of cinema in and beyond Puerto Rico. Trelles's early work focuses on the study of female directors, and has resulted in two important volumes: *Cine y mujer en América Latina: directoras de largometrajes* (1991) and *Nostalgias y rebeldías: Cinco directoras latinoamericanas de cine en Europa* (1992). In his 1996 book *Imágenes cambiantes: Descubrimiento, conquista y colonización de la América Hispana vista por el cine de ficción y largometraje* he analyzes the colonial discourses of dozens of films

---

[11] The 1985 Ley de Sociedades Especiales provided economic incentives for private investment in the island's film industry and encouraged the participation of Puerto Rican banks through credits and other incentives. Similarly, the 1994 creation of the Fondo de Cine de Puerto Rico became one of the most important initiatives for financial support for the production of feature films on the island (Trelles Plazaola *Ante el lente* 99-100).

from Spain, Argentina, Mexico, Cuba, Perú, Venezuela, Great Britain, France and Germany, pointing to the ways that historical contexts and colonial experiences influence the cinematographic representation of the past. Whereas, due to a lack of Puerto Rican films dealing with the subject of colonization,[12] no island productions were included in this book, in *Ante el lente extranjero: Puerto Rico visto por los cineastas de afuera* (2000) Trelles Plazaola exclusively addresses the representation of Puerto Rico. The book is divided in four parts, which chronologically study the representation of the island, whether as a setting or as used as a shooting location without being identified as Puerto Rico, in foreign and domestic films made with foreign capital or crew. The value of the book lies not only in its elucidating analysis of films that use Puerto Rico as part of the plot or as a location, but also in that, by providing a chronological overview of foreign film industries' presence on the island, he also addresses and critiques the United States and the Puerto Rican governments' lack of consistent and cohesive policies promoting the development of a Puerto Rican national film industry. This situation has led to the need to make co-productions with foreign capital, in which Puerto Rican writers, directors and actors have little control over the way that the island and its population are portrayed. He points out that "con demasiada frecuencia, Puerto Rico sigue siendo un lugar fácilmente intercambiable y su verdadera identidad, tan definida, antigua y caracterizada, se pierde para el cine" (Trelles, *Ante el lente*, 102). Even though at first sight these words reiterate the image of a cohesive Puerto Rican identity, they also critique the island's exploitation by foreign filmmakers who tend to use it only as an exotic exterior or as a generic "Latin American" setting.

Ironically, Banco Popular's *Idilio Tropical*, an edited collection of essays on Puerto Rican cinema whose title references the island's tropical location, does much to dispel the image of Puerto Rico as an exotic site. Puerto Rico emerges as a place with a developing film industry and talented professionals skilled at scriptwriting, editing, directing and acting. The collection's introduction addresses the social impact of cinema since its inception, considers

---

[12] This was true until the 2006 release of *El cimarrón* (dir. Iván Daniel Ortiz), the first Puerto Rican film set in the Spanish colonial period, and the first to emphasize its historical significance. It uses the conventions of melodrama and romance to address issues of race, power, slavery and revolt.

the ways in which it enriched the discourse of modernity and progress, and rethinks the symbolic significance of the space of movie theaters:

> Las salas de cine transformaron la fisonomía de las ciudades en Puerto Rico. Se convirtieron en espacios de modernidad que rivalizaban con las sedes públicas tradicionales: las plazas, las iglesias y los teatros. En las próximas décadas [post-WWI] los edificios para cine presentaron propuestas arquitectónicas novedosas que se alienaron junto a las vetustas construcciones del centro de ciudades y pueblos. La presencia del cine dinamizó los barrios urbanos y modificó las rutinas de todos (Álvarez Curbelo, "Pasión" 3).

This cultural impact is only one of the themes discussed in the seven essays that compose the collection, which addresses issues previously neglected in Puerto Rican film history and criticism, such as the tradition of animation and experimental cinema.

*Idilio Tropical* is exemplary of another type of resource that documents the developing film industry in Puerto Rico, namely collections on different aspects of Puerto Rican cinema, in the absence of monographs on specific topics, beyond historical overviews like those of García and Trelles. Another such project is Raul Ríos Díaz's and Francisco González's *Dominio de la imagen: hacia una industria de cine en Puerto Rico* (2000). The editors begin with the premise that much remains to be done in order for a mature Puerto Rican film industry to exist, and ask, "¿Qué hace falta para hacer realidad la gran ilusión de una industria de cine puertorriqueña?" (Ríos Díaz 7). The book compiles interviews with directors, distributors and producers, and gradually constructs an image of the realities and the problems that the Puerto Rican film industry faces in its struggle to expand. A project that uses a similar interview approach and that addresses some of the same issues in the case of Puerto Rican filmmakers in the United States is Ana María García's *Made in the U.S.A.*

One of the figures that have contributed much to the collection and preservation of Puerto Rican cinema on the island is scriptwriter, director and actor Roberto Ramos-Perea. The National Theater and Cinema Archive (Archivo nacional de teatro y cine), which he chairs, contains the most significant collection of Puerto Rican films, plays and literature on film and theater. In addition, the Archive's *Bulletin*, whose publication he also supervises, has systematically featured articles on Puerto Rican cinema, from historical documents such as early film announcements (*Boletín* No. 1) to artist filmographies and film criticism (*Boletín* No. 3).

Other contributions to the literature on Puerto Rican cinema include collections and catalogues like that of the Archive of the Moving Image (El archivo de imágenes en movimiento), the catalogue and screening schedule of the CineSanJuan Festival, or the publication of the script of Jacobo Morales's celebrated film *Linda Sara*, which includes the director's production diary, which provides insights into the process and the difficulties of being a film director in Puerto Rico, from casting to the limited funding that obliged him to complete the film in 25 days (Morales 24).

The historiography of Latin American cinema hardly ever puts Puerto Rico on the cinematographic map. Michael Martin's *New Latin American Cinema* is the collection that has devoted the most attention to Puerto Rican film, as in Frances Negrón-Muntaner's unique exploration of women's film and video production on the island. In contrast, other important books like Deborah Shaw's *Contemporary Latin American Cinema: Breaking into the Global Market* focuses on Mexico, Cuba and Brazil, while *Magical Reels*, one of the canonical books on Latin American cinema, discusses Puerto Rico only briefly, recognizing that the island "has witnessed the growth of a sophisticated film culture in recent years, escaping from the stereotypes imposed by US cinema of the 1920s which projected the island as a site of tropical romance" (King 228). The Puerto Rican film industry is grouped together with Central American film, in a final chapter that seems to encompass "the others," the countries and regions whose film industries do not merit independent sections of the book. In the case of Puerto Rico, the two main feature films that emerged after the 1970s trend towards a "critical, national, documentary movement" (King 230), *Isabel la Negra* (1979) and *Dios los cría* (1980) are discussed briefly in a single paragraph, pointing out the lack of commercial success of the former and barely noting the release of the latter: "Jacobo Morales's *Dios los cría* (*God Makes Them*, 1980) was much more assured, offering five vignettes of middle-class Puerto Rican life, receiving widespread critical acclaim" (King 230). This is only one example of the invisibility of Puerto Rican cinema, and even of acclaimed directors like Jacobo Morales, Ana María García or Sonia Fritz. Even though Puerto Rican cinema has much in common with the development of the cinematic industry in other Caribbean and Latin American countries, and in spite of the fact that since the 1950s it has systematically addressed social and cultural issues ranging from community formation and modernization[13] to the legacy of slavery and colonization, studies of Latin American cinema outside Puerto Rico tend to acknowledge its existence only briefly, and, with few exceptions,[14] rarely embark on thematic or stylistic explorations of Puerto Rican film. The chapters that follow intend to help fill that gap by addressing the issues of space, gender and nation in a variety of fiction, documentary and short films that offer critical perspectives on the power relations that construct the Puerto Rican national imaginary.

## CHAPTER OUTLINE

The book takes as a starting point the spatial aspect of the *gran familia puertorriqueña*, that of the family house dominated by a father figure that maintains the traditional patriarchal order in the symbolic national family. Chapter 2, "Building the Nation: Women's Productive and Reproductive Labor in the Factory," analyzes the intersection between space, gender and sexuality in texts that precede the cultural nationalist project of the 1940s and the 1950s, anticipating some of the criticism that inspired the authors studied in subsequent chapters. Responding to a socio-economic reality in which, from the 1910s to the 1940s, the cigar-making factory and the needlework workshop were the main spaces of occupation for women outside the home, this chapter examines the complex and contradictory roles that the factory has played in the construction of Puerto Rican national identity in relation to gender, sexuality, race and class. It studies texts in which the factory is an instrument of official discourse, and others, in which it is a space of opposition from which Puerto Rican working women have staged a resistance to exclusionary practices and discourses. Luisa Capetillo's work as a reader and union organizer in tobacco factories, and two documentary films–*Luchando por la vida*, about female tobacco leaf stemmers and

---

[13] See Jack Delano in *Idilio Tropical* and Rafael Cabrera Collazo, "La DIVEDCO y el cine en el Puerto Rico de los cincuenta."

[14] See for example Catherine Benamou's analysis of *La Gran Fiesta* in *Cineaste* 16.4 (1988): 47-50.

*La operación*, about women's productive labor and reproductive rights–frame the analysis of gender and sexuality in the factory.

Chapter 3, titled "Rethinking *la gran familia puertorriqueña* in the Family House," critically analyzes the space of the family house dominated by a father figure that maintains the traditional patriarchal order in the symbolic national family. It examines how, through alliances and through the politization of space, Puerto Rican writers and film directors subvert the association of the family house with Puerto Rican national discourses and propose alternatives to the familiar patriarchal national imaginary. It focuses on the alternative families that dominate novels like Ferré's *The House on the Lagoon* and García Ramis's *Felices días, tío Sergio*, as well as films like Orzábal Quintana's *Maruja*, Morales's *Dios los cría*, and Paco López's video to Rubén Blades's song "Ligia Elena."

In Chapter 4, "Gendering and Queering the Beauty Salon," my focus shifts to the subversive potential of a uniquely "feminine" space. It argues that the interplay between performativity, desire and the gaze genders and queers the beauty salon, constructing female solidarities that challenge the patriarchal order of Puerto Rican cultural nationalist discourse. Two short stories by Lugo Filippi, the story "Hebra rota" by Mayra Santos-Febres, and Fritz's eponymous film are the matrix for the analysis of the ways in which the gendering and the queering of the space of the beauty salon disrupts cultural nationalist ideas of heteronormativity and cohesion, to propose alternative family configurations.

Chapter 5, "Locating Power on the Margins: Gender and Sexuality in the Brothel," demonstrates how the patriarchal figure is decentered by that of the Afro-Puerto Rican prostitute Isabel la Negra, who transforms the space of the brothel into an alternative community, challenging previous representations not only of gender and sexuality, but also of racial and class identities. The texts discussed in this chapter–Ferré's "Cuando las mujeres quieren a los hombres," Ramos Otero's "La última plena que bailó Luberza," López Neris's film *Life of Sin*, and Santos-Febres's novel *Nuestra Señora de la Noche*–reveal Isabel as a figure that inverts gender and sexual hierarchies, exposes the contradictions of the model of the gran familia puertorriqueña and reconfigures of the idea of the national family through the space of the brothel.

The book's conclusion synthesizes my analysis of Puerto Rican gendered geographies and of the complex ways in which gender and sexuality are continuously negotiated in everyday spaces, through creative feminist agencies and coalitions.

The next chapter analyzes a series of texts whose purpose is to construct, contest or rethink the gendered geographies of national identity from the space of the factory, a space that has had a long, complex and often contradictory relationship to gender and sexuality, labor and national discourses.

CHAPTER II

# BUILDING THE NATION: PRODUCTIVE AND REPRODUCTIVE LABOR IN THE FACTORY

## GENDER AND LABOR IN PUERTO RICO

THE spaces represented in the work of early feminist authors like Luisa Capetillo were work spaces directly related to the feminist and labor struggles of the early 20th century–working conditions, union organization, education, and gender relations. As between the 1910s and the 1940s the tobacco and the needlework industries were the most frequent domains of occupation for women outside the home, the cigar-making factory and the needlework shop were the spaces in which many of these texts were set. This early literature critiques women's marginalization in the discursive construction of the Puerto Rican nation by relating women's labor to the nation-building process, responding to the female laborers' realities of the time, and also anticipating the criticism of the patriarchal model of *la gran familia puertorriqueña* by rejecting its masculine narrative and by privileging female voices and spaces of articulation.

Over the course of the 20th century, after the decline of the cigar-making and of the needlework industries, authors and filmmakers have revisited the relationship between gender, labor and nation in the cigar factory and in the needlework workshop. In contrast to Capetillo's early texts, some of the documentary films produced at the height of the cultural nationalist project represent, albeit problematically, the factory and women's labor as instrumental in the construction of ELA's national model. Other, more recent texts, take on the task of uncovering and condemning the violent practices that made women the backbone, but also frequently the victim, of the cultural nationalist model of *la puertorriqueñidad*. Through an analysis of the work of writers and film directors like Luisa Capetillo, Sonia Fritz, José Artemio Torres and Ana María García, this chapter traces the trajectory of the representation of the space of the factory in relation to gender, sexuality, race, class and national discourse, beginning with the decade of the 1910s. In this manner, it also sets the stage for the discussion, in the following chapter, of the space of the family house, which, beginning in the 1940s, became the principal cultural trope of the Estado Libre Asociado's national discourse.

In contrast to the other spaces analyzed in this book, the factory has been the focus of few fictional accounts, whether literary of cinematic (one example would be the sporadic references to female factory workers in Ángel Lozada's novel *La patografía*), but abounds in autobiographical accounts, political pamphlets and articles, like Luisa Capetillo's texts and Margaret Randall's recorded testimony of factory worker and reader Dominga de la Cruz. More recently, several documentary films and docudramas have referenced studies of factory work in Puerto Rican history. Of these, the most notable are the documentary films *Luchando por la vida: Las despalilladoras del tabaco y su mundo*, directed by José Artemio Torres, *Comerío: 180 Años de historia*, directed by Benjamin López (the first addressing entirely, and the second only marginally the tobacco industry in Puerto Rico), and *Tejedoras de vida: Puerto Rico, España y New York*, directed by Sonia Fritz, on the transnational connections of the needlework industries. Another film by Fritz, the docudrama *Luisa Capetillo: Pasión de justicia*, loosely based on Valle-Ferrer's biography of the historical figure, uses reenactments and Capetillo's writings to depict her work in tobacco factories, as a political activist and union organizer.

These documentary films have urged debates over subjectivity vs. truth, leading critics to note that all historical representation is "manipulated"–incomplete, selective, and at the service of particular interests–and that the value of cinematic representation lays in its capacity to "engage the issues, ideas, data and arguments of [the] ongoing discourse" (Rosenstone 128) of history, through "images that are at once invented and might still be considered true; true in that they symbolize, condense or summarize larger amounts of data; true in that they carry out the overall meaning of the past which can be verified, documented or reasonably argued" (128). This perspective emphasizes film's capacity to rethink "official" history by using cinematic conventions like editing and reenactments. Consequently, the analysis of these documentary texts poses a number of questions: Why were tobacco factories the first to employ women in large numbers, and the first to "produce" feminist labor organizers like Capetillo, who combined the occupations of worker, reader, journalist and union activist? How did the factory enable the creation of a working-class and feminist consciousness? How did women in tobacco factories develop a political consciousness different from that of women doing needlework in the home, and how did this difference shape feminist and class discourses of the Puerto Rican nation?

### HISTORY AND REPRESENTATION: TOBACCO AND THE CIGAR-MAKING FACTORY

Up until the mid-19th century, Puerto Rican tobacco was processed in workshops by means of a Spanish method that involved the handcrafting of tobacco leaves by artisans, individually or in workshops that employed a small number of craftsmen, no more than four in most cases (Quintero-Rivera, "Socialist" 24). The emergence of the tobacco industry in Puerto Rico in the late 19th century "formed part of the transfer of Cuban cigar making to other countries as manufacturers attempted to participate in the bonanza of the Havana cigar by imitating its production" (Baldrich, "From Handcrafted Tobacco" 153). As a consequence, cigar-making factories began to operate in cities like New York, Key West, Tampa and San Juan, at first employing men, and soon thereafter, women. Even though the tobacco industry prospered in Puerto Rico after 1898, "a pesar de que el cultivo del tabaco era de pequeña escala y predominaba la propiedad puertorriqueña, alrededor de 80 a 85 por ciento de la fase manufacturera del negocio lo controlaba el capital norteamericano" (Dietz *Historia* 135). Companies like the Puerto Rican-American Tobacco Company and the New York Tampa Cigar Company employed workers and dictated hourly wages and working conditions in cigar factories on the island. This economic control would later impact the emergence of class consciousness and of the labor movement in Puerto Rico.

As tobacco factories grew in size and capacity, they represented a progressively larger part of the Puerto Rican economy. By 1910, "74.6 percent of all industrial tobacco workers were employed in centers with more than a hundred employees" (Quintero-Rivera, "Socialist" 31), while factories that employed over a thousand workers at a time "were found only in the tobacco industry, and these employed 35.9 percent of all cigarmakers" (31). The expansion continued in the second decade of the twentieth century, and by 1918 "el tabaco pasó a ser el segundo renglón más importante de la exportación, reemplazando al café" (Dietz *Historia* 133). This growth produced a demand for workers so great that factory owners found themselves in need of employing women, who, up until that point, had only worked in the home, as laundresses, domestic servants, or in the needlework industry, which was still based in the house.

The early data on the incorporation of women in the salaried workforce is contradictory. While studying the occupational distribution in Utuado, Fernando Picó notes that very few women "dirigen sus propias tiendas, fincas y negocios. La documentación administrativa tiende a reforzar la visión de la mujer pasiva en la sociedad agraria puertorriqueña del siglo XIX" (F. Picó "Al filo del poder" 174). At the same time, island-wide data recorded in the 1899 census shows that "más de 60,000 mujeres de todas las edades trabajaban fuera de su hogar pero la gran mayoría de ellas lo hacían en calidad de criadas (18,453), lavanderas (16,855), modistas y costureras (5,785). Solamente 3,910 fueron clasificadas por el censo como obreras" (I. Picó 23). Part of the reason for this disparity might be the nature of the historical records and the tendency to diminish women's salaried labor until the latter part of the 19th century.

The tobacco industry expanded the salaried labor opportunities for women in the aftermath of the U.S. invasion of Puerto Rico, and in the context of foreign capital's need for cheap labor (I. Picó 23). In the tobacco factories, women's employment as "stemmers and leaf-classers represented, for the most part, their first contact with capitalist relations of production" (Baldrich, "Gender and Decomposition" 108). In the first decade of the 20th century, nearly 80% of tobacco workers were women (Dietz *Historia* 145), a number comparable only to the needlework industry, in which women occupied 85% of the workforce (145). While the majority of women in the tobacco industry were employed in large factories, some continued to work in local chinchales (Baldrich, "Gender and Decomposition" 116), where they were paid even less than leaf-strippers or leaf-classers employed by U.S. companies (Quintero-Rivera, "Socialist" 24).

Even though the incorporation of women in the salaried workforce and in the tobacco industry in particular provoked profound social and economic changes, it would be erroneous to think of their work outside the home as an indication of gender equality. In addition to tobacco factories, "los salarios por debajo del nivel de subsistencia y el exceso de horas laborales eran comunes en todas las demás labores realizadas en talleres y fábricas" (I. Picó 28-29). This was especially true in the case of women in the needlework industry, in which the levels of exploitation reached an infamous peak, as evidenced in Dominga de la Cruz's description of her experience with needlework in the early decades of the 20th century: "you can't imagine what work was like. We worked by the light of the lantern until two in the morning, day after day. And we were poorly nourished" (Dominga de la Cruz, quoted in Romero-Cesáreo 783).


The Home as Factory: Women in the Needlework Industry

Even though the cigar-making factory was one of the principal workplaces for women at the end of the 19th and at the beginning of the 20th century, it was not the only one. In the domestic space, traditionally associated with unpaid feminine labor, women began to enter a different section of the salaried workforce, involving piecework, in particular needlework in the garment industry.

The needlework industry in Puerto Rico was born out of the necessity to expand the geographical area in which fine garments were produced. Its origins "lay in the commercial crisis brought on by World War I, which forced a halt in the export of finely sewn and embroidered garments and linen from Europe" (Boris 36), mostly to the United States. This complemented the devastating effects of the San Ciriaco hurricane that hit the island in 1899, destroyed crops and forced many to move from rural to urban areas, augmenting the cheap urban workforce (Arcelay Santiago 27). The types of products of the needlework industry encompassed a broad range of items: "Los artículos de algodón que se exportaban eran vestidos, faldas, blusas, ropa interior y pañuelos y otros artículos en cantidades más pequeñas" (Dietz *Historia* 136). The work was part of a hierarchical system in which women were usually supervised by male contractors and subcontractors (Dietz 136) who benefited from the women's work more than the women themselves.

The Puerto Rican government made a conscious effort to incorporate women in the needlework industry, in part because of the demand from the US, and in part because needlework was seen as a "feminine" occupation.[1] In order to prepare girls for piecework, "in 1918, the public schools in Mayagüez adopted a needlework curriculum for all of its schools" (Boris 36). This education began in elementary school, and occupied about half of the girls' curriculum (Dietz *Historia* 136). This early preparation for women's insertion into the labor force was part of the development of capital, as "las exigencias del capital han transferido el trabajo doméstico a la esfera del mercado de trabajo asalariado y han elaborado una división del trabajo acorde con la socialización política sexual, asociando estos trabajos como 'trabajos de mujeres'" (Ostolaza Bey 70). In the case of Puerto Rico, the early education of girls into the craft of the needlework "era parte de un proceso más amplio en el que los Estados Unidos, como estado colonial, ofrecían el adiestramiento, las destrezas y el conocimiento necesarios para la acumulación de capital y la producción lucrativa para los capitalistas norteamericanos y para los pocos empresarios puertorriqueños que se asociaban a ese proceso" (Dietz *Historia* 136)–in other words, even though girls and young women were the main producers in the needlework industry, they were the ones who benefited the least from their labor.

The statistics associated with piecework reveal the level of exploitation in the industry. The majority of women–75% in 1935-1963–were between 16 and 35 years of age (Boris 41), young and in a physical condition that allowed them to work during late hours, with little light, and in harrowing conditions:

> Most of these workers lived in cramped and drafty shacks in outlying mountain regions, on sugar and tobacco haciendas, and along the swampy outskirts of towns. Receiving their bundles of

---

[1] It is hard, if not impossible, to find any record of male workers in the garment industry, other than contractors and subcontractors. In an isolated testimony in the documentary *Tejedoras de vida*, a man hesitantly admits that he knows of men that knew how to make mundillo, the elaborate lace for which Puerto Rico has become famous.

work from subcontractors known on the island as comisionistas, homeworking needle women labored for piece rates equivalent to one or two cents an hour in order to eke out cash in an economy that offered them few other opportunities (Boris 35).

In her testimonio Dominga de la Cruz depicts similar conditions, and alludes to "the double exploitation" by foreign factory owners and by Puerto Rican intermediaries, exploitation characterized by long hours, poor nutrition and night work (783). The abuse of female labor occurred not only in factories, under direct supervision from the factory owners, but also in women's homes, due to women's unpaid domestic work, and due to the insufficient pay and the appalling working conditions.

The name most frequently associated with the exploitation of women in the needlework industry in Puerto Rico is, ironically, that of a woman, María Luisa Arcelay, first a teacher in Mayagüez, then a garment workshop owner that employed women and children, and the first female elected official in Puerto Rico (elected to the Legislature in 1932 and 1936). While Carmen Arcelay Santiago's biography of María Luisa Arcelay presents a rather idealized perspective, references in other historical accounts claim that "she showed no interest whatsoever in women's issues" (Barceló-Miller 138) and offer a glimpse at the exploitation to which the women working in her workshop were subjected.

According to Arcelay Santiago, María Luisa Arcelay offered an opportunity to women and children to work and earn wages that they otherwise would not have had. Hers was one of the first workshops to open in Mayagüez, in 1917, and at its peak it employed up to 400 people (Arcelay Santiago 32). In 1939 she used her power as an elected official to introduce Law 663, which insisted on the implementation of a "reasonable minimum wage" (103)–ironically, without demanding a specific minimum wage. Every workshop owner was obliged to consider what would be a reasonable wage for his or her workers. While in the context of the proposal this was justified as a step towards the fair treatment of workers, in reality it responded to the protests of factory and workshop owners and subcontractors, who threatened to close their shops should a minimum wage be written into law. In this sense, Arcelay used her access to political power to cement her economic status and the dominant position of her social class.

What this biography doesn't mention are the strikes organized by Arcelay's workers, and the violence with which the Puerto Rican authorities at that time confronted them. While Arcelay Santiago depicts Arcelay's relationship with striking workers as one of reason and understanding, and even presents her as a victim ("María Luisa salió de su taller a explicarles a las manifestantes que las trabajadoras no se unirían a la manifestación. Los huelguistas le tiraron con piedras a María Luisa," 61), Eileen Boris testifies as to the way in which "Police called to protect employer property, ended up killing and wounding strikers who had stoned the workshop of Representative María Luisa Arcelay" (Boris 39). This episode refers to the violence and exploitation to which workers, mostly women, were subjected in the needlework industry, as they worked in conditions that threatened their health and as they received wages that hardly responded to the amount, the duration and the nature of their work. It is out of such reality that social and feminist activists like Luisa Capetillo emerge to critique the hierarchy of labor and the relationships between workers, factory owners, and the Puerto Rican state.

## GENDER, LABOR AND THE INTERSECTIONALITY OF OPPRESSIONS

The unjust and often violent labor practices to which female workers were subjected in the tobacco and needlework industries were a result of what Patricia Hill Collins has called intersectionality, or "particular forms of intersecting oppressions, for example, intersections of race and gender, or of sexuality and nation. Intersectional paradigms remind us that oppression cannot be reduced to one fundamental type, and that oppressions work together in producing injustice" (Hill Collins *Black Feminist Thought* 18). According to this theoretical framework, "Intersectional paradigms view race, class, gender, sexuality, ethnicity, and age, among others, as mutually constructing systems of power [that] permeate all social relations" (Hill Collins *Black Sexual Politics* 11). As part of this paradigm, patriarchy is complicit with racism and classism in the reproduction of a hierarchical system of power relations that encompasses the symbolic and the everyday manifestations of women's work, rights, and access. In a poignant example, Hill Collins notes that, "Historically, many White families in both the middle class and working class were able to maintain their class position because they used Black women domestic workers as a source of cheap labor" (Hill Collins *Black Feminist Thought* 74). This case is representative of a long tradition of subordination based on class, race and gender, as the domestic workers to which she refers are always female, black and working-class.

In the context of female Puerto Rican factory workers, an analysis through the prism of the intersectionality of oppressions reveals the ways in which, as Ramón Grosfoguel explains, female workers were incorporated into the expansion of the capitalist world-system, which was "structured and reinforced" over the course of the 19th century "together with a gender, sexual and racial hierarchy" (Grosfoguel). This expansion perpetuated "what has been called 'the new racism' in the reproduction of imagined historical borders that excludes colonial people from access to equal rights within the core of the capitalist world-economy" (Grosfoguel), and maintained "a colonial labor force that served as cheap labor" (Grosfoguel). Female Puerto Rican factory workers were seen as second-class citizens because of their gender and race, in a context that already constructed them as second-class colonial citizens. Race and gender only contributed to their exploitation and to the difficulty in resisting a global system that reproduced itself through rigid social hierarchies.

Puerto Rican historians, sociologists and cultural critics have brought to the forefront the intersecting oppressions that Puerto Rican women have faced over the course of the 20th Century, and in the island's specific colonial context. By studying "how the once-again colonized laboring poor of this island became constructed as the wayward of criminal subjects of the new colonialist law and order through the deployment of socioeconomic, political, and signification systems" (Santiago-Valles 5), Kelvin Santiago-Valles explains how social antagonisms were racialized in 1920s Puerto Rico:

> disorder not only unfolded as always already feminized and sexualized within many of the textual practices of the Creole propertied and educated classes: it also materialized as metonymically racialized in terms of being hidden, shadowy, dark. Once again, like children, all females, and the impoverished majorities in general, the black and mulatto laborers of the coast and urban areas would accordingly incarnate similar tropes. 'They' became cast as native, innocent, and dependent including corollary attributes such as ignorance and vulgarity (Santiago-Valles 105).

By calling the subjects that he studies "dispossessed laborers" and "colonized laboring classes" (144) Santiago-Valles emphasizes that elite rhetoric constructed them in terms of both class and gender, representing them as subdued or dangerous, as was needed or convenient for the reproduction of the social hierarchies.

In relation to women, intersecting hierarchies and structures of oppression were evident in the controversy that surrounded the women's suffrage movement, which was opposed by elite Creole male sectors that saw working-class women's illiteracy as an inherent disqualifying characteristic. At the time, critics of the movement worried that giving poor women then right to vote "signified making suspect the dignity and rank of 'our mothers, wives, and daughters' insofar as the latter would be sharing the identical social space of the common whore. This also raised questions about the manhood of the Creole (man) incapable of (paternalistically) protecting 'his' women from being confused with streetwalkers" (Jiménez-Muñoz 162). As Jiménez-Muñoz explains, this type of discourse equates lower-class women with prostitution, and implicitly with blackness and with transgressive sexuality. It also explicitly mentions space, the separate spaces that upper-class and lower-class women were to occupy in the fragmented space of the nation. Such rhetoric uncovers yet again the multiple hierarchical structures against which Afro-descendant, working-class Puerto Rican women had to struggle. Their social worth was questioned on the basis of their gender, but also on the bases of their class position, which, in many cases, was constructed alongside corresponding images of race and sexuality.

The intersectionality of oppression also offers a theoretical matrix for understanding the structures of domination that the women in the Puerto Rican cigar-making and needlework industries faced. Their work was gendered–in the case of the *despalilladoras*, they were given what factory owners understood as "female" work within the industry, just as the labor in the needlework shops or in the women's homes was defined as more "domestic" and intrinsically female. However, this work was not done by upper-class white women. It was the domain of lower- and working-class women, the majority of whom were black or of mixed race, and whose race, class, and gender were what positioned them in the factories, in the *chinchales* and in the workshops operated by local and foreign capital. This intersectionality of racial, class and gender oppression spread across generations, for a variety of reasons. On the one hand, it was structurally perpetuated, as public schools in different cities adopted a curriculum to teach girls at the elementary level the skills of sewing and embroidery (Dietz *Historia* 136). On the other, it was a reflection of the limited options that black, working-class women had when entering the salaried workforce. In that sense, the subsequent sections on women's labor mobilization, on Luisa Capetillo's work as a union organizer and an intellectual, and on the response to mass female sterilization in factories sketch "a map of the various ways that practices of dominance are simultaneously knitted into the interstices of multiple institutions as well as into everyday life" (J. Alexander 4), and introduce some of the strategies of resistance that women have elaborated to respond to these intersecting sources of oppression.

## Union Organization, Women's and Workers' Rights

The increase in the employment of women in factories and workshops in a variety of industries came during the wider process of the proletarization of "urban workers [whose identification changed] from artisans to proletarians, mainly in the development of large tobacco-processing establishments" (Quintero-Rivera, "Socialist" 19). While it was men who first began to organize in unions, women soon joined the fight for fair treatment, working conditions and compensation.

The inclusion of women in the factory workforce and their subsequent (albeit gradual and difficult) struggle for labor rights, resulted in a situation in which male workers, female workers and unions entered a complex relationship defined by conflicting interests. Men understood that the incorporation of women in the union system affected them in both positive and negative ways:

> Class pulled women together while gender pushed them apart. Class brought them together as workers in their common opposition to the fabricant. Gender kept them apart because cigar-making became a male domain once men excluded women at the beginning of the factory system during the last quarter of the nineteenth century. Cigar-makers' unions reflected these conflicting tendencies. Unions encouraged women to organize as stem-

mers, classers, and the like. Men did not stimulate women to become cigar-makers and had misgivings before accepting them in the occupations of the reorganized craft (Baldrich, "Gender" 107).

While the FLT (Federación Libre de Trabajadores, the largest union organization at the time) and other cigar-makers' unions recruited women, men opposed women's employment in factories as "part of their own [men's] struggle against capital. Their uneasiness with women in cigar-making was tinged with the same paternalism that manufacturers considered in hiring them: the devaluation of labor" (119). As a consequence, women faced not only the systems of capital and colonialism (in that the factories often operated with U.S.-based capital), but also a perception of female work as less valuable, resulting in men's fear of and opposition to women's salaried employment.

In spite of these obstacles, women solidified their participation in factories and their involvement in labor unions, traveled around the island to raise consciousness among workers in different regions, and voiced their dissatisfaction with their working conditions. As early as 1911, "hay noticias de huelgas de despalilladoras en Utuado por aumento de sueldos" (F. Picó "Al filo del poder" 180). These initiatives inspired the development of class consciousness and the transformation of the relationship between gender, class, national belonging and the space of the factory.

The incorporation of women in the workforce signified at least a partial shift away from women's association with the space of the home:

> para muchas mujeres solteras el trabajo asalariado en los talleres, a diferencia del trabajo remunerado por tarea de las lavanderas o planchadoras, o el trabajo como criada, muchas veces residente, de las cocineras, representó una independencia relativa respecto a la estructura de la vida doméstica tradicional. También puso en contacto cotidiano a las trabajadoras con sus pares en el taller, y las inició en una serie de luchas reivindicativas (F. Picó "Al filo del poder" 194).

In spite of these changes, women's incorporation in the salaried workforce was not a sufficient condition for the de-feminization of domestic work. It also brought about "una carga dual para muchas mujeres, puesto que ellas son igualmente responsables de las labores domésticas y del cuidado de los niños (Safa "Conciencia" 159). Women were still expected to perform the tasks commonly identified as "feminine" and "maternal." While the space of the factory became feminized, the home did not become associated with masculinity.

For both men and women, the transformation of the space of the factory included the introduction of *lectores*, of factory readers, who contributed to the construction of workers' socialist and anarchist consciousness by introducing them to political and philosophical texts and ideas. In most cases, they were hired directly by the workers, and their position was more egalitarian than most, as both men and women could occupy it.

The readers became an institution in the cigar-making factories in the latter part of the 19th century. The biography of Luisa Capetillo, one of the most notable readers in Puerto Rico and later in New York and Ybor City, describes the setting and the interaction between readers and factory workers:

> El lector se sentaba o se paraba frente a un podio y leía en voz clara y alta para que los obreros que despalillaban las hojas de tabaco, y aquellos que manufacturaban los cigarros, los escucharan. Era costumbre que los obreros, si deseaban que el lector repitiera una o más veces cierto pasaje pegaran con sus instrumentos de trabajo o el tenedor de despalillar en la mesa, y el lector podría repetir infinitamente un pasaje en particular (Valle Ferrer 60).

The texts were chosen carefully, after a democratic vote among the workers. The hall would elect a president, who would propose and submit to a vote the texts that would be read in the factory the following day. Among the texts that became well known on the factory floors were socialist newspapers like *Social Future*, *Democracy* and *Labor Union*, which often "published passages about or by outstanding women in the socialist and feminist struggles: names like Madame Roland, Clara Zetkin, and Rosa Luxembourg were frequently mentioned" (Romero-Cesáreo 778). Among the texts were "classic essays on anarcho-syndicalist or socialist politics" and "chapters from a novel selected by the workers and read serially over several days" (Hewitt 123). The variety of texts and themes gives an idea of the rich education that the workers received and of the readers' significance in the space of the factory. Through the *lec-*

*tores* and the *círculos de studio* (workers' discussion groups), factory workers, including illiterate ones, became "one of the best-informed and best-instructed groups in Puerto Rican society" (Quintero-Rivera, "Socialist" 27), a reality that was even more important for women, who rarely benefited from the same formal education as men (Sánchez-González 24).

Even though factory owners were hostile to the political leadership of factory readers, "cigar workers made it clear they would fight as vehemently for their right to employ readers as they did for higher wages, better working conditions, and union recognition; and by the 1910s, the institution had become entrenched (Hewitt 129). The owners' opposition and the workers' insistence on preserving the practice of factory reading bear witness to the significance that readers had in both male and female cigarmakers' lives.

The development of the Puerto Rican feminist movement, which had originated in the 19th century, was closely related to the workers' struggle for equality in the factories:

> La modernización de la industria tabaquera no sólo proletizó a los artesanos, sino que a su vez incorporó tanto a niños como a mujeres en todas las etapas de la producción del cigarro. No es casual, en ese sentido, que los primeros fermentos del feminismo en Puerto Rico se dieran en las fábricas de cigarros, bastante antes que se consolidara el movimiento sufragista en las décadas del veinte (Ramos, "Luisa Capetillo" 238).

Ramos situates in the space of the factory the emergence of Puerto Rican feminism as an organized, political movement. The first reason for that is the concentration of women who shared a reality of economic struggle and gender inequality in the home and in the workplace. The second surely involves the mention of children–an organized struggle for women's rights would improve the treatment of children both in the workplace and in the home, whether through better working conditions and the regulation of child labor, or through the women's increased salaries and healthier work environment.

Beyond the struggle for equality, women's work in the cigar-making factories had the broader political implication of allowing women the opportunity of economic emancipation. The origins of the struggle for women's rights and for the recognition of the value of women's work "emerged as women began to participate directly in the productive process and enjoy an independent status in economic life. This began, at least on a significant scale, with the growth of the tobacco-processing industry during the first decade of the twentieth century" (Quintero-Rivera, "Socialist" 24). This economic independence then paved the way for the incorporation of women in other areas of labor, beyond the factory floor.

As Jacqui Alexander has argued, the kind of critical consciousness that emerged in the tobacco factories in Puerto Rico "bespeaks the different ways in which women have reinscribed work with dignity. This consciousness takes concrete shape as daily practice within organizations that brings both individual and collective self-definition to women as workers" (Alexander 104-105). A significant aspect of this self-definition involves the ways in which the process of women's incorporation in the workforce gradually transformed the relationships between male and female workers in the tobacco factories. Labor solidarity against exploitation "overrode the traditional differentiation of sexes as they developed together a common struggle" (Quintero-Rivera, "Socialist" 25). One example of this common struggle can be seen in the change of the attitude of male workers towards female workers. Instead of thinking of women as an enemy in the fight for fair pay and working conditions, men began to see them as "comrades," a name used "not only among the new female proletarians, but also among their male fellow workers and among the traditional groups of artisans with whom they shared their daily community life" (25). As women's common purpose became evident through their involvement with unions and workers' rights, the way in which male workers saw them also began to change, gradually resulting in solidarity and in a common fight for justice in the workplace.

## LUISA CAPETILLO, GENDER AND WORKING-CLASS CONSCIOUSNESS

In the course of the 20th century, Puerto Rican female writers have looked beyond the national imaginary to envision alternative communities organized around equality, justice and women's rights. Among the first of these writers was Luisa Capetillo, a socialist and self-proclaimed anarchist who worked as a journalist and a reader in tobacco factories in Puerto Rico and in the United States.

Capetillo was born in Arecibo, Puerto Rico, in 1879, in a progressive family that valued education at a time when it was not readily available to women. Her association with the labor movement began in the early 1900s. Her first participation in organized labor protests dates back to 1907, when she took part in a tobacco workers' strike (Golden and Findlen 36). She joined the Federación Libre de Trabajadores "via one of its strongest affiliates, La Federación de Torcedores de Tabaco (FTT), the tobacco workers' union. [She] became immersed in the radical politics embraced by its members and their counterparts throughout the Caribbean" (Hewitt 123). Her work as a journalist was as an indispensable part of her struggle for workers' rights. In 1910 she began writing for *Unión Obrera*, the FLT's newspaper (Hewitt 123), and in the same year founded her own newspaper, *La Mujer*, dedicated to women's rights. Her work as a labor organizer in cigar factories in Puerto Rico, New York, and Ybor City, Florida, positions her not only as a Puerto Rican, but also as a Latina and international thinker and activist who steps outside the traditional understanding of the relationship between space, gender, sexuality and labor, and who connects island and metropolis, labor rights and women's rights, and Puerto Rican and other Caribbean workers in spaces like the factory, the tribune and the newspaper.

Capetillo wrote four books: *Ensayos libertarios* (1907); *La humanidad en el futuro* (1910); *Mi opinión sobre las libertades, derechos y deberes de la mujer* (1911); and *Influencias de las ideas modernas* (1916). In these books, she emphasizes the importance of her involvement in the factory, in labor unions like the Federación Libre de Trabajadores, and her passion for the defense of women's rights, causes she sees as universal rather than restricted by national boundaries and affiliations. She confronts traditional paternalist discourse, and morality and marriage as its technologies of power (Foucault), using the language of the working class: "Mujeres de todas las posiciones defendeos, que el enemigo es formidable, pero no le temáis, que según es el tamaño es su cobardía!" (Ramos 195). By rephrasing the international worker's slogan, Capetillo links the factory to gender and at the same time denounces the marginalization and the perceived inconsequentiality of women in Puerto Rican society. She emphasizes the connection that exists between women's rights and workers' rights through their labor, claiming that both must be recognized and defended not just nationally, but universally.

The problem of space is fundamental for Capetillo's discussion of class, gender and nation, as in her work "class relations could be understood as having a spatial form. The geography of social structure is a geography of class relations" (Massey 22). In Capetillo's writing, space fulfills a variety of functions–of marginalization and exploitation, but also of resistance and of the creation of a consciousness intended to build educational, labor and women's rights. She depicts class relations through a series of spaces and suggests that the anarcho-socialist model that she proposes has a spatial dimension that conditions the shift in class and gender relations that Capetillo imagines.

The four spaces that interact to construct the relationship between gender, sexuality, space and the Puerto Rican nation in Capetillo's work are the factory, the public forum, the home and the page, from which she constructs her philosophy of labor and women's rights, and ultimately her own notion of an ideal society. These spaces form "a complex web of relations of domination and subordination, of solidarity and co-operation" (Massey 265) that constructs Capetillo's model of society.

Capetillo's ideas about workers' and women's rights emerge alongside her critique of the traditional gender roles at the level of the family, of the symbolic space of the family house, and of the Puerto Rican nation. Even though Capetillo disidentifies from the discourse of *la gran familia puertorriqueña*, a notion that was already familiar in the late 19th century, her critique is directed at a set of hierarchies associated with that social model.

Capetillo's rejection of the model of the national family originates with a critique of the institution of marriage sanctioned by the state and by the Catholic Church. Unlike other early feminists, she rejects the artificiality and the oppression of marriage. She explains that "Para formar matrimonio no se necesita sanción de las leyes ni seguir costumbre alguna establecida. La voluntad de dos seres humanos de ambos sexos es suficiente para formarlo y construir un hogar" (Capetillo, *Mi opinión* 138). For her, the traditional catholic and state-sanctioned marriage is hypocritical: "En la actual sociedad la mujer se casa por seguir la costumbre. Y el hombre á veces para tener una ayuda ó esclava" (161). Instead, Capetillo proposes the concept of free marriage, without civic or religious laws, based on "leyes naturales" (164), as an expression of her anarchist ideas that insist on "rechazar toda atadura legal que proviene de las leyes creadas por el Estado, como las de la educación y las del matrimonio" (da Cunha 55). Free marriage appears to be the only way in which a man and a woman can enter or terminate a relationship that might not satisfy their emotional needs:

> Y si es la mujer la que está aburrida y cansada de su esposo, y este a pesar de conocer ó comprender que molesta, que fastidia; persiste en la idea de retenerla por que la quiere, pero no ha sabido ó no ha querido captarse sus simpatías ó su cariño, ó no ha querido, ó le ha sido indiferente, creyendo que por que ella está casada con el tiene la obligación de aceptarla sin haberla conquistado, es un . . . grosero, y esta mujer está en su derecho y deber natural de repararse por todos los medios y no engañarse a sí misma, ni engañar a los demás (Capetillo *Mi opinión* 150).

Similarly, according to the author, in the case of infidelity, "La mujer tiene derecho á separarse del marido infiel" (Capetillo *Mi opinión* 142). This relationship epitomizes what Capetillo calls "free love," the only union that a woman should accept.

As a way of critiquing the traditional family and marriage norms, Capetillo distinguishes between love and marriage, and between love and desire, approaching the topic of sexuality in a manner more open than any of her predecessors. She warns, "Que no se confunda el amor con el matrimonio. El matrimonio es una convención social; el amor es una ley natural. El matrimonio es un contrato; el amor es un besar. El matrimonio es una cárcel [. . .]. El matrimonio es la prostitución del amor (Capetillo, *Mi opinión* 172). With this warning, she implicitly rejects the traditional (and in her time already familiar) notion of the *gran familia puertorriqueña*, by attacking the normalization of the institution of the family, the basic unit of the nation governed by the interests of the state, and introduces an alternative concept of the national family that thrives in anarchism and for which the law of the state is an unnecessary limitation.

Capetillo also critiques the patriarchal establishment for keeping the woman in the house, as a mother and housewife, by claiming that her absence from the home would imperil the wellbeing of her children and her marriage, thus privileging middle- and upperclass families, in which women don't necessarily need to work outside the home. She notes that, "el hogar protegido por las leyes, y las riquezas, se beneficia y se protege más y se olvida el hogar pobre. Se olvida que la familia pobre, en vez de enviar á sus hijos á la escuela los utiliza vendiendo frutas ó los tiene que alquilar, ó hacer trabajos superiores á su edad" (155). *La gran familia puertorriqueña*, in her view, excludes working and lower-class families who cannot afford to abide by the traditional model (in which women and children are positioned in the home), and who are marginalized by a national model that they inevitably support through their labor.

Instead of marriage by law, Capetillo proposes desire as the bond of "free marriage": "El amor es la comunión completa de dos cerebros, de dos corazones, de dos sensualidades. El deseo no es más que el capricho de dos seres que una misma voluptuosidad reúne. Nada es tan pasajero ó poco estable como el deseo; no obstante, ninguno de nosotros se escapa de él" (Capetillo, *Mi opinión* 177). She insists that both people have an equal obligation to fulfill their duties to one another in an exclusive relationship, and just like the woman is devoted to the man, the man should be devoted to the woman. In case that he doesn't fulfill his obligations, Capetillo poses a rhetorical question: "¿Si ese hombre no sabe ó no puede cumplir con los deberes de marido, por qué exije a su mujer que los cumpla? ¿Qué moral es ésta?" (Capetillo, *Mi opinión* 142). In this sense, the periphrasis of the international workers' slogan ("¡Mujeres de todas las posiciones defendeos, que el enemigo es formidable, pero no le temáis, que según es el tamaño es su cobardía" Capetillo, *Mi opinión* 161) acquires a new meaning. By using it as a call to solidarity and resistance, Capetillo empowers women by telling them that they already possess the power to resist patriarchal oppression. She disidentifies herself from the model of the *gran familia puertorriqueña* and proposes a different community model, based on free choice instead of law, rights and obligations.

Even though Capetillo critiques the stereotypical association of women with domestic space and labor, she emphasizes the importance of motherhood as a factor for their education and their social liberation: "Para Luisa Capetillo, la maternidad es una de las funciones más hermosas reservadas por la naturaleza a la mujer. Opinaba que se sentía un ser humano por haber parido" (Valle Ferrer 57). Capetillo uses motherhood to argue for women's education, noting that, "La mujer madre es la primera que educa, dirige al futuro monarca, como al ministro y presidente; al útil bracero y el inteligente educador. Ella forma, modela cuidadosamente, pero de un modo á veces equivocado, por falta de educación, casi siempre los futuros lejisladores y revolucionarios" (Capetillo, *Mi opinión* 143). This passage reproduces certain stereotypes of gender roles (the woman as mother who takes the principal care of children, and the male gender of the leaders that she mentions), associating mothernhood with domestic care and with unsalaried, if not always emotional labor. At the same time, she promotes women's access to education and wider social participation, demanding "the kind of education and social services that would allow women to act effectively in public as well as private spheres" (Hewitt 125), as "la madre instruída" (Capetillo, *Mi opinión* 144) is not educated only at school, but also through public participation. By positioning the mother as a teacher, Capetillo transforms the space of the house into a space of instruction, a necessary complement to the traditional school, and associates the space of the family house with the struggle for gender equality.

Capetillo's struggle for gender equality is inevitably connected to the fight for equal rights for workers, and the need for solidarity across social classes:

> Puerto Rico's first published working-class feminist is also the first to insist on elaborating class divisions between women, which she argues are habitually rationalized in Puerto Rican culture. Capetillo was especially intolerant of those women who feel entitled to their relative luxury while seeing others in their immediate vicinity–even women working long hours in their own homes–suffer for lack of the most basic necessities (Sánchez González 27).

Capetillo's understanding of the class hierarchy inspires her to make a direct call for solidarity to confront gender and labor oppression. In this sense, she transforms not only the space of the family house, but also that of the workplace–whether factory, workshop or the home as workplace–by identifying gender and class as two complementary axes of identity and bases of social resistance.

Capetillo elaborates her critique of the nation and of the national family by juxtaposing the space of the house against a series of other spaces–the factory, the newspaper and the public stage–and by emphasizing how class differences and solidarity point to the contradictory nature of the idealized Puerto Rican national model.

The space of the factory is present in Capetillo's writing through the figure of the worker. Her identification with workers in the cigar-making factories inspires her class consciousness that makes her claim that socialism, more than state institutions or nationalism, can be the solution for inequality and exploitation, and can lay the foundations of an egalitarian society: "Socialista soy, porque aspiro a que todos los adelantos, descubrimientos á invenciones establecidos, pertenezcan á todos, que se establezca la socialización sin privilegios. Algunos lo entienden con el estado, para que este regule la marcha, yo lo entiendo sin gobierno. [. . .] Socialismo ácrata" (Capetillo, *Mi opinión* 291). In Capetillo's society, "no son los intelectuales, ni los clérigos, ni los burgueses los que se transforman, sino que son los obreros los que transforman a la sociedad mediante una revolución pacífica del pensamiento y acción para convertir luego a los demás" (da Cunha 59). The space of the factory then becomes the source of new ideas on class, equality, justice and nation, according to a configuration that Capetillo sees as ethical and necessary in Puerto Rican society.

The space of the factory also becomes the matrix for the critique of the model of society that privileges a middle-class patriarchal identity. For Capetillo, "una nación no sería moderna mientras excluyera a la mayoría de sus ciudadanos de la sociedad y de las cuestiones de gobierno" (da Cunha 56). The main technology of marginalization and exclusion, according to Capetillo, is that of labor exploitation and unequal pay, a reality that the author equates with slavery in an allusion to the historical legacy of labor exploitation on the island: "La esclavitud del salario es la esclavitud moderna, que oprime y ha hecho y hará más hambrientos y criminales que la esclavitud de razas y la de la época colonial. Es más cruel, más injusta" (Capetillo, *Mi opinión* 295). As a result, the factory would become the site of a "revolución pacífica" (da Cunha 53) that would inspire a socialist-anarchist egalitarian community in which nationalism and state government would prioritize the rights and needs of workers, women and other previously marginalized groups.

The construction of gender and of the national imaginary occurs simultaneously on the public stage and in the newspaper, two spaces that can be understood in both literal and figurative ways.

During her involvement with La Cruzada Ideal (Capetillo, *Mi opinión* 298) Capetillo uses the public stage to educate factory workers, to raise consciousness and to organize them along axes of needs, rights and class identity. Her writing often resembles her speeches. She addresses workers and peasants directly, posing rhetorical questions, making appeals to them to see through the system of exploitation and to build a network of resistance. This tone is consistent throughout her work, from her earliest essays in *Ensayos libertarios* to *Mi opinión*:

> ¡Trabajadores! [. . .] ¿Dónde está el producto de vuestro trabajo? La Hermosa riqueza que producen el trabajo, el azucar y el café, dónde está? En las arcas del que os explota, que se ha hecho capitalista mientras careceis de concepto de ser humano. ¿Vuestro trabajo no produce? Y de donde extrae el que os explota tantos miles de dollars? ¿Qué es lo que produce? (Capetillo, *Mi opinión* 296).

From the metaphorical tribune of the page to the material stage she appeals for justice, as she again calls on the workers to "haced que los gobiernos que llevais a poder con vuestros votos, contraigan el deber de proporcionaros trabajo cuando no lo haya en otra parte" (260)–an example of her dedication to the construction of a nation that gives equal labor and education rights to women and working-class people.

Capetillo's use of the newspaper and the stage, and of the newspaper as a stage, situates her on the margin of the working class, as Julio Ramos has argued. Capetillo herself acknowledges and confronts this liminality in *Influencias de las ideas modernas*, in the essay "A un amigo barbero," recounting an incident in which she was told that "solamente los que aran la tierra son productores" (Ramos, *Amor y anarquía* 123). This apparent liminality, however, is also a step towards a social transformation, as Capetillo's access to the tribune and to the newspaper, her political consciousness and her education, were rights that she desired for all women and workers, not only for the select few with which some may have identified her. In this sense, her liminality, her position between the illiterate and the educated, the exploited, the socially conscious and active, is part of the process of social and political transformation in which she participated.

In her docudrama *Luisa Capetillo: pasión de justicia*, "una adaptación libre" (Fritz, *Luisa Capetillo*) of Norma Valle Ferrer's biography of Capetillo, Sonia Fritz employs the spaces of the page and the stage to comment on the construction of gender and nation in the author's work. As Capetillo is shown writing, a voiceover presents her ideas on workers' and women's rights, and as she reads to workers in the tobacco factory, the notion of "una nueva realidad" (Fritz, *Luisa Capetillo*) taken from Dostoyevski's *Crime and Punishment* alludes to her revolutionary feminist and socialist ideas.

In turn, the public stage emerges as a space that constitutes a complementary side of Capetillo's activist work. The film only alludes to this space through Capetillo's role in organizing factory strikes, but the space that substitutes that of the public tribune in the film is the theater stage. In addition to writing articles and political pamphlets, Capetillo was also the author of plays, whose themes ranged from the image of a utopian anarchist society to gender relations and social perceptions. The film presents Capetillo's life as a playwright whose ideas appeal to people in a way in which her essayistic writing does not always do. The play staged in Fritz's film addresses gender relations in a patriarchal society, and reaches its climax in a moment in which the main female character declares that "a mí no me interesa ser una señorita" (Fritz) and demands her freedom from virginity and from the expectation of marriage. The fact that the play is performed on the stage implies a certain degree of access and influence that the written page might not have had among workers with little formal education. In this sense, the stage becomes one more space where Capetillo builds "oppositional practices within and across multiple simultaneous sites" (Alexander 6). The stage emerges both as a site of representation and as a discursive space that allows the transformation of the relationship between gender, sexuality and the patriarchal family model of the Puerto Rican nation.

In Capetillo's work, the spaces of the factory, the home, the page and the stage interact with another space, that between Puerto Rico and the continental US, from New York to Ybor City. The diasporic space inhabited by Puerto Rican workers in the United States becomes a site for the critique of the national model and for the construction of a socialist and anarchist political identity. Her pamphlets and plays are among "the fin-de-siècle working class migrant generation's most avant-garde texts [and] comprise the foundational narrative enterprise of Boricua literary history" (Sánchez-González 21), along with activists and authors like Bernardo Vega and Jesús Colón. In this sense, it is important to recognize Capetillo as a transnational worker and writer, and as a Latina woman who offered an indispensable testimony of the life and work of the Puerto Rican and Latino community in the United States.

By crossing over from Puerto Rico to New York and Ybor City, Capetillo constructs a network of spaces that share common concerns of gender, sexuality, labor, rights and social justice. By taking her feminist and anarchist ideas from the factories in Puerto Rico to those in New York and Tampa, she imagines a common space imbued with the possibility of solidarity, of multiple axes of resistance, and of common goals of subverting a class hierarchy and of constructing an identity that prioritizes economic and social equality. The space of the factory is an indispensable part of this transnational space, as it is in the factories in Puerto Rico, New York and Tampa that her idea of justice crystallizes. Even though the workers don't share a common geographic space, the space of the factory acts as the common ground of their struggle for educational, economic and social justice.

## *Luchando por la vida*: Reenacting History in the Factory

In contrast to Capetillo's anarchist and anti-nationalist philosophy, contemporary documentary representations of the space of the factory have inserted women's work in Puerto Rican national history, positioning it as an integral part of the nation-building process. One such documentary is José Artemio Torres's *Luchando por la vida: las despalilladoras de tabaco y su mundo*, which focuses on the history of tobacco in the town of Comerío, and which makes women's factory work the primary instrument for the construction of Puerto Rican national history. The film is divided in two parts, the first providing the national context and the history of tobacco production in Comerío, and the second one consisting of interviews with former *despalilladoras de tabaco* (female tobacco stemmers), intertwined with a reenactment of women's labor in the factory.

The documentary's first section resembles an illustrated lecture on the history of the tobacco industry and on the intricacies of tobacco production and cigar-making in the town of Comerío. Much of the film's factual and statistical information comes from the work of historians Ángel Quintero-Rivera and Fernando Picó, who were also consultants for the film. With graphs and tables the documentary notes landmark years and numbers (annual quantity of production, rates of increase and decrease), and uses additional archival material to offer an overview of the history of tobacco production in Puerto Rico and to claim authority in its representation.

The film's claim to authenticity and veracity is enhanced by a number of elements of form and style, namely by the voiceover narration and by the editing. The male voice that recounts the history of Puerto Rican tobacco and its development in Comerío is intended to be that of the informed historian, the one who has the right to speak from and for the nation. Similarly, the juxtaposition of a variety of materials–from drawings of taínos using tobacco to photographs dating back to the early 20th century, to maps and pages from archival documents–adds a sense of authenticity to the narrative that is the context of the history of women's work in cigar-making factories.

The two spaces with which the film engages are those of the factory–the physical space and the memory of it, recreated through reenactments–and the space of the nation, also both material and symbolic, enabled by the factory and by women's labor.

The space of the factory is represented through archival photographs and through the reenactment in the final part of the film. The image of the tobacco factory that emerges through these representations is claustrophobic and crowded, characterized by restless labor. In the pictures and in the reenactment, the women are seated close to one another, in long rows behind tables on which piles of tobacco wait to be stemmed. As if to emphasize the traditionally perceived "feminine" quality of the space, the women gossip, tell jokes about pregnancy and motherhood, and discuss the fact that several generations of women in the same family have worked in the tobacco factory. These conversations construct a sense of community, of a shared space and of shared concerns, most having to do either with what the documentary understands as "women's" issues or with the work that women were performing in the factory. While some of the women, like Etelvina Rosario and Luz Falcón, do discuss the dismal working conditions and insufficient pay in the factory, the voice that provides the audience with the historical, political and economic reasons behind these conditions is the omniscient masculine voice of authority, of the historian who claims access to the truth. This presents a striking difference with the representation of the factory in the writings of Capetillo, whose feminist voice addresses economic and political problems. Consequently, the documentary filmmakers use the women's voices as examples and evidence, but not necessarily as the core of the history that they narrate.

Another difference, which at first sight appears curious, but in fact carries deeper implications for the representation of the factory and of women's work, is that, in the film, the institution of the reader is substituted with that of the radio. While this representation is "truthful" in the sense that most of the women represented in the film began working after the 1930s, when the *lectores* were no longer ubiquitous in cigar-making factories, it is notable for its implications for the representation of the women and of their political consciousness. While Valle-Ferrer makes extensive references to the variety of socialist and anarchist texts, newspaper articles on current events and politically charged literary works that the readers presented to the factory workers on a daily basis, the play that comes on the radio in the documentary is a melodramatic radionovela titled "Cuando amar es pecado" and protagonized by the actors Axel Anderson and Elena Montalbán, who were also the lead actors in the 1959 film *Maruja*, about a woman who comes to a tragic end because of her sexuality and desire to transgress traditional feminine roles. The fact that what the women listen to is a melodramatic radionovela that alludes to sinful love, and not a text associated with the politics of the times, is a sign of the film's desire to subdue certain issues associated with women's factory labor in order to facilitate their insertion in the cultural nationalist model by enforcing the consensus that lays in its foundations.

The filmmakers also recognize some of the contradictory, conflictive and exploitative aspects of factory work. Several women discuss issues like working conditions and low pay. In one of the most moving interviews in the film, Carmen Rosario (La Changa) even recounts an incident in which women stood up to a factory owner when he fired some of their coworkers, and refused to go back to work until he hired all of them back. Rosario recognizes the gender hierarchy involved in the confrontation–she remembers saying to the owner, "Sí, nosotras vamos a entrar. Por encima de usted que es un varón nosotras vamos a entrar" (*Luchando*)–but the interviewer's questions never take her story beyond the incident, to problematize the relationship between gender, class and labor. Instead, the victory appears more as a small act of conscientious workers, as a sacrifice that may have endangered their jobs, but which was resolved in a favorable way, through the owner's acceptance of the women's demands–yet another instance of consensus in the face of conflicting class interests.

In the documentary, the space of the nation also has two levels, a material and a symbolic one. The representation of the material, palpable, visible nation, the one that all viewers should recognize and with which they should identify, is quite traditional. It is based on images of land and maps, in which men either work the fields or map them, always in control of the form and of the representation of the "motherland". The maps, the long panning shots and the video footage of the countryside and of agricultural work are also examples of nostalgic images intended to allude to the island's history and to serve as triggers for a collective memory of a lifestyle that is disappearing.

As an extension of the material nation, a symbolic nation emerges from the space of the factory. By narrating the history of the tobacco factory and of the cigar-making process, and by presenting archival images of factories that employ hundreds of people, the films argues that the tobacco industry and the cigar factory acted as economic pillars of the Puerto Rican nation.

The space of the nation also emerges in the reenactments of factory work performed by the film's female protagonists. Reenactments offer the audience an idea of "how things were" but, in this case, are also problematic in that the perception is mediated first by the memory of the historical actors decades after the original events, and second, by the selectivity of the film editing that only allows on screen parts of what is reenacted. What most cinematic reenactments of history have in common, however, is that, like archival footage, they are intended to connect the present to the past, to bring the past to the present, always with a tinge of nostalgia and of longing for what was and for what might be lost. The juxtaposition of archival photographs of female factory workers with images of the contemporary reenactments serve to revive the collective memory by using the collective nature of factory work. In this way, the film evokes a common national history with which not only the women in the documentary, but also its viewers are invited to identify.

While it is true that the film addresses the working conditions and the insufficient compensation that *las despalilladoras* received, its ultimate goal is not to critique or to demand retribution. Instead, the film emphasizes the exploitation and the marginalization in order to represent them as necessary sacrifices and to depict the women not as victims but as martyrs for the national cause. This intention is most evident in the interview with Ana Gutiérrez Rosario, the daughter of a *despalilladora*, who explains that it is only decades after the fact that she understands her mother's sacrifice–the long working hours, the low pay and the daily separation from her children. Not coincidentally, the young woman is filmed standing outside, in the street, in the public space, in front of a car, a certain sign of modernity and progress which, the documentary suggests, were enabled by her mother's labor and sacrifice. This recognition, from daughter to mother and from woman to woman, legitimizes the factory work together with the context in which it was performed, and claims that, instead of looking at the women as subjects that were exploited, they should be regarded as (unconscious) builders of a sense of consensus and of a common national project.

The documentary rethinks women's protagonical role in the home, in the workplace and in the larger context of the nation. However, where it comes short is in its capacity to elucidate the exploitation that tainted their historical protagonism, and to expose the contradictions embedded in the apparent consensus of the Puerto Rican cultural nationalist model.

## Productive and Reproductive Labor in *La operación*

While Torres's film incorporates women workers into a cohesive national discourse, documentary filmmaker Ana María García critiques the state's abuse of women's productive and reproductive work, and the exploitation of their sexuality for the benefit of that same national discourse. Her documentary *La operación* uncovers the process of the mass sterilization of women of child-bearing age in Puerto Rico and examines the contraceptive pill testing conducted on working-class women from the 1940s to the 1960s. In García's analysis, Operation Bootstrap's discourse of "overpopulation [that] had to be controlled" (López 38) and the need for female labor in Puerto Rico after World War II served as the political justifications for the implementation of these practices, "consciously developed as a long-term solution" (38) to the island's economic problems. Some of the question that *La operación* poses are: What is the significance of the fact that a disproportionate number of sterilizations were done in the factories in which women worked, with the approval of their superiors? How does that fact transform the space of the factory, traditionally associated with production and capital? What does the film say about the relationship between gender, productive and reproductive labor, and the Puerto Rican nation?[2]

In the early years of the Estado Libre Asociado, sterilization became an official policy that claimed to allow women to move from the house to the factory and to assume new roles as workers and producers. As part of Operation Bootstrap, the new discourse on the family insisted that "para progresar había que tener una familia pequeña" (*La operación*). It was the reproduction of mostly lower-class women that had to be controlled, as "the programs aimed at bringing women into public birth control clinics target only the poor" (Safford 37). The responsibility of fulfilling the traditional roles of mother and housewife was not reciprocated by men's labor in the home. The notion of "progress" equated with fewer children and more income per capita per family was achieved through the control over women's bodies. Women became the instruments of the construction of the nation, but instruments in a process controlled by a patriarchal system that only allowed them to reproduce a specific national model. In this sense, state imposition of sterilization and population control to ensure women's participation in the nation is both ironic and violent. While it suppresses women's reproductive functions, rejecting the traditional image of the nation as a mother, it exploits their labor and their sexuality for the benefit of the very same nation-building process.

The use of the factory for the construction of the nation through the control of female labor was also a tool for the capitalist interests invested in the new national imaginary, and crystallized in the "causal relationship between the move to integrate women into the factory workforce and a government effort to promote the sterilization of women, which was free, and paid for by a US AID grant" (Falicov). In an interview for *La operación*, Dr. Antonio Silva, the notorious mastermind behind the sterilization campaign in Puerto Rico, explains,

> en las fábricas teníamos clínicas de planificación familial. Especialmente donde había un alto número de operarias mujeres. Entonces la companía les daba un break, de una hora, e iban a la

---

<sup>2</sup> For a discussion of reproductive rights in Puerto Rico, see Alice Colón Warren and Elsa Planell Larrinaga, "Silencios, presencias y debates sobre el aborto en Puerto Rico y el Caribe Hispánico" (2001).

> clínica de planificación familial. En la misma fábrica. Para que no
> tuvieran ni que ir al centro del pueblo. Y cuando los industriales
> se reunían en la asociación de industriales, yo iba y les hablaba y
> les decía, necesito la colaboración de ustedes. Y les teníamos nú-
> meros: miren, en los beneficios de maternidad que se ahorra la
> compañía nada más es para ustedes profitable dejar que esas mu-
> jeres dejen de trabajar una hora y vayan a la clínica de planifica-
> ción familial. Porque en el tiempo no solamente lo que le costaba
> a la compañía si tenía que pagarle el parto, pero los dos meses
> que la ley en Puerto Rico prescribe cuando una mujer da a luz,
> un mes antes y un mes después, que la productividad de esta per-
> sona que se pone en zero en esos dos meses, se significaba a la
> compañía millones de dólares (*La operación*).

His words are accompanied by scenes of women working in garment factories with a concentration that emphasizes their restless
labor and the need to earn a living–both elements exploited by the
desire for profit that transparent in Dr. Silva's narrative.

Dr. Silva's words make explicit the relationship between capital,
gender, and the control of space–by visiting family planning clinics
in the factory, women would not need to step out in the city, where
their time and their labor would be wasted. The quote also emphasizes the extent to which the capital needed for the construction of
the new Puerto Rican national model depended on the labor of
women–it was women who had to sacrifice having children in order
to make possible the ideal of progress. Dr. Silva also tacitly identifies working-class women with the foundations of the Puerto Rican
cultural nationalist model, as it is their labor, their time and their
national responsibility that foreign and domestic factory owners re-
quire to ensure the development of a number of industries needed
for the development of modernity and progress embedded in the
new Puerto Rican national imaginary.

The relationship between gender, colonialism and capital provides the organizing core of the documentary, but it has also been a
cause of criticism: "while the film is focused on a policy that affects
women as women (and very specifically, women's reproductive
choices), the film is not about women as gendered subjects in a patriarchy. Instead, it uses the stories of women as a metaphor to reveal
and critique U.S. colonialism on the Island" (Negrón-Muntaner, "Of
Lonesome" 240). Negrón-Muntaner sees this as part of a broader
trend in which "Puerto Rican women's film practices are deeply

rooted in a master narrative of anti-imperialism which impedes a gender specific analysis or an anti-colonial reading which questions its own nationalist premises" (241). While this has indeed been a trend in Puerto Rican women's filmmaking, and even though the gender-centered analysis is not paramount to the voiceover narration (which focuses on the historical context), the film's images and interviews do interrogate the gender-specific causes and implications of female sterilization. From discussions about men's refusal of vasectomies to images of women telling other women about the effects of the experimental contraceptive treatments, the film positions gender and sexuality in the center of the analysis of labor and nation, while the explanations of the relationship between Puerto Rico and the U.S. that Negrón-Muntaner critiques contextualize the complex mechanism of reproduction control in Puerto Rico.

The value of *La operación* lays not only in that it problematizes the intersection of gender, labor and nation in the factory, but also in that it serves as a historical document, as a testimony that gives voices and faces to the women that participated in the process of industrialization and nation-building, some of them willingly, others unwillingly and still others unwittingly. Even though the film uses archival material, still images and interviews with doctors and former government officials, a large portion of it is devoted to the stories of the women who worked in the factories and who visited the family clinics, where they were subjected to sterilization or given experimental contraceptive treatments with exaggerated hormone levels to their health's detriment. The women reveal the space of the factory not as a site of organized resistance (as in the case of Luisa Capetillo) but as a space of patriarchal control that they could only perceive as such years after the events, and to a great extent thanks to the director's provocative questions. In this sense, the documentary space of the film is juxtaposed against the space of the factory, and becomes in itself an instrument of denunciation of the exploitation of women that served the construction of the Puerto Rican cultural nationalist model.


CONCLUSION


The construction of gender, sexuality and the Puerto Rican nation takes place in a variety of spaces, of which the factory is one of the most problematic. At first sight, its relation to female work collides with its original association with masculinity, which goes back to the industrialization process of the 19th century. In spite of the factory's association with the male breadwinner, however, women have used that space to critique the gender hierarchies of the Puerto Rican nation. In response to these hierarchies, Puerto Rican working and writing women have re-gendered the space of the factory, "feminizing" it to construct a space in which women's rights can be reclaimed alongside workers' rights. Similarly, authors and film directors like Sonia Fritz and Ana María García have represented the struggles of female factory workers to critique the contradictions embedded in the Puerto Rican cultural nationalist model, and to propose alternative imaginaries. While some of these imaginaries maintain the possibility of building an egalitarian and just nation, others, like the one proposed by Luisa Capetillo, suggest an altogether different option–the idea that identities like class and gender can serve as the organizing axes of society, making the national model altogether obsolete.

The following chapter will focus on a series of novels and films that subvert the spatial trope of the house as the ideal model of the nation. It sets the stage for the subsequent discussion of spaces like the beauty salon and the brothel, and of their complex relationship with this national model, both as its matrices and as spaces of resistance that transgress the racial, gender and class hierarchies of Puerto Rican national discourse.

CHAPTER III

# RETHINKING *LA GRAN FAMILIA PUERTORRIQUEÑA* IN THE FAMILY HOUSE



## SPATIAL TROPES AND THE REPRESENTATION OF PUERTO RICAN NATIONAL CULTURE

THE family house has been the privileged setting of Puerto Rican texts that explore the intersections of gender, race, class, and nation. Since the late nineteenth century, authors like Manuel Zeno Gandía,[1] Antonio S. Pedreira,[2] René Marqués[3] and Edgardo Rodríguez Juliá[4] have depicted the house as the dominant site for the consolidation of traditional national models. Puerto Rican political and cultural discourse since the 1930s, in particular, has associated the space of the nation with the family house, often representative of a set of class and racial characteristics that cultural nationalism has identified with *la puertorriqueñidad*, the "authentic" Puerto Ri-

---

[1] In the tradition of late nineteenth-century naturalism, in *La Charca*, considered the first Puerto Rican novel, Zeno Gandía depicts a house fraught with violence and abuse, but uses these to critique the flaws of human nature.

[2] Even though the paternalist rhetoric embedded in the debates over the essence of Puerto Rican national culture predate Antonio S. Pedreira's *Insularismo*, his book is a prominent example of the early 20th century national cultural imaginary, characterized by specific racial and gender components, and pertaining to an elite section of the society of the 1930s.

[3] Marqués's play *Los soles truncos* uses the image of a family house in ruins, to critique the illness of colonialism, while his novel *La víspera del hombre* idealizes the house as a patriarchal space. For further analysis of these texts, see Juan Gelpí, *Literatura y paternalismo en Puerto Rico*.

[4] Rodríguez Juliá's recent novel *La piscina* evokes a sense of melancholia, loss and defeat in the aftermath of the death of the family patriarch.

can character. This association was formalized in the 1940s, when Luis Muñoz Marín's cultural nationalist ideology elaborated a discourse of national consolidation, making the family a metaphor for the cohesion of national culture, and the family house its symbolic space. Cultural nationalism constructed the national house through "la retórica del paternalismo [que] a menudo remite a las relaciones familiares, y su metáfora fundamental consiste en equiparar a la nación con una gran familia" (Gelpí 2).

This paternalist rhetoric was part of the cultural nationalism that foregrounded the constitution of Puerto Rico as a Commonwealth, or as Estado Libre Asociado. The populist ideology of *muñocismo*, named after Partido Popular Democrático's leader Luis Muñoz Marín, was accompanied by a political and economic vision that proposed to transform Puerto Rico into a model of development for other Caribbean nations. While the initial intention of Muñoz's ideas was "lograr mayor justicia e igualdad social" (Dietz "La reinvención"179), progress, understood as industrialization, urbanization, economic development and infrastructure, soon took over as the main priority of the national project (Dietz "La reinvención" 192-193). As part of this objective, the Puerto Rican government instituted Operación Manos a la Obra, or Operation Bootstrap–a development project that involved facilitating the entry of foreign capital in the island by offering them tax breaks and incentives. While the project led to some early success, it failed the Puerto Rican working classes in a number of ways. Populist politics tried to "implantar métodos de producción capitalistas del exterior, ofreciendo una fuerza laboral dócil, aunque bastante bien adiestrada, a las empresas extranjeras como la material prima para 'explotar'" (Dietz "La reinvención" 202). The policies benefited foreign investors more than the Puerto Rican people, and, in the long term, made the island's economy dependent on that of the United States: "La estrategia de Operación Manos a la Obra ligó aún más la economía puertorriqueña a los Estados Unidos, pero no la integró. La oferta del status de Estado Libre Asociado hecha al PPD en 1950, y su aceptación desde 1952, unió aún más el gobierno local a los Estados Unidos" (Dietz "La reinvención" 199). In political and economic terms, this particular vision of the island's future accepted few dissenting opinions, using the trope of national belonging, or of *la gran familia puertorriqueña*, to incorporate discursively those that, in practice, felt excluded, or who did not necessarily benefit from the country's economic direction at the time.

In his book *La memoria rota* Arcadio Díaz-Quiñones criticizes ELA's populist reliance on foundational myths in search of "una historia que uniera y no dividiera; una historia no conflictiva del 'pueblo' puertorriqueño" (Díaz-Quiñones *La memoria* 26-27) that would facilitate the national consensus that was the basis of ELA's proposal. Díaz-Quiñones blames these myths (the myth of 1940, and, I would suggest, the myth of *la gran familia*) of creating what he terms "una memoria rota" (26), a broken, incomplete memory of 20th-century Puerto Rican history that ignores and obscures the key contradictions of Muñoz Marín's political project. In order to problematize this broken collective memory, in recent decades historians and cultural critics have examined how, beginning in the late 1960s, PPD's cultural nationalist discourse entered in a crisis that had both economic and socio-cultural dimensions. In economic terms, "ya a finales de los años sesenta, el 'milagro económico' empezaba a desmoronarse, y en los últimos años entró en una crisis política, social y económica que ha llevado al país a una sombría frustración" (Díaz-Quiñones *La memoria* 122). Cultural institutions "desfallecieron intelectual y moralmente, o se consolidaron como estructuras antidemocráticas al servicio del poder, cerrando el paso a toda alternativa renovadora" (120), leaving little opportunity for debate or critique from within. And socially, "la crisis social interna–el aumento de las tasas de desempleo, la violencia imparable en las ciudades–despertó una nueva y voraz pasión por un pasado más complejo, y construyó otras reglas y otros espacios de validación intelectual y política" (66), through what Rubén Ríos Ávila has called the need to recuperate "la memoria de la historia olvidada" (Ríos Ávila *La raza cómica* 102). Ultimately, the crisis was expressed in multiple social domains, and affected the island in a variety of ways:

> De la crisis del 'modelo' hablan con elocuencia algunos hechos: la reducción dramática en la inversión industrial; una tasa de desocupados de más del 20%, según cifras oficiales, y a pesar de la emigración masiva; la dependencia cada vez mayor del programa federal de subsidios para la alimentación; la marginalización de amplios sectores de la población, el aumento espectacular de la delincuencia, la drogadicción y la violencia; la nueva militancia sindical y universitaria que han tenido que ser duramente reprimidas (Díaz-Quiñones *La memoria* 122).

In the realm of culture, this all-encompassing crisis led to a desire to rethink the intellectual pillars of cultural nationalism by questioning its voices of authority and authenticity. In the late 1960s and the early 1970s, critics and authors who positioned themselves outside ELA's project began to ask important questions about who constitutes the Puerto Rican nation, and who has the right to speak for it. One of the most productive proposals that emerged out of these debates was José Luis Gonález's idea of the four-storied house of national culture, and of *plebeyismo literario*, which exemplified his intent to empower critical voices that were marginalized in ELA's official discourse.

José Luis González was among the first to challenge the populist representations of Puerto Rican national culture and of its dominant symbols, mapping geographies of labor, resistance and agency. In 1979, his book *El país de cuatro pisos* transformed the literary configuration of the nation, arguing that the African component formed the foundation of a multilayered Puerto Rican nation (González 21-22). González called for a fundamental reexamination of the intersection between class and race, center and marginality that had defined that nation. Even though in González's work the house is still "una imagen sólida que no puede ser transmutada sin perder su estructura de significación" (Irizarry 163), it challenged the privilege of middle-class whiteness as the national model, and urged for a counterhegemonic alternative to the cultural nationalist discourse.

José Luis González bases his idea of *plebeyismo*, or of a view of Puerto Rican culture "from below" on a historical analysis, explaining that, after the arrival of U.S. capitalism, the Puerto Rican creole bourgeoisie, the class that, through the19th century, had fulfilled the role of leader and model for Puerto Rican society, began to lose "las bases materiales en que se asentaba su hegemonía cultural" (94). It was no longer "generadora y conductora de lo que ya podía concebirse como un destino nacional" (95), now determined much more by US economic interests. The loss of this prestige translated into the loss of a model that the popular classes had strived to emanate for centuries. However, it was also a moment of crisis that inspired the need for the creation of new models and images of national identity, a moment of crisis that fuels the process of plebeyismo that leads, as González argues, to the development of a true Puerto Rican popular culture: "la masa popular puertorriqueña, huérfana en grado cada vez mayor de la 'ejemplaridad' de una clase dirigente capaz de ofrecerle modelos válidos de creación artística como los que le ofreció en el pasado mediato e inmediato, empezó hace varios lustrous a 'vivir por sí y desde sí,' a 'nutrirse de su propio jugo e inspiración' plebeyos" (99). González adds that, "Plebeyismo es creación de modelos desde abajo y su imposición hacia arriba" (99). It is this political, intellectual and artistic crisis that inspired the cultural production that, beginning in the 1970s, would challenge the traditional models of nation and identity by bringing to the forefront the intersections between gender, race, sexuality and class, and by situating the tensions and negotiations between these axes of identity in everyday spaces that challenge the privileged trope of the family house. In this sense, with few early exceptions, it is only in recent decades that Puerto Rican writers and filmmakers have subverted the patriarchal model of the family, the space of the traditional family house and the figure of the father, to propose critical perspectives on the articulation of Puerto Rican national discourse, and to affirm alternative national imaginaries.

In contrast to the proposals that developed as direct criticisms of muñocismo and of populist discourse, in the late 20th and in the early 21st centuries the debates on the symbolic representation of Puerto Rican national identity and culture departed from class- and race-based analyses. Instead, they adopted a postmodern perspective that claimed that Puerto Rican national culture has been subsumed by post-fordist capitalism, which has turned national symbols into "un producto cultural y comercial sumamente rentable para el capital transnacional que se ha trocado en 'puertorriqueñista'" (Pabón 35), putting nationalism at the service of consumerism, and privileging new spaces of representation characterized by fragmentation and subservience to capital. These skeptical views of the possibilities of national culture ignore the fact that "local cultural identities continue to be salient mediums for political mobilization and serve to promote a variety of other interests, not limited to issues of sovereignty and independence" (Dávila 3), and not conformant to the "acceptable" cultural nationalist identity. Similarly, in the Puerto Rican colonial historical context, political scientists, sociologists and historians continue to reassert that the use of national tropes speaks to the existence of "a Puerto Rican nation in spite of, and because of, almost five centuries of colonialism" (Carrión 68), and point to the manifestations of an island "culture" contrasting with that of the metropolis (Carrión 69) in literature, art and cinema, as evidence of the vitality of Puerto Rican national identity.

More recently, critics, writers and artists like Yolanda Martínez San-Miguel and Mayra Santos-Febres have highlighted the need to rethink race, class, gender, sexuality, language and the migratory experience as markers of fluid identities and as sources of social and cultural opposition that impact Puerto Rican national culture. While they destabilize the traditional image of the national house, they continue to use it to propose axes of alliances that create communities built not around a traditional patriarch, but around female or Afro-Puerto Rican symbolic figures and solidarities. As Myrna García has eloquently argued in her recent study of *las casitas* in New York, the house can also come to represent "la afirmación de un espacio físico propio" (García 266) in the context of migration, diaspora and marginalization away from one's national home.

This chapter responds, on the one hand, to a traditional Puerto Rican cultural nationalist imaginary that envisions the nation as cohesive and uniform, particularly as it relates to gender and sexuality, and on the other, to recent feminist geographers' conceptualizations of the relationship between space and issues of gender, patriarchy and the everyday. It analyzes the house as a national trope, but also as a material and gendered space, that both constructs and is constituted by relationships of class, race, sexuality and desire.


## THE TROPE OF THE HOUSE IN FEMINIST GEOGRAPHY


The texts that I study in this chapter critique the family home as a site of patriarchal control, a space that, even though "usually thought to be gendered feminine, has also traditionally been subject to the patriarchal authority of the husband and father" (Duncan 131). This conscious association of the home with femininity is part of the social and spatial configuration of the "separate spheres," an ideology that relegated women to their domestic functions and men to public roles. In Latin America, "the basic distinction between the casa, or the home, the domain of women, and the calle, or the street, the domain of men" (Safa *The Myth* 47) emphasizes the intersection between gender and the spatial dimension of the separate spheres. In the Caribbean context, evidence of this association of gender with particular spaces goes as far back as the 17th century, when "the choice for criollo women lay between two highly controlled states–matrimony and the convent" (Franco 27), as opposed to the privileged masculine spaces of the pulpit and the confessional (Franco xiii). Even though in the past four centuries the modalities of women's identification with the domestic space have changed, women's negotiation of agency and sexuality maintains a spatial dimension, evident in recent debates on motherhood, on gender violence and on the control over women's bodies.

The traditional association between domesticity and femininity crystallizes in the division of social space, and, as part of that, in the construction of physical, material spaces. Feminist architects have noted how "architectural language and thinking about domestic space are partly structured around a series of gendered binaries in which the preferred term privileges the dominant forces within architecture and society and has masculine connotations" (Walker 823). This problem is evident in the modern house, in which the space of the kitchen "encierra en una habitación la actividad de cocción de alimentos, desconectando al protagonista del espacio de otras áreas domésticas" (Pérez Rodríguez 46), creating borders that alienate women from the rest of the house, its inhabitants and their activities. This separation is important because "living spaces both reflect and shape ideals of family life" (Edwards 27), both of the nuclear family and of the family as a metaphor of the nation. Domestic design constructs gender hierarchies, "reproduce[s] them as part of the natural order" (Dowler 7), and enhances the social internalization of the spatial relations of power in and through the space of the family house.

These discussions, often initiated by feminist geographers, highlight a need to rethink common representations of the intersections between domesticity, gender and sexuality through the space of the house. In recent years, Puerto Rican writers and filmmakers have engaged in this process of deconstructing and subverting the spatial tropes of Puerto Rican national discourse from the standpoint of gender and sexuality. The following sections address the trope of the house, traditionally representative of *la gran familia puertorriqueña*, and the ways in which it has been imagined, configured, constructed, destroyed and rebuilt in Oscar Orzábal Quintana's film *Maruja*, in Rosario Ferré's novel *The House on the Lagoon*, in Magali García Ramis's *Felices días, tío Sergio*, in Jacobo Morales's short film *La otra* and in Paco López's short animated video "Ligia

Elena." Even though these literary and cinematic works present four different visions of the Puerto Rican nation, what they all share is the significance of gender and sexuality in the construction of the national house and in the negotiation, whether ultimately reaffirming or subversive, of traditional patriarchal relations of power.

## The Fallen Housewife: Gender and Patriarchy in *Maruja*

Since the establishment of the Estado Libre Asociado in 1952, Puerto Rican and foreign filmmakers have explored the construction of Puerto Rican national identity in relation to gender and sexuality by employing the trope of la *gran familia puertorriqueña* and its privileged space, the family house. One of the first feature films to depict the negotiations of gender, sexuality and space in the context of the Puerto Rican nation was *Maruja* (1959), directed by Oscar Orzábal Quintana. The story of an unfaithful wife who seduces several men in the same town (including the mayor, his son and a foreigner visiting another distinguished family), *Maruja* condemns some aspects of the gender hierarchy of the national discourse, while upholding and reproducing others, ultimately reaffirming traditional models of dominant masculinity and of submissive femininity.

*Maruja* constructs gender and sexuality in a variety of spaces, the most prominent of which is the house. The film introduces the house that Maruja shares with her husband Lorenzo in a scene that establishes the gender relations that dominate the space. In a scene that suggests Lorenzo's satisfaction with his marriage and with his own masculinity, he gets out of bed in the morning and begins his exercise routine after a happy glance at his young, beautiful wife. As the camera's point of view shifts, it reveals that Maruja only pretends to be asleep. Bored and unhappy, she remains in bed until her husband leaves and she can have the house to herself. In this introductory scene, the family house's symbolic potential as a national trope is frustrated by Maruja's disdain for gender models. At the same time, the house remains a gendered space in which femininity is silenced so as not to challenge or openly discredit masculine authority, whose sense of power and self-worth must remain intact.

In the film, the house interacts with other spaces–the barbershop, the street, the church, and other houses–that draw different axes of negotiation of gender and sexuality in relation to Puerto Rican national identity and belonging.

The space that immediately borders Maruja's house is Lorenzo's barbershop, one of several "discursive spaces . . . of cultural exchange" (Alexander) in which masculinity and community, race and class are constantly constructed and negotiated. Located below Maruja's house, the barbershop is a gendered space that also acts as an instrument of spatial control. Men gather there not only to receive the shop's services, but also to play dominoes, to socialize and to discuss politics. The only woman who occasionally enters the barbershop is Maruja, who must pass by in order to enter and exit her home. Her presence in the barbershop is an exception and disturbs the traditional configuration of the space. At the same time, as a male space located between the home and the street, the barbershop positions Lorenzo and other men in a privileged location from which they can police Maruja's social and spatial mobility. Her access to the home and to the street is mediated by her husband's gaze, by his assistant Dionisio, and by their clients. Their vigilance requires that Maruja invent excuses to gain access to the city, lest her presence in the street be deemed unreasonable and suspect. By finding ways to circumvent this control and by carrying out the affairs with Don Teo, with his son Angel and with the Martinican Jean Pierre Duprey, Maruja challenges the patriarchal spatial order and gender hierarchy traditionally associated with the barbershop.

The house and the barber shop border the street, a public space of access and mobility, but also a space in which the female body can be observed, controlled and objectified by the male gaze. The street is constitutive of agency, of geographies of female and queer liberation, but also of repression. It "serves as a metaphor for sites of resistance that are part of a rhizome-like process of deterritorializing and a progressive opening up to the political system" (Duncan 129), offering the possibility for resistance that the privacy of the home often denies women, homosexual people and other groups that struggle against patriarchal oppression. At times this agency comes literally at a cost—consumption is often one of the main factors that allows women and queer people to claim the space of the street as their own and to contest "the boundaries of sexual citizenship" (Binnie 196), opening possibilities that enclosed, private, domestic spaces may deny to those marginalized by patriarchal social norms.

Just as it is true that the street has enabled the social integration of some groups and has provided a venue from which they have claimed rights and visibility, "the concentration of these movements and subcultures in urban space has made it easier to both demonise and control them" (Knopp 149). In a striking example, Marta Cruz-Janzen remembers growing up black in a white neighborhood in Puerto Rico, and points out the pressure that the space of the street and the desire for access to that space exerted on the family: "[My grandparents] were the only blacks in the neighborhood, always conscious of their neighbors' watchful and critical eyes. We were careful never to set foot outside the house unless we were impeccably groomed" (Cruz-Janzen 169). In her case, the street becomes a space of control and of the reaffirmation of the "proper" racial models of the Puerto Rican national imaginary, framed by the politics of private vs. public spaces.

In the film the street is a space in which both men and women reproduce the patriarchal pedagogy of gender. This reaffirmation of normative sexuality occurs throughout the film, from the initial scene, in which Virginia gossips about Maruja's infidelities, to the scene in which, upon seeing Maruja across the street, Don Porfirio describes her to Jean Pierre Dupuy as "otro bello tipo de arquitectura" and as "una exposición para todo el pueblo y un fomento para el turismo" (*Maruja*). The street is a male space in which women are allowed if they must, for they,

> do not usually walk in an obviously purposeless way [. . .] their badge of respectability (that is usually vital for their safety) is that they are nearly always either carrying something or pushing something. This pushchair, bag, case, or letter may aid the necessary self-permission for the idle, pleasurable intention of going for a walk. To stop safely, I have to buy space (in a café or a cinema) or look as though I am at least a potential purchaser in a shop, or possess a pass to gain admission to a library, museum, club, etc. (Scalway 166).

By strolling purposelessly down the street, Maruja "becomes more dangerously feminine" (Wigley 335) by exposing herself to the male gaze, which constructs her integrity, honor and purity as suspect. The difference between her and Scalway's image of women, though, is that Maruja displays her body consciously, for a reason–she looks for a man who would take her away from the small town that has trapped her in its monotony. She transgresses the space of the street by walking leisurely, and in this way claims access to a space that is traditionally marked as masculine, challenging the patriarchal framework of the housewife.

In the street, gender and sexuality intersect with race to construct a body that is identifiable as subversive in both racial and gendered terms. Maruja is a light-skin mulatta woman, and her race is fundamental for the analysis of the construction of gender and patriarchy in the film. All the men that are attracted to her are white, and her blackness, or her *mulatez,* is a constitutive element of the ways in which the male gaze(s) perceive, desire and marginalize her. Maruja's body is not simply female–it is a black female body, and her sexuality, as perceived by the male characters, is refracted through the lens of blackness. The fact that it is the overtly sexual, mulatta woman that gets killed is also important–it speaks to the ways in which blackness is marginalized, or even threatened, in the idealized model of national identity at the height of which the film was released.

The issue of race and its relation to national belonging become most evident in a scene in which Ismael Rivera, together with the popular band Cortijo y su Combo, perform the song "El negro bembón" on the street, in front of Lorenzo's barber shop and the house in which Maruja lives. The song's lyrics narrate the story of the murder of a black man who is killed precisely because of his blackness. The song "habla directamente sobre los prejuicios raciales [y] cuestiona el comportamiento del asesino, que ha matado sólo porque su víctima tiene un determinado rasgo físico al plantear que 'eso no es razón para matar al bembón,' acción que se explica por las normas sociales del discrimen" (Abadía-Rexach 5-6). The fact that the black musicians perform in the street, and that the song that they perform in the street is about the intersection of race, violence and exclusion, associates it directly with Maruja's character. Like the black man who is the song's subject, Maruja's blackness excludes her from the discourse of national belonging. In addition, the song serves a narrative purpose, as it foreshadows Maruja's own assassination minutes later. Even though they don't question the foundations of racism in Puerto Rico (Abadía-Rexach 6), the lyrics, together with Maruja's death, expose instances in which blackness is the target of violence, and implicitly condemn the structures that enable marginalization and exclusion in everyday discourse and in the political discourse of the nation.

The street allows Maruja access to a series of other places, traditionally patriarchal but similarly transformed by female agency. By arranging her first meeting with Jean Pierre Duprey in the church, Maruja challenges the space's association with traditional marriage, and appears to purposefully ignore its rigid expectations of gender relations. Several of the film's humorous scenes ridicule the priest's authority by putting his life at risk (of being run over by a bicycle, of being hit at a construction site), and by attributing to him the line "Es que quieren dejar al pueblo sin cura" (*Maruja*)–when the authority that he claims is only a surface below which infidelity, deceit, blackmail, murder–ills condemned by the Christian tradition–are the organizing forces of society. By using the church's association with chastity and honor as a disguise, Maruja uncovers layers of hypocrisy and deceit that the rest of the people in the town prefer to ignore, and exposes the church's powerlessness to prevent and punish these ills.

*Maruja*'s patriarchal geographies emerge through the contrast between Maruja's house and that of Don Teo, the mayor with whom Maruja has an affair. Don Teo's house is also inhabited by his wife Provi, and by their children, including Angel, who has just completed his university education in Paris, and whose attraction to Maruja threatens his engagement to the young, beautiful and modest Lisa. Don Teo's house is conventionally patriarchal–while he has a prominent public service career, Provi conforms to the image of the traditional housewife. In contrast to Maruja, Provi is only seen outside when accompanied by her husband. Don Teo, on the other hand, walks freely in the city, unpoliced by family or institutions of power. Reproducing the binary of *la casa* and *la calle*, the film maps an urban geography of gender, in which the street is a masculine domain, and the domestic space a feminine one, organized by patriarchal order.

The contrast between two female characters–Maruja and Lisa, Angel's lover and fiancé, respectively–illustrates the film's construction of patriarchal geographies of gender and its critique of female sexual agency. Maruja and Lisa are dissimilar in every way, from their appearance to their behaviors and to the ways in which they occupy different spaces. Maruja's tight dresses and high heels contrast with Lisa's modes attire. While Lisa is rarely seen outside unaccompanied and never without a reason, Maruja strolls leisurely, occupying public spaces in "inappropriate" ways. Most importantly, Lisa's devotion to Angel stands in stark contrast to Maruja's infidelity to her husband. While Maruja's murder exposes the violence of patriarchal authority and condemns male privilege, her actions are seen not as an expression of female independence or sexual agency, but as immoral and deserving of the consequences. The film's theme song reinforces that contrast with references to Maruja's sins, in lines like, "Sólo Dios en el cielo te perdonará / Maruja, Maruja, por tu liviandad" and in the reiteration of the concluding phrase, "Maruja ya pecó" (*Maruja*). This vilification of female sexuality is equally evident in the final scene, in which, after Maruja's death, Angel reconciles with Lisa, whose forgiveness becomes a vindication for female patience and virtue, qualities that Maruja lacks. The beach, the open space in this final scene of reconciliation, signifies the beginning of Lisa's and Angel's socially-sanctioned marriage, which conforms to the cultural nationalist model of the traditional and patriarchal *gran familia puertorriqueña*.

## *THE HOUSE ON THE LAGOON*: NARRATING THE NATIONAL HOUSE

Key in the process of rethinking Puerto Rican national discourses were the writers of the Generation of the 1970s, whose texts "hacen ingresar en los textos a los sectores postergados: la mujer, el negro, el mulato, el mestizo, el lumpen, el emigrado, el homosexual" (Sancholuz 578). The characters that had occupied a position of alterity in cultural nationalist discourse became central to the new national models conceived by the authors of this generation. Among these writers' most important contributions was the proposed centrality of gender as an analytical category, in the context of two broad historical processes–the feminist movement of the 1960s and the Puerto Rican independence movement. Rosario Ferré and Magali García Ramis, among others, do away with the hegemonic cohesive model of *la puertorriqueñidad* and "divide subjectivity into multiple, overlapping components" (Bost 191), insisting on the negotiation of various identities–racial, class, gendered, linguistic, sexual. Instrumental in this process of subversion was the appropriation and the resignification of the space of the house, one of cultural nationalism's indispensable tropes.

Rosario Ferré's novel *The House on the Lagoon* uses the space of the house as a privileged site for the negotiation of gender, race, class, and national identity. This negotiation occurs against the backdrop of other theoretical texts on Puerto Rican national discourses like González's *El país de cuatro pisos* and Gelpí's *Literatura y paternalismo.* While *The House on the Lagoon* challenges González's lack of discussion of gender in the Puerto Rican national imaginary, it also resists his view of a nation understood through its popular and Afro-Caribbean elements. In this sense, the house in ruins at the end of Ferré's novel reiterates the crisis of the national imaginary, this time stemming not only from the loss of a patriarchal, Hispanocentric view of Puerto Rico, but also from the renegotiation of class and race proposed in González's book.

*The House on the Lagoon* tells the story of four generations of the Monfort and Mendizábal families, centering on the relationship between Isabel Monfort and Quintín Mendizábal. The novel is set in their family house, custom made for Quintín's ancestors, and destroyed and rebuilt several times over the course of a century. The house is inhabited by the Monfort-Mendizábal family and by their servants, most important of whom is Petra, the old African woman who emerges as the matriarch of her own family in the city's outskirts. The plot focuses on Isabel's decision to write a family history, a secret manuscript that enrages Quintín because it uncovers a story that he would rather not reveal. As time passes, the house is transformed from a site of patriarchal domination to one of violence and discord, which result in the ultimate destruction of the house and of the patriarchal order that could no longer reproduce itself.

During the 1970s, José Luis González's essays "El país de cuatro pisos" and "Plebeyismo y arte en el Puerto Rico de hoy" transformed the dominant understanding of national culture. Instead of a culture based on Eurocentric models imposed from above, and instead of populist models that blurred social divisions and inequalities, González brought into the popular imagination the notion of *plebeyismo,* which he explained as a "creación de modelos desde abajo y su imposición hacia arriba" (González 99), "capaz de penetrar y conquistar los dominios de la expresión estética superior" (101). The notion of *plebeyismo* was based largely on González's image of the Puerto Rican nation as a four-storied house, in which Africans constitute the first, foundational floor. *Plebeyismo*'s racial and class implications "subvert the elitist and derivative national patrimony" (Flores 62), and offer a poignant critique of previous national cultural imaginaries.

In a 2000 interview Ferré distances her novel from González's *El país de cuatro pisos* by pointing out that his national house consists of four floors, and hers of two, the Spanish and the African

(Pino-Ojeda 105). In spite of these differences, Ferré's novel does benefit from a parallel reading of *El país de cuatro pisos*, not because of the specificities of the depictions, but certainly because its characters and its vision of Puerto Rican history follow a trajectory that, according to González, constitutes the blueprint of contemporary Puerto Rican national identity.

Ferré's indispensable revisions of González's depiction of Puerto Rican national identity include her emphasis on women as protagonists and narrators of the construction of the nation. In *El país de cuatro pisos* women are part of the Puerto Rican national "house" only insofar as they belong to a certain class or ethnicity, but are hardly mentioned as a group (or groups) with their own roles and needs in the development of Puerto Rican culture. The only time that González references women directly is in relation to his desire to interrupt a line of analysis that blames the US invasion for the perceived "loss" of Puerto Rican culture, pointing out that,

> así como sus valores culturales le sirvieron a la clase propietaria para resistir la 'norteamericanización,' esa misma 'norteamericanización' le ha servido a la masa popular para impugnar y desplazar los valores culturales de la clase propietaria. Pero no solo a la masa popular [. . .] sino incluso a ciertos sectores muy importantes de la misma clase propietaria que han vivido oprimidos en el interior de su propia clase. Pienso, sobre todo, en las mujeres. ¿A alguien se le ocurrirá negar que el actual movimiento de liberación femenina en Puerto Rico–esencialmente progresista y justo a despecho de todas sus posibles limitaciones–no es en grandísima medida un resultado de la 'norteamericanización' de la sociedad puertorriqueña? (González 36).

Beyond this comment, there is no discussion of patriarchy in Puerto Rican culture, no critique of the traditional image of women in the Puerto Rican literary canon, nor of the ways in which women's increased participation has challenged the patriarchal order.[5]

Ferré's response to the absence of women in the four-storied house is to make them protagonists and speakers, and to emphasize their agency in the narration of the nation. In that sense, *The House*

---

[5] For critical analyses of the social roles and cultural representations of women, see the work of Yamila Azize Vargas, María M. Solá, María del Carmen Baerga, Marcia Rivera and others.

*on the Lagoon* exemplifies the ways in which "Women's attempts to plot themselves as protagonists in the national novel become a recognition of the fact that they are not in the plot at all but definitely somewhere else" (Franco 146). This approach emerges from Ferré's previous work, in which she had used–and subverted–female prototypes like the figure of the doll, the double, the disabled or the hysterical woman, in order to question patriarchal power and female marginalization (Roses 281). One way in which the author makes a claim for the inclusion of gender in the Puerto Rican national imaginary in *The House on the Lagoon* is through another such motif, that of Isabel's manuscript, which re-writes Puerto Rican history from a particular gendered, racial and class perspective.

Isabel begins writing her manuscript in secret, eager to uncover the silenced history of the Mendizábal family, yet anxious about the possibility that her husband Quintín might discover it. When Quintín finds the pages hidden in the walls of the house, he is outraged, but instead of confronting Isabel, he begins revising the manuscript in the margins. Isabel's manuscript, together with Quintín's revisions, results in a fragmented, palimpsestic work, in which "the insistent doubling of the narrative self constantly questions the nature of the author and the constitution of the authorial voice" (Barak 33). In this case, Isabel's and Quintín's voices question each other, in an effort to subvert the historical claim to authority characteristic of national discourses.

The struggles over the manuscript's gendered histories depict the domestic space as a space of marginality and secrecy. The fact that Isabel writes the manuscript in secret from her family, and above all from her husband, is a sign of the "unofficial" character of history written from a woman's perspective. In addition, the secret manuscript is also "a fundamental element of her literary deconstruction of patriarchy [that] includes an undermining of the masculinist values which are perceived as an integral part of the dominating system" (Fernández Olmos 43). Here, the values to which Fernández Olmos refers can be understood as the patriarchal characteristics of official versions of nation and history, as well as the perceived masculine quality of narrative authority. In fact, when Quintín discovers the manuscript, he is outraged. At first he reads it with condescension, counterposing his "official" history against Isabel's "fictionalized" (and therefore "untruthful") version of it: "As he read on, Quintín began to feel uncomfortable. The manuscript was an authentic effort at writing fiction; Isabel definitely intended it as a novel. But she had made up incredible things about his family and left out much of what had really happened" (Ferré, *House* 71). Subsequently, he accuses Isabel of altering history–"history" signifying his version of the past, unmarred by Isabel's interpretation: "But Isabel had altered everything. She was manipulating history for fiction's sake" (Ferré, *House* 71). Quintín's disbelief is in part the disbelief at the audacity of a woman who has crossed the limits of her discursive marginality and taken upon the task of rewriting the story of her family and her nation.

The second cause of Quintín's unease is that in her writing Isabel exposes family secrets that allude to the hypocrisy of the official history regarding issues of race, class and gender. Quintín's preferred version of history is centered on "a discourse that strove to create a national family, unified and homogenized through its submission to a patriarchal order that valorized the Spanish inheritance to the exclusion of all others" (Russ 156). Isabel subverts that discourse by revealing stories that the family prefers not to remember, like those of the importance of the Bloodline Books, which people consulted before marrying, to make sure that there was no non-white blood in the bride or in the groom's family, or anecdotes about Quintín's predecessor Buenaventura Mendizábal, his self-righteousness and authoritarian character. Through these stories Isabel's manuscript "departs from traditional patriarchal discourse by favoring the orality of the oppressed [. . .] by telling a story that, in many cases, has been suppressed by the powerful yet survived in the form of gossip and oral accounts among poor people, women and slaves" (Henao 75). It is precisely through gossip and secrets, "female" linguistic practices traditionally marginalized and not considered part of official history, that Isabel subverts the patriarchal master-narrative of the nation.

It is debatable whether simple curiosity about Isabel's imagination or a fearful desire to discover aspects of a past that he had himself repressed is what keeps Quintín from destroying the manuscript, but the fact is that instead of burning it, he takes upon the task of disproving its story by writing his version in the margins. In Isabel's version of history, then, the "marginal" voice is that of the patriarch, who now loses his authority and can only offer "other" or "alternative" versions of a history that someone else–a woman–is writing. This results in an inversion of gender roles in relation to the power to construct and narrate a Puerto Rican national discourse.

The manuscript's potential to invert traditional gender relations is realized through the representation of space and through the gendered geographies that the novel maps. Isabel hides the manuscript in the family house that Quintín built, on shelves and behind books, as if it were part of the house's walls. On the one hand, "the place where Isabel hides the manuscript suggests her belief that what she has written deserves the same status and legitimacy as both Quintín's dictionary and he Roman histories by Plutarch he translates with that dictionary" (Adjarian 177), as she makes an implicit comment on the worth of literature and history written by women. On the other, Ferré also incorporates her version of Puerto Rican history in the walls that carry the weight of the national house, whether González's four-stories house or a new version of it. The manuscript is not published, not official, but its subversive voice is part of the house, and even though hidden, it has the potential to speak.

When Isabel asks Petra to hide the manuscript in the cellar, it becomes part, at a literal level, of the foundations of the house, and figuratively, of the narrative foundations of national history. The space of the cellar is particularly important for what it implies "about the text's ultimate function as writing by a woman. As an underground utility area, the cellar suggests the stored and the hidden: a kind of metaphoric unconscious. Isabel's words thus come to represent what has been suppressed/repressed in the Mendizabal house" (Adjarian 178). It is an underground space that hides from view, but also keeps and preserves–supplies, bodies, secrets, stories. Finally, the space of the cellar also alludes to *El país de cuatro pisos* and to its emphasis of the first, African, floor. When in the end, thanks to Petra, the manuscript survives the house's demolition, it comes to represent "a victory for fiction and for Isabel, since it's her version of the story that prevails" (Kevane 67). It speaks to the historical transcendence of the female version of the Puerto Rican nation, and becomes a claim of authority for the woman's voice.

While José Luis González's *El país de cuatro pisos* does not address the issue of gender in the construction and the negotiation of the space of the house, it does discuss its racial and class composition and intersections. His class analysis emphasizes the presence of "dos culturas: la cultura de los opresores y la cultura de los oprimidos" (12) and he clarifies that "esas dos culturas, precisamente porque coexisten, no son compartimientos estancos sino vasos intercomunicantes cuya existencia se caracteriza por una constante influencia mutua" (12), which is defined by a relation of domination that results in the perception of a certain kind of "national culture": "la cultura de los opresores es la cultura dominante y la cultura de los oprimidos es la cultura dominada. Y la que se presenta como 'cultura general,' vale decir como 'cultura nacional,' es, naturalmente, la cultura dominante" (12). In González's analysis, racial categories coincide with class, and Africans constitute the first, foundational floor of the national house. González assigns particular value to this first floor, arguing that it is one of the main elements that bring Puerto Rico closer to its Caribbean neighbors, and thus makes possible Caribbean unity and solidarity.

The negotiation of race, class, and the space of the house in Ferré's novel in many ways coincides with González's image of the house, but, ironically, results in a very different statement about Puerto Rican culture and identity. The two books construct an image of the Puerto Rican national house that is both spatially and temporally defined by the relationship between race and class. Much like in *El país de cuatro pisos*, the first floor of the novel's house is occupied by Afro-Puerto Rican descendants of African slaves, now Quintín's and Isabel's servants. The second floor, that of the European migrants, is most prominently represented by Buenaventura Mendizábal, and the fact that the house did not exist before his arrival is quite telling. Buenaventura, and not the African slaves, lays the foundations of the national house. Petra and her relatives live in the house, and can be seen as "marginal members of the family" (Stoner 118), and even though they impact the course of the family's history, their status is that of servants who share neither the family's racial or class characteristics, nor the privileges that come with them. Contrary to González's version of Puerto Rican culture, here the first floor is a subterranean level that is only part of the national house insofar as its inhabitants support the house through their labor and service.

Petra, the one figure of authority at the first floor, is represented in a problematic way that does little to invert the relations of power in the house. Petra is the matriarch of her family in Las Minas and Lucumí Beach, but a servant in the big house. She occupies the house's cellar, which she has furnished "with an old set of wicker furniture which had originally been used at the house and which Rebecca had discarded. Her wicker peacock throne was an important feature of the sitting room. Every night she would sit on it, wearing her brightly colored bead necklaces and bracelets. She would listen to the servants' complaints, and give them advice" (Ferré *House* 236). The "throne" to which the author refers is a symbol of power, albeit an ironic one, as Petra still occupies the lowest level in the house, both spatially and symbolically. She has influence over Buenaventura and dares to threaten Quintín: "'Go ahead and disinherit Willie, then,' Petra said defiantly. 'But I swear to you by Elegguá–he who is more than God–that one day you'll be sorry!' And with that, she turned around and went back to the cellar" (Ferré *House* 372). However, her powers seem mystical, irrational, and inaccessible to Isabel's logic. Petra is the keeper of secrets that no one else knows, she miraculously recovers from an illness and her prophecy that Quintín will pay for disowning Manuel comes true faster than Quintín could ever imagine. After Buenaventura's death, when Petra's family members take over the house, they seem to bring chaos and disorder. Instead of the constructive element of the Puerto Rican nation that Petra would be in *El país de cuatro pisos*, in *The House on the Lagoon* she is a power to be feared by those that built the house of Puerto Rican national culture.

In the context of the Puerto Rican literature of the 1970s, this representation of Petra remains problematic. At first sight, Ferré depicts her as a devoted servant and as the ideal keeper of the family's secrets. This image, however, contains a series of contradictions that stem from a long tradition of narratives of the black "mammy" or domestic servant through the perspective of the (male or female) masters, a tradition often tinged with a misidentification of the servant's position within and relationship to the master's family.

Several studies of the representation of the domestic servant in modern Brazilian literature identify the problematic aspects of Latin American discursive constructions of the black female servant. Sônia Roncador's analysis begins with 19th century images of the black maid in Brazil as "portadoras de vícios morais e coenças contagiosas nos discursos médico-higienistas" (Roncador 10), as a counterpart to the white bourgeois lady of the house, as a docile and asexual black mammy (13), and as a black domestic worker in recent testimonial literature, in which her story remains excluded from the privileged genre of the autobiography. These representation have hardly ever been in service of the maid: "a doméstica foi discursivamente apropriada como signo de alteridade por excelência, servindo como contraponto às senhoras aristocrata e burguesa nos discursos hegemônicos de contestação das transgressões sociais e raciais e de formação das identidades nacional, racial e de gênero" (Roncador 8). Instead, they are representations necessary for the construction of gender and race in the white family and in a particular kind of national imaginary, in terms of both femininity and masculinity, through what Jossianna Arroyo has called "travestismos culturales," or the masks that white elites create in order to construct a cohesive image of the nation. In these narratives, the black "mammy" becomes a convenient element in

> las visiones culturales que construyeron la nación como un organismo. En la lectura de ese cuerpo nacional, el cuerpo del otro (o de los otros), en especial, el de las poblaciones negras, aparece como una parte integral de ese discurso, ya que, para organizar el imaginario subjetivo de la cultura o la subjetividad cultural, es necesario 'integrar' ese cuerpo al discurso nacional. Sin embargo, y a pesar de la presencia inminente y necesaria de ese cuerpo, estas narrativas conforman una serie de estrategias para contenerlo, discilplinarlo o sublimarlo. Con ese fin se manipulan estratégicamente la raza, el género y la sexualidad en la construcción del imaginario nacional de la cultura. (Arroyo *Travestismos* 5).

In the novel, Petra exemplifies both the otherness and the illusory family/national cohesion that Arroyo uncovers. In the house, her presence contrast with those of the other occupants: "She was six feet tall and her skin wasn't a watered-down chocolate but a deep onyx black; when she smiled it was as if a white scar slashed the darkness of the night. She wore brightly colored seed necklaces around her neck and steel bracelets on her wrists, and she went barefoot" (Ferré *House* 58). Her race and her traditional dress are identified with "las manifestaciones culturales de negros y mulatos [que] pasan a ser claves estratégicas de la representación" (Arroyo *Travestismos* 21) in the process of the construction of the national imaginary. Once in the house, Petra becomes part of it, even as she occupies the lowest, underground levels of the national structure.

In the family house Petra contributes to the construction of an idealized cohesive national model by both reproducing and challenging models of gender and sexuality. She is key in the construction of Buenaventura's masculinity as the master of the first house on the lagoon, and instead of resisting his power, she reproduces it: "Petra became Buenaventura's personal servant. She took care of his clothes, polished his shoes, cooked him special dishes, and would have kissed the ground he walked on had he asked her to. She worshipped him like a god" (Ferré *House* 63). She is also a counterpoint to the construction of Isabel's femininity–at the end of the novel, at Petra's funeral, Isabel thanks her "for everything she had done for us. Her name had suited her well: Petra means rock, and for the many years I had known her, she had been the rock on which the house on the lagoon had stood" (Ferré *House* 348). This rhetoric is contradictory, as Petra's representation as a cornerstone of the family house ignores the hierarchical relationship between her and Isabel, in whose case "custom directed that as wife she oversee the running of the household, including taking charge of servants" (Lauderdale Graham 91). The images of the black female servant and the *señora de la casa* mirror each other, entering in a relationship that constructs them reciprocally and that put limits on their agency within the house. On the one hand, the discourse silences Petra's voice and obscures her exploitation as a servant (over the course of the narrative, Rebecca lowers Petra's pay, Quintín rapes and impregnates a young member of her family, and later disowns the child, who is also Petra's offspring). The idealization of Petra's role and position in the family constructs Isabel as a successful mistress of the house, and validates her own femininity, at the expense of the visibility of the violence inflicted on Petra and the other servants. On the other hand, these words construct Isabel in her role as *señora de la casa* who is complicit with the racial and class hierarchies of the system in which she participates. In a sense, Isabel's tribute to Petra from her privileged position identifies her as the "sujeto de la escritura [que] se 'subordina' simbólicamente a la otredad para constituirse a sí mismo" (Arroyo *Travestismos* 20), to insert herself in the patriarchal discourse, imposing limits on her own agency to question and to subvert it beyond the pages of her manuscript.

Petra's character, as depicted in the novel, also contributes to the illusory national unity by establishing "uma falsa retórica de parentesco" (Roncador 12), by passing on to the children in the master's house the family history told to her by her mother. Isabel reminisces about the time when "Petra hadn't been born yet, but her mother told her the story of what happened to her grandfather on that day, and Petra passed it on to us" (Ferré *House* 61). Through these words Petra is revealed as a mother figure in the white children's imagination, a figure that is problematic, as its idealization of race and gender contrast with the exploitation of the black servant to which the children remain oblivious. Petra reciprocates the elite's need for her in the big house by welcoming them, at a certain level, into her own family history, transforming the relationship into one convenient for the construction of a unified, if illusory, national discourse.

In the context of those contradictions, Petra's character poignantly critiques the relationship between class, race and gender in the novel. In contrast to *Maldito amor*, where "Ferré uses language which echoes the class structure and gender of her characters" (Hintz 87), here Petra occupies a significant portion of the novel and often drives the plot, but the narrative voice to which the reader listens is not hers. Her character shares the problem of representation of several other "nanas negras" in the writing of Ferré and Olga Nolla:

> while the white, well-to-do female writers can tell and fashion their own stories, the same is not entirely true for the Afro-Caribbean women in the texts. Their stories are still being written by others, and even when they have a voice [. . .] they are told how to act. [. . .] The nanas negras are still in separate quarters that are different from those of the white protagonists who consider those spaces distinct and separate (Gosser Esquilín 61).

Consequently, the relationship between Petra and Isabel problematizes Latin American feminism in relation to privilege, as "class and gender, two classical social divisions, come together in the intimacy of the home" (Stoner 117-118). Isabel can write because she, like other writers, uses hired help for domestic chores, and it is that privilege that "allows her (Isabel) to explore her rights as a woman" (Henao 31). Petra is clearly marginal in the space of the house and in the articulation of the nation that the house represents. With the authority that the written word grants them, Isabel writes about Petra and Quintín offers an alternative perspective that seems to demonize her even more than Isabel's benevolent, yet fearful and detached descriptions (she mentions that there are times when she agrees with Petra but is afraid to stand up to Quintín).

From the standpoint of race, the juxtaposition of Petra's marginalization with the centrality of Isabel's narrative voice reveals a desire to subdue the racial hierarchies that structure Puerto Rican society. Regarding Isabel's whiteness, critics have argued that, "by plotting Puerto Rican ethno-nationality through the subjectivity of white women and their fundamental conflict with Puerto Rican white men, Ferré cancels out asymmetrical power relations between Puerto Ricans and Americans and reinscribes the supreme value of whiteness over racialized subjects" (Negrón-Muntaner, *Boricua Pop* 195). This argument is valuable in that it points to the multiple silences that permeate the text, including the absence of a historized account of race and colonialism on the island. These silences grant visibility to the privileged white characters, constructing a nation that ignores the marginalization of Afro-Puerto Ricans, as well as the colonial oppression of white Puerto Ricans, in order to create the illusion of a predominantly white, privileged society. In this sense, Negrón-Muntaner's words inscribe the problematic of race and gender in the Puerto Rican colonial context, and urge their reconsideration in the context of the United States' racialization of Puerto Ricans on the island and in the diaspora. The novel's protagonist speaks from a particular gender, racial and class position, which is far from representative of the spectrum of female characters in the novel, and which inspires the need to question the composition of the rebuilt and reimagined national house.

The negotiation of racial, class and gender categories occurs in the space of the house, which in reality encompasses several houses consecutively destroyed and rebuilt, making some critics question the viability of the concept of the nation in the novel. The ending of Ferré's short story "Amalia," (reminiscent of *The House on the Lagoon*, the house burns and the only survivors are a young girl and the Afro-Puerto Rican servants) suggests that the author challenges certain national imaginaries, as in her writing, "the idea of nation and national identity in her (Puerto Rican) context is highly problematic. [. . .] She even razes this 'conventional' type of nation down to the ground in her version of "Amalia" when the protagonist and her accomplices destroy the uncle's house in flames" (Lindsay 71). While the destruction of the house by fire can be interpreted as the end of nationalism, in "Amalia," as in the novel, there are characters that survive. It is the marginal characters–women, Afro-Puerto Ricans, slaves and servants–who cause the fire, and who emerge from it, alluding to the possibility of a new kind of family. Through the image of the house in flames and in ruins, Ferré challenges national cohesion and integrity, suggesting the need to constantly question and rethink the apparent authority of national discourse.

## GENDERED SPACES, QUEER NATIONS: THE PEDAGOGY OF GENDER IN *FELICES DÍAS, TÍO SERGIO*

The female narrator in Ferré's novel questions the national discourse on gender, but does little to challenge the construction of race and class in the "national house." In contrast, other authors reconfigure the space of the house by questioning the intersections of gender, racial and class hierarchies embedded in the model of *la gran familia puertorriqueña*. Magali García Ramis's *Felices días, tío Sergio*, set in a middle class family during the years of Luis Muñoz Marín's government, focuses on the relationship between adolescent Lidia and her uncle, and can be read as a coming-of-age story, "un bildungsroman femenino situado en la década de 1950 [que] feminiza la narración épica masculina" (Acosta Cruz 269). Its depiction of the gendered experience of space maps a feminine geography, becoming a "bildungsroman equívoco, que es sobre todo una novela de anti-aprendizaje" (Sotomayor 318), an un-learning of expectations of gender, sexuality, race and class in the context of the national microcosm that the family house represents.

Before uncle Sergio's arrival from the US, Lidia grows up in a family that succumbs rather uncritically to visions of prestige and progress that emerge from an eclectic mix of colonial and patriarchal interpretations of race, class and gender. There is a simple yet inviolable line between what is perceived as "good" and "bad," and the children are always expected to consider this binary:

> Del lado del Bien estaban la religion Católica, Apostólica y Romana, el Papa, Estados Unidos, los americanos, Eisenhower, Europa, sobretodo los europeos finos, Grace Kelly, la gente preferiblemente blanca, todos los militares, Evita Perón, la ópera, la zarzuela, todos los productos de España desde las mantillas hasta los chorizos y Sarita Montiel, y absolutamente todo lo germano y lo suizo, desde el vino del Rin hasta los relojes cucú (García Ramis 28).

A similar list for "el lado del Mal" includes communists, atheists, masons, Protestants, Nazis, the newly-formed African nations and Puerto Rican nationalists (28). These lists, schematic and exaggerated as they are, offer an idea of the kind of knowledge and prejudices that the narrator would later have to reexamine, inspired by Sergio's lessons.

The irony explicit in the above binary knowledge stems from the realization that *la enseñanza*, the reproduction of the colonial, patriarchal, racist and classist order that constructs an imaginary of the Puerto Rican nation and that prescribes Lidia's place in it, unfolds in the absence of a patriarchal figure. The novel demonstrates how patriarchy can thrive without a patriarch, in a house in which Mamá Sara "dominaba en espíritu el hogar sin hombre de nuestra familia" (García Ramis 11). Years after Lidia's grandfather and father have died, her grandmother continues to arrange the table by placing her "silla alta, como de reina, que ponía a la cabecera de la mesa del comedor e insistía que la del otro lado se dejara vacía para que allí se sentara el Hombre, que podía ser, según quien estuviera de visita, el tío Roberto, el monseñor Serrano o aún el primo Germánico" (10). The male figure is phantom, and any man can fulfill the criteria for occupying the empty chair, just by virtue of being a man. This is symptomatic of "colonial dynamics which cause the protagonists to internalize and identify with the colonial mentality to the point where they protect and perpetuate the very oppressive systems and relationships of which they are victims" (Henao 13). Patriarchy does not need a man in order to exist in the house–centuries of colonial rule, the word of the Catholic Church, and in the immediate context of the novel, the paternal (yet almost ghostly) figure of Luis Muñoz Marín have solidified the patriarchal order and the gender roles that it prescribes.

The women in Lidia's house reproduce the patriarchal order in different ways. As Mamá Sara and Lidia's aunts reiterate a discourse of accepted and unacceptable gender roles (regarding men, women, homosexuality and heterosexuality), Lidia, Andrés and Quique internalize those models, even when they don't understand them or as they try to consciously resist them.

Gender and sexuality are among the aunts' principal causes of concern with regard to the adolescent girl, and to make clear to her the limits of "acceptable" behavior, they make constant and explicit references to what women and men are not allowed to do. Lidia encounters the issue of gender inequality upon her uncle's arrival, when she is told not to question what he does because "Él es un hombre, y a los hombres no se les va detrás preguntándole qué hacen o qué dejan de hacer" (García Ramis 9). These words are meant to teach a lesson about the limits of feminine authority in patriarchal societies like Lidia's. Religious discourse reinforces patriarchy, as the aunts use Catholicism to explain the essence of the institution of marriage. When Lidia asks whether two people who live together without marrying would go to hell, her aunt Sara F. responds: "Bueno, de todas formas es culpa de la mujer. [. . .] Las mujeres que se portan mal son viciosas, lo hacen por vicio, en cambio, los hombres, muchas veces no pueden evitarlo, el hombre tiene el lobo por dentro . . ." (García Ramis 29). In this case, the woman reproduces the religious concept of female vice and original sin, and uses it to justify and reinforce patriarchal notions of femininity and masculinity.

The patriarchal norms that organize the space of the novel also impose rigid limits of sexuality that the children learn at the family house. There, the expectations of heterosexuality and marriage are reinforced by the restrictions by which the children are expected to abide, and which correspond to their future roles of patriarch and housewife, respectively. While Lidia's mother and aunts reproach her for not keeping clean and for being a *marimacha* (a tomboy), threatening that she will never find a husband, they approve of Andrés's interest in a white upper-middle class girl: "Todos estaban felices de que él se fuera haciendo hombre y hubiera escogido bien a su novia" (Garcia Ramis 117). The young boy is condoned for acting "like a man," while the young girl is reprimanded for not conforming to traditional norms of femininity.

Similarly, the limits of sexuality are drawn through a discourse on homosexuality, as when Lidia overhears a conversation that condemns homosexuality, which provokes questions that remain mostly unanswered: "Sí hombre, pato, le salió pato ese muchacho a la pobre Tati Almeyda. Ajá, pero ya lo mandó para Estados Unidos, allá lejos, a California que dicen que allá es que los están mandando a todos" (García Ramis 31). On the one hand, comments like these serve a pedagogical purpose, as lessons for acceptable norms of sexuality; on the other, they expose the hypocrisy of the notion of the cohesion and uniformity of the *gran familia puertorriqueña* around which the national discourse of the 1950s was built, by suggesting that the presumed uniformity is possible only because difference is silenced, erased or expelled, often through forced migration.

The children's response to the discourse on gender and sexuality is multifaceted and often contradictory. They internalize and reenact the prescribed identities, while at the same time resisting some of their underlying principles and everyday manifestations. They reproduce images of femininity and masculinity through their games, a process evident in the girl's description of the children's reenactment of Tarzan: "Si yo quería ser Jane me tenía que quedar al pie del árbol, en la casa de la selva, cocinando y cuidando a Quique, que era Boy. Como quería tanto trepar yo también, la mayoría de las veces transaba mi identidad humana por la de mona" (García Ramis 15). At first glance, such a gesture on Lidia's pat is logical–in the game, she is under pressure to perform femininity, and while she does not have the option of playing the male character of Tarzan, she negotiates and subverts gender expectations by avoiding the human roles altogether. At another level, however, Lidia's adoptin of the role of the monkey can be interpreted as a veiled expression of her own sexuality, as critics like Lawrence La Fountain-Stokes have argued: "Lidia conceptualizes her state of non-femininity as one of savagery, the only state that seems available as an option for resistance" (La Fountain-Stokes "Tomboy Tantrums" 51-52). Not only does it propose "the marimacha as an authentic figure of resistance and female emancipation" (La Fountain-Stokes "Tomboy Tantrums 53), but is also an allusion to her own homosexuality, subtly referenced in episodes like the game and in her overt attraction to female actresses like Sophia Loren.

When faced with traditional models of the Puerto Rican nation, of which she is expected to be a productive part, Lidia struggles to understand the prescribed behaviors and the imposed boundaries. She finds an alternative order in her uncle Sergio, a communist, independence supporter, and homosexual, who returns briefly from New York, and whose presence disturbs the order in the traditional family house. Sergio's homosexuality, inferred from the sotto-voce references to "patos" and to his "ojos enormes, de pestañas largas casi de mujer" (García Ramis 7), is a reason for his marginalization, but also one of the "lines and parallels between Lidia and Sergio" (La Fountain-Stokes *Queer Ricans*), as the narrator's own lesbianism is implied in numerous incidents, from her fascination with Sofia Loren to the constant accusations of her being a marimacha.

In this sense, "además de ocupar el lugar del padre ausente, [Sergio] representa un contrapunto ideológico al resto de la familia" (Acosta Cruz 271). Whether or not Sergio is meant to represent a missing paternal figure is in fact arguable, as his character diverges from the traditional model of the patriarch in numerous ways–he is only present in the house briefly, and the knowledge and the education that he brings never manage to defeat the dominant discourse. However, the significance of Sergio's character lies in his ability to impact the two aspects of Lidia's transformation–the politics of gender and the politics of nation–and to offer a kind of education contrasting with what the girl receives at home, emphasizing the importance of Puerto Rican history and of (often unspoken) national heroes that stand as alternatives to Luis Muñoz Marín.

One such incident occurs shortly after Sergio's arrival. When Andrés is curious about a school named after Segundo Ruiz Belvis, Sergio responds: "fue un hombre muy importante en nuestra historia, un abolicionista, ayudó que hubiese más justicia en Puerto Rico, estaba en contra de la opresión . . ." (García Ramis 60). The silence with which Lidia's aunt responds to the uncle's explanation indicates to the girl that "había pasado algo malo" (García Ramis 60), a suggestion that what Sergio considers important in Puerto Rican national history, and the lessons that he teaches the children, clash with the ideology according to which the family brings them up. By revealing this sort of "secrets" and by giving voice to the silences of the Puerto Rican past, Sergio becomes "el sustituto de maestro de historia nacional, [y] un libro de información que nunca hubo en la sala de la familia Solís" (Díaz Basteris 166). He voices "la percepción de la historia nacional puertorriqueña desde los ojos de quienes no hacen historia: los integrantes marginales de la sociedad" (Días Basteris 164) and unveils a version of history alternative to the cultural nationalist ideology that dominates the populist regime of the Puerto Rico of the 1950s and of its *gran familia*.

In contrast to Sergio's consistent ideological education, his stand on gender and sexuality is much less overt. His tendency to privilege the political over the gender identities represents the "equívoco de la generación de independentistas y nacionalistas [. . .] con una limitada capacidad para reconocer que la problemática del mundo no se limita a lo ideológico y que alcanza la identidad sexual (al eros) de los sujetos en la sociedad" (Díaz 332). The book's emphasis on the pedagogy of gender and on the gendered spaces that the narrator struggles to negotiate critiques this omission of gender and sexuality from the political discourse and envisions the female narrator's agency and coming to consciousness as the basis for the construction of a new national identity along axes of gender and sexuality, together with those of political and cultural identification.

The family house in *Felices días, tío Sergio* is the matrix for the construction of patriarchal geographies that uphold traditional norms of national and gender identity. The house, in relation to the neighborhood, on the one hand, and to the city of San Juan, on the other, denotes spaces of inclusion and exclusion that stand for contrasting ideologies, and represent different approaches to the construction of gender and national imaginaries.

The inside and the outside of official national discourse are marked, quite literally, by a wall that divides spaces that engender contrasting ideologies. Lidia's house neighbors that of Don Gabriel Tristani, an old nationalist and independence supporter who lives with his daughter, la Margara, "una mujer callejera, mala" (García Ramis 3) who is about to have a baby out of wedlock. The children are forbidden to go to Don Gabriel's house or to speak to la Margara, a prohibition that they promptly transgress in one of the opening scenes of the novel. Don Gabriel doesn't conform to the children's simplistic, exaggerated, caricaturesque image of nationalists, of whom Lidia is taught to think as unkempt, long-haired unreasonable men. In contrast, "Don Gabriel no era así. Era un viejito de ojos azules y mucho pelo blanco; era muy limpio y callado" (33). Even at this rudimentary level, the girl realizes that the image that her family has constructed of nationalists does not correspond to her perception, especially after, guided by her uncle, she gets to come in close contact with the elderly man.

The wall that divides Lidia's family from that of Don Gabriel also connects the two houses and thus represents both the divisions and the proximity of classes and national ideologies in 1950s Puerto Rico. In the opening passages, Lidia laments her inability to see, learn and cross to the other side: "Su casa colindaba con la nuestra por detrás, pero la pared enorme que dividía los lotes de la calle nuestra de los de la de él, no permitía que nos viésemos nunca" (García Ramis 33). As the novel progresses, the children find ways to get closer, to look over the wall, even as the space of Don Gabriel's house remains a taboo: "Andrés y yo nos trepábamos sobre [las conejeras] y nos guindábamos de las ramas del palo de pana para tratar de mirar a casa de la Margara, pero apenas si alcanzábamos. [. . .] Pero sabíamos que vivían ahí; ella pasaba con su barriga frente a nuestra casa, ellos existían como algo prohibido, y queríamos verlos" (García Ramis 73). Lidia's gaze both differentiates and acquaints the children with the prohibited space and discourse of independence. It also illustrates how the spaces, the social classes and the conflicting discourses in the novel constantly interact: "los espacios exteriores e interiores dialogan entre sí; tras la casa de los nacionalistas y la casa de Lydia (sic) los patios se enlazan" (Sotomayor 319). By suggesting the possibility of "crossing over," the novel identifies Lidia as the possible symbolic female representative of an independence discourse in terms of both gender roles and political ideology.

At a narrative level, uncle Sergio is the children's guide to the house of Don Gabriel, and symbolically, he leads them on the path to understanding and identifying with Puerto Rican national identity. Sergio "funciona como sustituto del padre ausente que le lleva [a Lidia] la patria desconocida u ocultada" (Bourasseau Alvarez 785), in a manner that in many ways challenges the idea of puertorriqueñidad upheld by Luis Muñoz Marín in the 1950s. It occurs almost by accident, and, significantly, when Lidia's aunts happen to be out of the house, when their patriarchal voice is temporarily suspended. The first time that Sergio takes the children to Don Gabriel's house, they feel the excitement and the fear of doing something forbidden: "Pero no podíamos evitar el altruista gesto, el dramático gesto, el retador gesto de acompañar al Tío como en secreta cofradía, a la casa del Nacionalista ese, de la mujer perdida esa, del hijo natural ese–porque allí no se salvaba nadie del rechazo de mi familia y mi clase" (García Ramis 111). This initial emotion transforms into an understanding and an identification with *la puertorriqueñidad*, and makes the children part of another kind of *familia puertorriqueña*, not the cohesive, united family imagined by Muñoz Marín, but instead one that stands for independence from colonial and neocolonial power:

> Para Quique y para mí el descubrirnos como puertorriqueños nos dio cohesión, nos permitió ubicar todo lo que habíamos comenzado a aprender, nos dio una identidad con la realidad coti-

> diana del mundo que vivíamos y nos hermanó, por primera vez, con gente que no era nuestra familia sanguínea sino de otra familia más amplia, más grande, toda nuestra (García Ramis 152).

This culminates the protagonist's process of coming to consciousness, alludes to her liberation from her family's patriarchal norms, and signifies her capacity to distance herself from the populist and moralizing cultural nationalist discourse of the 1950s (but also from Sergio's model) ultimately resulting in a discovery of her political self.

The process of coming to consciousness has not only an ideological, but also a spatial dimension. Space denotes the contrast between discourses that operate inside and outside the house–the house as a dominion of a patriarchal order that leaves space for very few transgressions of norms of gender and national identity, juxtaposed against the outside, the street on one side and Don Gabriel's house on the other. When at the end of the novel Lidia looks for a way to understand Sergio's departure and her own loss, she needs to leave the confines of the house and step out to the patio (which borders Don Gabriel's house) in order to think: "El día que Tío Sergio se fue, cuando llegamos a casa, me fui a caminar por el patio a tratar de entender cómo era posible que a uno le cambiaran la vida, se la cortaran en dos, en un sólo día, en tres días, en un momento" (García Ramis 136). The spatial position of the protagonist suggests that she has reached the moment when she is able to step out, literally and figuratively, of the family house in which patriarchy continues to restrain her politization, and has taken a step towards her political transformation in terms of both gender and national identity.

As in *The House on the Lagoon*, the construction of the nation in *Felices días, tío Sergio* extends beyond the house of the metaphorical national family. In García Ramis's book it is again imagined as territorial, but instead of encompassing numerous locations on the island's map, it is delimited by a small stretch of the capital city, in the area of Santurce, which appears self-contained, self-sufficient and again marked by specific racial and class characteristics:

> Nuestro mundo hasta entonces era uno medible y perfecto. Abarcaba unas veinte cuadras desde la Parada de Guaguas número 20 a la 15 a lo largo de la Avenida Ponce de León, la más importante en aquel tiempo, y sus calles laterales. Tenía Plaza de Mercao, edificios de Gobierno, bancos, cafeterías, iglesias, reposterías y nueve cines (García Ramis 12).

In the 1950s, characterized by the urge for progress, by urban development and by a modified, cultural-nationalist ideology of nation-building, the security and the identity of the white, middle class national imaginary find themselves threatened by the gradual incorporation of the lower classes into the urban context, often facilitated by the construction of housing projects in the proximity of middle-class neighborhoods. The novel alludes to the way that this proximity represented a threat to the perceived values of the utopian middle class to which Lidia's family belongs. In response to the announcement of the creation of a new housing project, Lidia's aunt fearfully says, "Ahora se dañará todo. La gente del caserío va a dañar las propiedades, empezarán los robos" (García Ramis 125), unequivocally positioning "self" and "nation" against clearly defined "others." Otherness, in this case, is engendered by racial and class characteristics that are undesirable in the imaginary–but also in the territory–of the white middle class, which perceives itself as the rightful model of national identity.

The white, middle-class, self-contained national model is constructed and reproduced through a rigid pedagogy of gender and class: "Casi nunca nos dejaban salir a jugar con los niños del vecindario. A mí porque no había niñas y a Andrés para que no fuera a coger las malas costumbres porque los varones de su edad no eran de familias educadas" (García Ramis 48). Curiously, Lidia's education seems to be more concerned with gender norms than that of Andrés, whose most important responsibility is to represent the behavior and the education of his class, looking forward to the moment when he will be one of the men in charge of it. The nation's gendered, reproductive function is ascribed to the young woman, while its leadership to the young (white, middle class) man, its future leader–a situation that reaffirms patriarchy and feminizes the nation. Lidia's capacity to transgress the gender roles and sexual norms that form part of the cultural nationalist imaginary positions her as an agent of possibility and as a potential protagonist of the construction of an alternative national imaginary with respect to gender and sexuality.

*Felices días, tío Sergio* subverts the patriarchal aspects of cultural nationalism and, through the figures of the uncle and of the young female protagonist, uses gender and sexuality to oppose national discursive associations with a feminine nation governed by a patriarch characterized by heterosexual masculinity and virility. In this sense, Lidia's coming-to-consciousness by the end of the novel puts her character forth as an alternative figure–in terms of political affiliation, gender and sexuality–to the background populist, cultural nationalist model.

## TWO WOMEN, TWO HOUSES, ONE PATRIARCH IN *DIOS LOS CRÍA*

In the 1970s and the 1980s Puerto Rican cinema remained a privileged medium for the construction of space, exploring the trope of the house in relation to gender, race, class and nation. While feminist artists continued to question traditional expectations of gender and normative configurations of gendered spaces, others pushed back against the feminism of the 1970s, implementing humor and satire to reinstate and reaffirm the patriarchal spatial order through the cinematic medium. The following sections focus on spaces simultaneously gendered and racialized in two short films: *La otra*, part of Jacobo Morales's film *Dios los cría*, and "Ligia Elena," the animated video to Rubén Blades's well-known song. These films use similar motifs, dichotomies and stereotypes to reconfigure the relationship between gender, space and nation. At the same time, they make contrasting arguments regarding the space of the Puerto Rican nation and the places to which it relegates women from different class and racial backgrounds. While *La otra* seemingly inverts gender stereotypes only to reaffirm traditional gender roles, "Ligia Elena" recasts the relationship between nation, gender and space in Puerto Rico and more broadly, in Latin America.

Thanks to its representation of contemporary Puerto Rican social issues, Morales's *Dios los cría* is commonly recognized as the film that marks the beginning of contemporary Puerto Rican cinema, the period in which "el cine puertorriqueño alcanza su madurez" (Torres Ortíz 97). *Dios los cría* is a collection of five short films, each dedicated to a situation in the life of upper-middle class Puerto Ricans. It begins with the eponymous short film *Dios los cría*, about the fight for the inheritance of a dead patriarch, followed by *Negocio redondo*, which critiques the materialism and hypocrisy of the Catholic Church. The third short, *Entre 12 y 1*, is set in an elevator in which three people admit to infidelity. The fourth, *La gran noche*, follows an aging prostitute, and finally, *La otra* depicts a love triangle that crystallizes power hierarchies and the contrast between the expectations and the reality of gender roles.

*La otra* is organized around two images–of women and spaces–represented through two corresponding dichotomies–a wife and a lover situated in their respective houses. The representation of the two female characters exploits viewers' stereotypes about what constitutes a "typical" wife and a "typical" lover. The film opens with a sequence in which a beautiful woman (the actress Gladys Rodríguez)–presumably the lover–is depicted in front of a mirror, in a scene that visually alludes to The Snow White fairy tale. The use of colors like red for her hair and white for her robe is not accidental; it suggests the promise of pleasure behind apparent but deceptive innocence. As the woman asks the mirror, "¿quién es la más bella?" the camera catches details of her face and mouth, creating a sense of seduction and desire, while the three consecutive sexual acts with the male protagonist (played by Morales himself) imply a desire that most audiences would associate with an extra-marital affair rather than with marriage. It is also significant that, in contrast to the second female character introduced shortly thereafter, this first woman has no name, suggesting that the film's title alludes to her, "la otra mujer," or "the other woman." This representation builds on social preconceptions of marriage as monotonous, of sex as hidden or forbidden, of the female lover as secret and as stereotypically beautiful, and of the affair as an appealing dream.

The space in which these initial scenes are situated again exploits audience expectations and enhances the stereotypical image of a female lover and an extramarital affair. The setting is the apartment's bedroom and the mise-en-scène is such that the bed occupies the center of the frame, dominating the space and making an explicit suggestion about the woman's role as a sexual object. The bed is in a big, elegant apartment with large windows, with the white color again dominating the interior. Since the woman is always seen in the bedroom and there is nothing to suggest that she works–or, for that matter, that she ever leaves the home–the implication is that her main role is that of fulfilling the protagonist's sexual desire. The combination of the setting, the slow motion and the lighting suggest a sense of luxury, of a man who can afford to maintain an affair with a beautiful woman.

The dichotomous representation of women in this film is completed with the introduction of the second female character, Josefina (Norma Candal), whose image is that of a "typical" wife and housewife, an image that once again builds on common preconceptions and gender stereotypes in Puerto Rican society. Josefina cooks, serves the male protagonist and worries about his health. Her appearance differs from the first woman's–she is somewhat older and doesn't project the same sense of glamour.

The spatial setting of this second part of the film and the space that this second female character occupies once again play upon the audience's internalization of common social preconceptions about marriage and traditional gender roles. The film leads one to believe that Josefina is the protagonist's wife by situating her in the space of the kitchen, fulfilling a traditional role and reproducing gendered relations of power. In contrast to the bed in the first scene, here the object that occupies a central area in the mise-en-scène is the table where the male protagonist is having dinner. His initiative to bring Josefina her plate and relieve her of her domestic duties is an evident exception, a situation made clear by the woman's surprise and discomfort. Instead of inverting gender roles, this romantic scene elucidates what is normally lacking in this relationship–namely, equilibrium in the domestic obligations.

The relationship between Josefina and the protagonist reaffirms gender roles and stereotypes through the distribution of work, both domestic and salaried. While Josefina maintains the house, she is not allowed to have a salaried job. The male protagonist insists that, "¡Seré yo quien provea cuanto haga falta en esta casa!" (*Dios*), exercising patriarchal power to prevent the woman from leaving the house and from providing for herself independently. (Ironically, in the final part of the film he is seen in his office in the Milla de Oro banking district in Hato Rey, as a professional whose job is in quite a precarious position.) The fact that Josefina and the protagonist go to bed without the desire that characterized the first scenes of the film emphasizes the different quality of his relationship with Josefina, where the focus on sex is replaced by love and care–yet another stereotypical dichotomy on which the film builds. This second relationship and the space in which it develops present another side of the traditional masculine imaginary–that of the "breadwinner," of the family responsible for taking care of a loving, submissive wife and of a traditional house.

Both relationships are introduced with no small portion of irony, evident at the narrative level in the exaggeratedly rigid stereotypes that the feminist movement has critiqued since the 1960s. At the formal level, slow motion, the easily perceivable contrast in color palettes and in motifs like the bed enhance the sense of irony and of a certain distance from the dichotomous reality depicted in the film. However, the irony never reaches the point of denouncing the traditional gender roles, and instead frequently (as in the final sequence) flirts with the possibilities that these gender roles open for a reaffirmation of patriarchy.

The film's climax, in which the protagonist's two worlds inconveniently collide in his office, offers what the audience is led to believe is the story's resolution. It becomes clear that the red-headed woman is in fact the wife, while Josefina is the secret lover. The wife's derision of the less attractive Josefina (who appears in the office with homemade cake, in contrast to the wife's bottle of champagne) is confronted with the emphatic words, "Eras esposa solamente en el aspecto romántico, amoroso" (*Dios*), suggesting that true love and affection are manifested in everyday actions like cooking and mending his socks. While at first sight this might seem a denunciation of traditional gender roles and of the sexualization of the female body, in reality it reaffirms another type of stereotype–of the reproductive role of women and of their restriction to the domestic sphere.

*La otra*'s brief epilogue, which constitutes the second major role inversion in the film, reaffirms the gendered power structure through the man's capacity to continue manipulating the relationships with the two women. In the film's final moments he marries Josefina but is seen dancing in a bar with his former wife. On the one hand, this sequence exposes the hypocrisy of a certain social character, middle-class, white and male, similar to the protagonists of the other short films that constitute *Dios los cría*. More than a denunciation, however, the absurdity of this final scene constructs a rather heroic depiction, implying that the deception will be carried on indefinitely, without much chance of a true equilibrium of gender roles in Puerto Rican society.

This final scene also allows for a rereading of the short's title, and of a new way of understanding it in relation to the other four vignettes. While at first glance a gender-referencing title like "la otra" would allude to the protagonical role of a woman, the film quickly makes it clear that this is not the case, and that the women's significance in the film results only from their relationship with the male protagonist. It is he who decides who is the official partner and who is the "other" woman, imposing otherness in the context in which women have little agency. He assumes a position of power that seems absolute, undisputable, and socially accepted, and at no point do the women or other characters question his relationships. On the contrary, as the last scene shows, even after discovering the truth, both women remain in relationships with him, only in roles that are deceptively inverted.

More broadly, the situation that unfolds in *La otra* can be read as an allegory of gender relations in traditional Puerto Rican national imaginaries. As the film constructs the Puerto Rican nation through the image of the house, the two houses in which it is set can be seen as contrasting yet complementary, and ultimately reproducing a patriarchal national discourse. In addition, the film reaffirms the authority of the institution of marriage, and of the man's power to determine the rules that organize that institution. The woman, whether participating in the marriage as a wife or as an "other," is always loyal and accommodating, rarely leaving the house or the limits imposed by her position as a wife or as a lover, while the man is characterized by his liberty to cross the boundaries between the two worlds that he controls. While the irony with which the male protagonist is represented might imply that the film assumes a critical perspective regarding gender relations in the Puerto Rican national imaginary, this irony does nothing to empower women or to give them the tools to change the status quo. This is the case even when *La otra* is read in the context of the overall film's title, as "dios los cría" ("y ellos se juntan") is hardly an oppositional statement. It is rather one of observation and acceptance of a situation, of a kind of people, whose behavior might be reproachable, but which the speaker has no intention of attempting to change. Consequently, the film's representation of women and gender relations in the Puerto Rican nation ultimately reaffirms and reestablishes a traditional, male-dominated power structure.

In an interview that focuses on the Puerto Rican film industry and on his own cinematic work, Jacobo Morales reiterates the need for authenticity in film, an authenticity that he claims forms the nucleus of *Dios los cría*: "la autenticidad es lo que le brinda el mayor potencial de universalidad a una película" (Ríos Díaz 15). While the notion of authenticity is problematic in film analysis, in that it implies a compound, yet debatable set of cinematic characteristics, including the provenance of funding, director, actors, themes, locations, and, just as importantly, ideologies and representations,

Morales's words indicate his understanding of the responsibility that he bears for the development of a national film industry, one that he hopes would one day be able to transcend the island's borders. While the merit of *Dios los cría* is undeniable, in that the film "refocus[ed] Puerto Rican cinema by looking at things Puerto Rican–subjects, history, characters, idiosyncrasy–and drawing on that reality to propose an original, nationally-rooted definition of this art form" (Rodríguez 69), it is difficult to use the word authenticity to describe it, as its focus is limited to a certain cross-section of society, and is hardly representative of Puerto Rico's social and cultural complexity. While the film is a powerful indictment of the "greed, hypocrisy, deception, personal interest placed before human relations, and rejection of those who won't follow established ways" (Rodríguez 69-70), it can hardly be called "authentic" if one were to examine closely what it excludes. While, scene by scene, mostly white and middle-class characters expose their weaknesses and excesses, the film contains almost no references to working-class people, Afro-Puerto Ricans, women who resist patriarchal power, or to a notion that there is a Puerto Rican society beyond the satirized middle classes that Morales depicts. In the film, González's four-stories house, schematic and problematic as it might be, has been reduced to a single level, motivated the hypocrisy, the materialism and the desire for power that haunt its scenes.

## "La sociedad" vs. "la vecindad": Race, Gender, and Urban Space in "Ligia Elena"

In contrast to *Dios los cría*, "Ligia Elena" presents a much more multifaceted and conflicted racial and class composition of Puerto Rican society. "Ligia Elena" tells the story of a white, upper middle-class young woman who escapes with a poor black trumpet player, and of her family's consequent disappointment and panic at their daughter's "betrayal" of their hopes for her future. The song's–and even more so the video's–representation of a predominantly white, Hispanocentric, patriarchal model of the Puerto Rican nation uses many of the same motifs, stereotypes and dichotomies as Morales's film. However, in contrast to *La otra*, Paco López's video to Rubén Blades's song results in a poignant indictment of traditional racial and class hierarchies, and constructs a national model founded on equality, acceptance and social integration.

The video focuses on two sets of parallel yet contrasting spaces, each representing different associations with class and race. The first consists of the urban spaces that the protagonists inhabit, beginning with Ligia Elena's town, with its orderly, wide, straight streets and neatly painted houses, suggesting a well-maintained middle- to upper-middle class neighborhood. In contrast, the arrabal, the poor area where the musician takes Ligia Elena, is depicted as a chaotic area with winding streets, implying that the order that governs the town in which the girl's family lives does not apply there.

The second set of spaces consists of the houses that the family and the young couple inhabit. The parents' house is large, spatious, and contains elegant furniture that evokes certain (stereotypically upper-middle-class) values. In contrast, the trumpet player's house (which, ironically, can be seen through the parents' window, suggesting that the distance between the two worlds is not that great) is small, apparently consisting of a single room, messy and disorganized, but emitting a sense of joy lacking in the big house. Instead of luxurious furniture, what can be seen in the musician's house is a large bed, reaffirming the sense of desire and pleasure that is absent from the family house. These two contrasting spatial representations, with their corresponding associations of freedom vs. conservatism and adherence to traditional social norms, construct two different models of Puerto Rican (and more broadly, Latin American) society—one patriarchal and hierarchical, and the other one modern and integrated.

As each space becomes associated with certain racial and class identities, the song and the video offer a critique of the traditional national ideal of whiteness. Even if in Latin America (and in Puerto Rico in particular) the imaginary of the predominantly white nation has been critiqued for decades, there is still an underlying racism that remains evident both in everyday practices and in linguistic expressions. Through the representation of characters like Ligia Elena's mother, the video critiques whiteness as the traditionally ideal model of the Puerto Rican nation.

The contradictions embedded in the character of Ligia Elena's mother become the video's principal source of indictment of racism. The regret and the panic that emerge from her words, "a mí lo que más me choca es que esa malagradecida, yo pensaba que me iba a dar un nietecito con los cabellos rubios, así como Troy Donahue, y viene y se marcha con ese tuza [gentuza]" ("Ligia Elena"), exaggerated as they are in the song, are treated with unequivocal irony in the animated video. The visual representation of the blond grandchild takes the ideal of whiteness further, as the song as sung in the video describes him as a "nieto con cabellitos rubios, con los ojos rubios, con dientes rubios," ("Ligia Elena"), accompanied by the corresponding visual image of a blond-haired, blond-eyed, and blond-teethed baby. This picture of a white, blonde child complements the mother's exaggeratedly high blonde hairdo, but stands in contrast to her light brown skin. The song's lyrics never mention her race or ethnicity, but the way in which her attitude towards race contrasts with her own racial identity of a mulata points to a contradiction, to a "bourgeois logic of the racial inferiority of blacks [that] underlies the colonized and colonizing ideal [. . .] and the expectations regarding a white, racially exclusive upper-class sector" (Aparicio 88), seemingly internalized by a wide spectrum of Puerto Rican society. By making the mother the carrier of this traditional racial ideal of whiteness, by having Ligia Elena fall in love with a black musician, and have a mulatto baby, the video uses gender to critique the reproduction of a patriarchal colonial social order, and emphasizes the young woman's subversive agency in the construction of a racially inclusive model of the nation that also crosses class lines.

The video's critical standpoint on race and gender intersects with a similarly subversive commentary on the question of gender and class. According to the song's lyrics, Ligia Elena and the musician come from opposing ends of the social hierarchy–while she is "de la sociedad," he is "de la vecindad," implying a class incompatibility that is problematic in the eyes of the girl's well-to-do family. The stand that the song takes in defense of class integration through the young couple's relationship is evident in the futility of "regaños, ni viajes ni monjas / ni las promesas de amor que le hicieran los niños de bien" ("Ligia"), and in the power of the "humilde trompeta" whose freedom and love end up being more appealing than the promise of a luxurious life.

The video proposes a progressive and integrated social imaginary represented through the blending of the spaces represented in the videoclip. It is important to note the critique that the song and the video direct at hierarchical discourses of race and gender–at the end, the trumpet player is seen among high society people, who move away in an unequivocal gesture meant to put distance between themselves and the black musician. Meanwhile, the poor area that he inhabits does not reject Ligia Elena, even though she comes from a different background and a different social sphere. Consequently, the space seen as a space of possibility for the transformation of the Puerto Rican national imaginary is not the one commonly accepted as a model of Puerto Rican culture–upper-middle class, white, and patriarchal–but the one associated with African roots, popular culture (music, in this case salsa, long seen as a transgression of traditional Spanish genres like la danza) and racial mixing that result in a transformation of national discourses of whiteness and Hispanic identity to propose an alternative Puerto Rican nation.

## CONCLUSION

In recent decades, artists have subverted the predominantly white, elite, masculine, heterosexual and patriarchal Puerto Rican national imaginary, and have highlighted the roles of previously marginal groups–Afro-Puerto Ricans and women, among others. The trope of the house has been instrumental, both as a setting and as a metaphor, for the construction and for the negotiation of alternative national geographies, some of which reaffirm, and others that subvert traditional patriarchal models of the nation.

The analysis of race, class and colonial relations in the work of authors like José Luis González and Juan Gelpí helps map the gendered geographies that emerge from the literary and cinematic work of writers and filmmakers like Rosario Ferré, Magali García Ramis, Jacobo Morales and Paco López. While *The House on the Lagoon* opens possibilities for transforming the relationship between gender and nation, it also reaffirms racial and class hierarchies that have ordered national discourses founded on notions of whiteness and on the island's colonial legacy. *La otra* similarly reaffirms gender hierarchies by constructing a feminine nation governed by a patriarch who polices gender and sexual norms in the national imaginary. García Ramis's more critical approach presents the family house as a place that the protagonist needs to escape in order to understand and subvert the gendered relations of power at play in the cultural nationalist discourse out of which *Felices días, tío Sergio* emerges. Even more poignantly, "Ligia Elena" uses a set of parallel but contrasting spaces, again exemplified by the trope of the house, to construct an alternative geography and to negotiate racial, class and gender hierarchies in order to propose a national discourse based on social integration.

While some of the texts discussed above address the spatial division of masculine and feminine labor and the relationship between women's productive and reproductive work, the following chapter will focus on another space of female labor–that of the beauty salon–as a gendered and a queer space that enables the construction of a national imaginary that challenges the heteronormative cultural nationalist model.

## Chapter IV

# GENDERING AND QUEERING THE BEAUTY SALON

## Feminine Geographies, Gender Politics and Emotional Labor in the Beauty Salon

Puerto Rican cultural nationalist discourse constructed the spaces of the factory and the house through a patriarchal logic that projected "acceptable" female models–dedicated mothers, faithful wives and selfless workers. Other spaces, however, have evaded this representation and have become sites for the creative subversion of traditional gender relations. Since the 1970s, feminist writers and directors have set their literary and cinematic texts in beauty salons and brothels, and from these locations have voiced eminent critiques of the patriarchal models of *la gran familia puertorriqueña.*

This chapter focuses on the gendered geographies and the feminist solidarities that emerge in the face of patriarchal and capitalist hegemonies in the work of authors like Carmen Lugo Filippi, Mayra Santos-Febres and Sonia Fritz. These writers and film directors have used the space of the beauty salon as a site for the construction of subversive models of gender and sexuality that resist and critique those put forth by Puerto Rican cultural nationalism. Through the relationships that develop between women in the beauty salon, and through the interactions between the beauty salon and spaces like the street, the strip club, the church and the family house, the protagonists of Lugo Filippi's stories "Milagros, calle Mercurio" and "Pilar, tus rizos," of Santos-Febres's story "Hebra rota" and of Fritz's eponymous short film, politicize the space of the beauty salon, both gendering and queering it. In this way, they challenge some of the spatial tropes associated with Puerto Rican cultural nationalist discourse and propose axes of feminist and queer solidarity that form the basis of new models of community.

In Puerto Rican literary and cultural production, the beauty salon is one of the spaces constitutive of the gendered maps of domination, resistance and feminine agency. The common association of the beauty salon with femininity may obscure the fact that one of the main functions of the salon is the construction and the performance of gender identity, which "always varies according to space" (Black 86). Salons have always been spaces in which "identity is performatively constituted" (Butler 25) and in which women negotiate racial, class and sexual boundaries. Inevitably, they are also spaces of contradiction, unveiling possibilities for solidarity and political consciousness, while bearing witness to the reproduction of patriarchal norms of femininity, and to the capitalist exploitation of labor, gender and sexuality. These tensions foreground in context-specific ways the negotiations of gender and racial identities in beauty salons in the Caribbean.

More than spaces like the house and the factory, the beauty salon enables a critical analysis of the negotiations of race, and of its intersections with other axes of identity in that space. This occurs both in the Caribbean and beyond, often in contexts in which racial hierarchies are a defining feature of society. It is notable, for example, that Afro-Caribbean beauty salons in the UK tend to cater to one of several groups of clientele–white, Afro-Caribbean, and Asian women–which leads her to conclude that "the salon may be seen as a relatively homogeneous space in terms of the gender and ethnicity of its clients" (Black 10). Even so, race, in terms of its construction through hair and in terms of whom the salons cater to, remains indispensable for understanding the space and the interactions that take place in the beauty salon. In the case of Puerto Rico, even though a salon might not cater only to white women, factors like its location and the cost of its services might exclude, or present an unwelcoming environment, to working-class or to Afro-Puerto Rican women living in certain areas. In other contexts, the negotiation of race in the beauty salon may help women navigate the transnational, racial and ethnic complexities of the immigrant experience. The Dominican beauty salons in New York do just that, as they become "an important socializing agent that facilitates the immigrant and transmigrant adaptation to New York City and helped to sustain Dominican ethno-racial identities as Indo-Hispanic" (Candelario 28-29), enabling women to negotiate changing notions of nation, race, ethnicity and gender. Similarly, the "management" of race in the Hispanic salons in Newark that Ramos Zayas analyzes reveals the ways in which blackness, whiteness and national belonging intersect and transform the beauty salon into a space of exclusion and inclusion, of the demarcation of racial lines and of the construction of communities.

The negotiation of race in the beauty salon reveals the space's potential as a site for various practices of political organization in different cultures and in different historical moments. During the civil rights era African American beauty salons became sites of encounter and of political consciousness-raising. In the early to mid-20th century African American beauty salons transformed into important community sites for the dissemination of information about the civil rights movement and for the organization of political resistance (Black 37-38). At the intersection of race, politics and gender, through "a combination of economic opportunity, philanthropy, and institution building, the black beauty industry shaped a broad and inclusive view of black political activism that allowed them to encourage a wide range of black women to get involved in their communities" (Gill 34). Salons remain spaces of political discourse and practice into the present, bringing national and international struggles to local communities, and inspiring workers' organization for labor rights, best studied in the context of workers' protests in Asian nail and beauty salons (Kang). By focusing on different geographic areas and ethnic communities, these studies reveal how the beauty salon has emerged as an active and creative site for political activism around axes of race, gender and modalities of feminine labor.

These racialized geographies of gender and labor constituted through the space of the beauty salon often carry a class dimension. By virtue of being a space partly defined by labor, the beauty salon is also, by default, a site of the negotiation of class identities. As with other workplaces, the role of beauty salons in the construction of class identity seems to be quite complex. Because beauty salons are "a significant source of female self-employment" (Black 104), ownership of a salon enables women's economic self-sufficiency, and becomes a step towards upward social mobility and financial independence. However, class hierarchies may also govern the relationships among the women that work in the salon, as when the owner's upper-middle class upbringing determines the treatment of her employees, the kinds of tasks that they are asked to perform, etc. In a telling example, Ginetta Candelario depicts the class relations between the owner and the employees of a Dominican salon in New York: while Lamadas's owner prefers to eat her delivered meals undisturbed, most of the women gather to eat around the massage table, while two of them, unable to afford the delivery, bring more economical food prepared at home.

In other cases, employment in the beauty salon could represent the only available way out of a situation of marginalization and abuse. Often, however, this escape does not necessarily result in upward social mobility. For young Brazilian transvestites who have been forced to leave their homes, for example, working in the beauty shop does not necessarily provide a permanent way out of abuse and exploitation, as some of them end up abandoning the salon for prostitution (Kulick 137).

Employment in the beauty salon, while benefiting some women, might be detrimental to others' economic status, health and wellbeing. This is the case of women who have no control over the hiring practices, the administration of work hours and adequate compensation. For them, "long hours and low pay are endemic in the industry. Despite being subject to laws concerning health and safety, and workers' rights, the industry is poorly regulated and generally non-unionised, which contributes to these abuses of employment standards" (Black 105). Consequently, women's labor in the beauty salon is not only a factor contributing to social mobility, but might also be the target of exploitative labor practices.

The gendered geographies of power and resistance that emerge in the salon are complicated by the fact that there are multiple kinds of labor that women perform in beauty salons, and only a portion of their work is recognized as skilled and therefore salaried. A large portion of the work that women do on a daily basis in the beauty salon is emotional labor or counseling. Beauty therapists, hairdressers and other women who work in beauty salons frequently discuss the fact that clients come to the salon to share personal stories, and that they often expect a response that might range from that of "an intimate yet detached listener" (Black 117) to thoughtful and considerate advice. Beauticians would have to respond to women's interest in discussing "topics that ranged from their assessment of local, national and international politics and happenings to the provision of information about how to negotiate local institutions and bureaucracies and the emotionally and physically taxing terrains of romantic relationships, health issues, and workplace experiences" (Candelario 208). This creates expectations that beauty salon employees not only do the work for which they were trained, but also embody characteristics that they are "supposed to" have by virtue of being women and working in the beauty salon.

The reason that this kind of emotional labor presents a burden for the stylists is that their interactions with clients are always inevitably based on services that take place in the arena of capitalist exchange. This double burden of labor presents a contradiction: "Therapists experience an ambivalent relationship with clients encompassing the role of the trained professional offering advice, and also the service worker being paid to give the client what she wants" (Black 117). The issue of profit, inseparable from the interaction between stylists and clients, affects the labor and the adequate compensation of the worker. Even though she is not trained or paid to give emotional and personal advice, if she does not fulfill the client's expectation that she do so, the client might react with dissatisfaction, which in turn might affect the employee's pay or job security.

The expectation for emotional labor and emotional services is normalized by the physical proximity of the beauty therapist to the clients. Unlike most other professions, that of the beauty therapist involves closeness that often consists of contact with the client's hair or body, which might result in different reactions and different kinds of expectations on the part of clients:

> Beauty therapists are aware that touch is a powerful indicator of intimacy. If the client finds that intimacy difficult to handle, then the therapist must find tactful ways of handling her unease. If that intimacy is welcome, as several interviewees noted, then touch may unleash communication on other levels; the therapist may be required to handle feelings that are not initially and obviously to do with bodies, as, for example, when clients confide about their family or marital problems in the course of treatment (Black 124).

Thus, close physical contact, inherent in the beauty therapist's work, becomes the cause for expectations of emotional services and emotional labor on the part of the employees of the beauty salon.

The intimacy involved in the work of the beauty salon alludes to a degree of homoeroticism that few authors have engaged extensively in their studies. When Candelario explains that Chucha and Leticia, the owner and the manager of Lamadas (from "las dos amadas") are a lesbian couple, she quickly clarifies that "their sexuality was unnamed and explicitly unacknowledged by them and by staff and clients. No one called them a couple, much less a lesbian couple, or even 'partners'" (Candelario 195). Even though sexuality is continuously constructed in the beauty salon, this story suggests that space is governed by a hierarchy, according to which heterosexuality is visible and constantly referenced, while homosexuality remains invisible and excluded.

In the case of Puerto Rico, there are a number of context-specific issues that attribute to the beauty salon a particular role in the construction of the politics and the discourses on gender, sexuality, class, race and nation. One such context-specific issue is the interpretation of the *alisado*, or hair straightening (particularly among Afro-Puerto Rican women), a practice that involves complex negotiations of gender and national identity. Thanks in no small part to traditionally racist discourses on racial mixture that tend to prioritize white and indigenous heritage and to marginalize African features, "la celebración de la mezcla no es arbitraria, sino selectiva en tanto favorece unas combinaciones y no otras" (Godreau 107). As a consequence, Afro-Puerto Rican women straighten their hair not necessarily because "el alisado imita una estética occidental/blanca y que la mujer negra que se alisa está, por ende, negándose a sí misma" (84) but in order to approximate the dominant stereotype of *la puertorriqueñidad*, and through it to claim belonging in the Puerto Rican nation. In the process, these women also subvert "the ideology of *blanqueamiento* (whitening or bleaching) [that] continues to permeate Puerto Rican national culture" (Duany 182), an ideology that they no longer associate with the desire to be white, but instead with a belonging to a specific model of Puerto Ricanness.

This analysis suggests that an important function of the beauty salon is the adaptation to exclusionary national discourses, in response to the contentious question of national belonging. This leads the analysis away from the notions of "false consciousness" and "Puerto Rican inferiority complex" that often enter the discussion of Spanish colonialism and US imperialism on the island in relation to issues of race and class. At the same time, it is important to recognize that the space and the services of the salon facilitate a differentiation between "Puerto Rican national subjects" and their "others," "aquellos que se consideran 'negros' o 'menos mezclados.' Desde una perspectiva puertorriqueña, éstos pueden incluir a los afro-americanos, los dominicanos, los haitianos o a las personas del Caribe inglés" (96). Since it is almost exclusively women who straighten their hair in an attempt to approximate an ethnic and racial national ideal, the women who choose not to straighten their hair are the ones that remain outside the national imaginary. In this sense, the beauty salon has the potential to become a space of belonging, but also of the creation of "otherness" that doubly marginalizes women.

Racial and gendered citizenship is intimately related to sexual citizenship, and to the relationship between consumption, gender, and culturally specific notions of femininity. While consumption is often a form of manipulation that benefits the flow of capital, "beauty consumption" can also be seen as a "form of emancipation from the constraints of everyday life" (Quiñones Arocho 110). The transformation of the body that takes place in the beauty salon thus becomes an expression of agency: "denied economic equality or even political power, women celebrate the techniques and products that offer them control of their lives" (123). In this analysis, consumption is conceptualized not as weakness, but as conscious agency in the control over one's body and self.

The question perhaps most relevant to the analysis of the literary and cinematic texts in this chapter is that of the possibility of constructing gendered geographies of resistance and female solidarity in the beauty salon, around shared concerns of race, gender, sexuality, family and labor. How does the interplay between patriarchy and gender differ in the space of the beauty salon and in other spaces of female labor? What is the potential that consumption and intimacy have to germinate strategies of resistance around axes of race, class, gender and sexuality in the salon? If female interactions resist patriarchal notions of the salon as a space of apolitical aesthetics, what are the alternative geographies that women construct, and that contest patriarchal images of female labor in the salon as devoid of social impact or political potential?

In the beauty salon, solidarity often emerges as a result of interpersonal relationships–both discursive and corporeal–that develop during processes like hair straightening (Godreau 85). During this beauty ritual, women share "contacto íntimo entre mujeres que se dejan tocar, halar y lavar por otras, ya sea a cambio de un pago, o simplemente porque sí. En el proceso, se intercambian cuentos, chismes, preocupaciones, y también se construyen solidaridades" (Godreau 121). The possibility for solidarity accompanies the emerging sense of sisterhood: "el ideal de belleza compartido en el beauty hermana y acerca a las mujeres, suavizando distinciones sociales en el trato personal" (124). *Hermanar*, to create sisterhood, is a powerful notion that speaks to the possibility inherent in any space, including the beauty salon, in which women have the freedom to interact while shielded (at least to an extent) from patriarchal expectations of feminine discourse and behavior.

The possibility of solidarity also emerges through the conversations between the beauty salon's female clients. As one of the women says, "That's why I come here, to fix myself up and to forget my troubles in life" (Quiñones Arocho 116). What is important in this line is the women's need to "come here," to go to the physical place that provides them with the capacity to address their everyday reality. Thus, as women share their frustrations and give each other advice on topics as intimate as family and sexuality, they construct a community that empowers them to resist some of the mechanisms of patriarchal oppression.

At the same time, the idea of solidarity in the salon should resist idealization, as at times that space reproduces certain social hierarchies. In a revealing example, Quiñones Arocho narrates an incident in which a client, Berta, asks for another client's opinion of a manicure design. In what follows, "Yolanda looks at her with great surprise and immediately approves the manicurist's work. The minute Berta walks away, however, Yolanda makes a gesture of repulsion, and her other friends laugh" (121). This incident suggests that the beauty salon is not immune to the tensions that traverse its customers' society, and calls for a cautious analysis of the extent of these solidarities offer the female protagonists of the texts analyzed here effective instruments of resistance, liberation and the subversion of patriarchal national models.

The rest of this chapter takes these issues as starting points, focusing on literary and cinematic representations of the space of the beauty salon, and on the ways in which the interactions that it enables–intimate contact between women, resistance to patriarchy in a particular material space, the construction of the body, and gendered negotiations of urban space–constitute a productive approach to the reconfiguration of the interplay between space, gender and community.

## "Milagros, Calle Mercurio": Gendering and Queering the Beauty Salon

"Milagros, calle Mercurio" focuses on the relationship that develops in the beauty salon between Marina, a hairdresser, and Milagros, a young woman who is one of her clients. Marina first notices Milagros as the girl and her mother walk to church. She is intrigued by the beautiful girl and curious about her mother's constant vigilance. One day the mother brings Milagros to the beauty salon looking for help with her daughter's hair, which has begun to fall. Gradually, Milagros gains Marina's trust, which allows her to turn to Marina after the events in which the story culminates: the police discover Milagros dancing in a strip club, she suffers severe punishment at home and decides to escape, but not before asking Marina to cut off all her hair.

The story develops in a variety of urban spaces, and addresses feminist geographers' concerns regarding the relation of space to gender, patriarchy, power and desire. Marina and Milagros move from Madrid to Isla Verde to Ponce, from the street corner to the strip club, and in all these spaces they challenge the power of patriarchy and traditional norms of gender and sexuality. In the process, they also trace new geographies of gender, defying social constructions of space, gender and nation, feminizing and queering both physical and metaphorical spaces in order to question patriarchal and heteronormative imaginaries of the relationship between gender and nation.

The first set of spaces that the story encompasses are the cities that the protagonists inhabit–Madrid, Isla Verde and Ponce, with their houses, streets, and beauty salons, in the case of Marina, and Ponce's streets, church and strip club in the case of Milagros. Marina, the story's narrator, reminisces on her marriage to Freddie, identified only by his military occupation and by the monotony that he brings into her life. She follows him to a military base outside Madrid, but soon her dreams of traveling give way to the burdens of domestic work deprived of social and cultural activities: "Cuando la nena cumplió un año ya me encontraba al borde de una neurosis. La rutina doméstica me aplastaba, necesitaba respirar otros aires y más que nada hablar con aguien que me comprendiera" (Lugo Filippi, "Milagros" 28). The city is inaccessible to Marina, whose confinement to the domestic sphere results from a patriarchal social order (she moves because of her husband's job and is left to take care of the home and of their child), as much as from the interaction between imperial and military structures of power (her husband's service in the U.S. army, which controls their patterns of spatial and social mobility).

It is not surprising, then, that the narrator seizes the chance to work at a beauty salon as her only opportunity to leave home and to perform labor that is not domestic and that in some sense satisfies her need for self-realization. Through her work in the salon Marina finds "a feminised space away from external demands upon the woman, and a place where pleasurable attention to the body and the emotions may be obtained" (Black 87). Even though she remembers those years with irony, inventing a French-sounding word–"me inicié en las artes peinoriles" (Lugo Filippi, "Milagros" 28)–Marina recognizes that it was the desire to escape domesticity, to encounter pleasure and an opportunity for social participation that took her first to the salons in Madrid and San Juan, and then to her privately-owned salon in Ponce.

The space of the beauty salon, even though presented as an alternative to domesticity, is hardly unproblematic. It is saturated with a variety of tensions–of race, class, gender and sexuality–that the story introduces into the characters' relationships. In the salon in Isla Verde Marina confronts demonstrations of superiority by her upper-middle class clients, whom she calls "perfectos monigotes con ínfulas de grandes damas" (29). Such descriptions challenge the perception of the beauty salon as a feminine space of solidarity "que se forma entre hermanas, amigas y vecinas al compartir, cotidianamente, el ritual del embellicimiento" (Godreau 120), revealing instead the inequality that saturates this capital-dependent space of labor and of service. It illustrates the argument that the salon uncovers wider social relations (Black 10), in this case of a society traversed by rigid class and racial lines. What Godreau describes as solidarity enabled by the space of the beauty salon is not impossible, but through the relations of power between employees and clients, in both cases women, the short story problematizes the beauty salon as a space intersected by complex axes of capital, class and patriarchy, and highlights these same hierarchies in Puerto Rican society.

It is in part the lack of independence, and in part her mother's insistence, that drives Marina to open her own beauty salon, this time on Mercurio Street in her hometown of Ponce. The salon is decorated according to Marina's taste: "Lucía coquetón el lugar con sus paredes recién empapeladas, sus collages de cortes y peinados que yo misma había ideado sobre planchas de plywood negra y sus tres secadoras idénticas, alineadas frente a un gran espejo de marco sencillo (detestaba los pretenciosos ribetes dorados de los espejos de Woolworth's)" (29). The most important part of this description is in fact what it leaves out–the silently constructed class identity of the space, evident in the narrator's desire to demonstrate good taste through the matching hairdryers and the simple (but presumably more elegant) mirror frame. Marina positions herself in contrast to other women who would have preferred Woolworth's products, and evokes a sense of style that gives her salon a desired class identity. Yet again, the descriptive details point to the need to think of the space of the beauty salon as a site for the construction and the intersection of gender and class hierarchies, reproduced by the very women that own and manage or that use the services of the beauty salon.

Surrounding the beauty salon in Lugo Filippi's story are a number of places that collectively construct the image of a city and a nation defined by interlaced experiences of gender and sexuality. The space most prominently present in the part of the story that takes place in Ponce is the street, with the possibilities that it offers women for resistance, and the limits that it imposes on them by virtue of being an open space, accessible to the scrutinizing gaze of power and authority. In texts like *Maruja* (analyzed in Chapter 2), the street is a masculine space in which the male gaze was the instrument of a pedagogy of gender that reaffirmed traditional feminine and masculine roles and behaviors. In Lugo Filippi's story, the street is a similar site for the reproduction of normative femininity. Marina first notices Milagros as the girl is walking down the street with her mother, and it is Marina's gaze and access to the street that construct an image of Milagros and her mother that initially identifies them with traditional gender models: "Fuiste tú, Marina, el clavo caliente que se apostó en el balcón para observar la peregrinación crepuscular de Milagros. La madre avanzaba a trancazos, la

Biblia bajo el brazo [. . .] A un pie de distancia, Milagros las seguía sin alterar en lo más mínimo su rítmico trote" (31). Later on in the story, it is again in the street that Marina hears gossip that Milagros has been detained in a strip club where she was performing: "No se puede creer en nadie, nena, la Milagros tan seriecita, tan mosquita muerta y mira lo que hacía cuando salía de la escuela, na menos que esnuándose en un club de la carretera pa Guayanilla, esnuándose, oye eso, y que esnuándose!" (35-36). The street becomes the space in which gender is scrutinized and controlled, in this case by women who act as agents of patriarchal power.

The gossip in which Marina finds herself participating is one of many "cautionary verbal and nonverbal messages about the dangers of transgressing the boundaries of heteronormativity" (Asencio 3) and of "appropriate" femininity, turning the street into a site of objectification and of the reproduction of norms of gender and sexuality that emerge in the interplay between the gaze and the performance of identities that it imposes on women. By participating in gossip in the street, Marina affirms her own conformity to heterosexual gender norms, disguising her own sexuality and using passing as "an act of self-protection and safety and a strategy often adopted to maintain familial approval" (Torres 237), sparing herself public condemnation and social rejection.

The relationship between the gaze and the performance of gender roles in the space of the street is part of a larger issue, that of the interplay between patriarchal power and urban space. In the modern world, patriarchal models and expectations of gender also limit women's access to urban space. The city "was gendered in the very general sense of the distinction between public and private. [. . .] The public city which is celebrated in the enthusiastic descriptions of the dawn of modernism was a city of men. The boulevards and cafés, and still more the bars and brothels, were for men–the women who did go there were for male consumption" (Massey 233-234). As a result, women's limited access to public space and their confinement to the home was a way of controlling both space and gender by tacitly limiting women's access to material, everyday urban space. Cities were (and many still are) gendered spaces, masculine and patriarchal, that impose rigid restrictions on gender and sexuality, especially when it comes to physical mobility and social inclusion and participation.

Reading the story as a map of the gendered geographies of access, agency and repression calls for a closer look at one of the climactic episodes of Lugo Filippi's story, in which a policeman detains Milagros in a strip club and takes her home to be punished by her mother. Here, the road (*la carretera*) and the strip club act as sites of patriarchy and male privilege, as the men's presence in the strip club (both the clients' and the policeman's, whose professional duty is confounded by a fascination and attraction to Milagros's nude body) is never questioned, while Milagros suffers verbal condemnation and physical abuse for performing in the strip club. Milagros, just like "toda mujer que intente cruzar la línea de lo socialmente vedado para ella será castigada, marginada como poco femenina o como diabólica" (Palmer-López 252). The metaphor of "crossing the line" is especially opportune for this analysis, as for Milagros, the limits of gender and sexuality are not only those of "acceptable" behavior, but also of access to space. In specific spaces, the expression of female sexuality is criminalized and condemned, while male agency and demand for spaces like the strip club suffer no repercussions.

What comes into play in this episode is not only Milagros's, but also Marina's sexuality and its relation to space. Marina's fascination with Milagros soon becomes a subtle attraction, as the narrator begins following the girl and reenacting in her mind the scene in the strip club. While the policeman is allowed to participate in the events in the strip club, as a woman Marina has no access to the physical space, and consequently imagines the scene as it might have happened. Luz María Umpierre analyzes this episode through a "homocritical" perspective (309), arguing that "la escena no deja de estar cargada de sexualidad" (314), even though Marina is forced to perform a more traditional "female" role in the scene (to participate in gossip and condemnation on the corner in front of Milagros's house), and to suppress her desire for Milagros.

Umpierre's homocritical perspective is also useful in analyzing Godreau's description of intimacy and of the relationships that develop between women in the beauty salon. Godreau notes that the salon is characterized by "tiempo compartido y de contacto íntimo entre mujeres que se dejan tocar, halar y lavar por otras, ya sea a cambio de un pago o simplemente porque sí" (Godreau 121). Even though this particular description of the interactions that take place in the salon does not explicitly reference sexuality, it is fundamentally homoerotic, even if it leaves out the element of desire that defines Marina's relationship with Milagros in the salon.

Godreau's and Umpierre's descriptions of the beauty salon, as well as Lugo Filippi's fictional account, challenge ethnographic studies derived from other cultural and social contexts that argue that in the salon, "heterosexuality operates as a default position, presumed and uncommented upon" (Black 98). In contrast to Black's account, sexuality is an inextricable part of the interactions in the beauty salon in Puerto Rican anthropological studies and in fictional texts like "Milagros, calle Mercurio," whose protagonists transform the space of the beauty salon through desire, presenting the possibility for both gendering and queering it.

The relationship between the story's female protagonists redraws the patriarchal conception of space through the prism of a gendered, but also of a queer geography of silence, repression, desire and agency. Just like "the heterosexing of space is a performative act naturalized through repetition and regulation" (Valentine 146), so is the queering of space the product of desires, gazes and other performative acts that transform the identity of the space and the relations that develop in that space. In the salon, Marina's "lesbian body configures a particular kind of spatiality" (Binnie xiii), as the narrator not only transgresses gender and sexual norms by transforming Milagros's hair and self, but also queers the space of the beauty salon as she encounters, observes and desires Milagros. In the process, Marina does more than challenge norms of gender and sexuality. Her desire for Milagros, and the way in which she subverts common associations of the beauty salon with female heterosexuality, "change[s] the way we understand space by exposing its performative nature and the artifice of the public/private dichotomy" (Valentine 154). Marina defines the public space of the salon by lesbian desire, and in this way turns the private, marginalized and silenced experience of desire into a powerful instrument of subversion and transformation of social norms and of the construction of public space.

The challenge to particular constructions of gender and space is realized also through the trope of the double, represented through the parallel experiences of Marina and Milagros, and the similar challenges that the two women have to confront. On a narrative level, the parallels that the story draws between the two protagonists culminate in the final scene, in which Marina sees Milagros's reflection in the mirror, as the girl enters the beauty salon:

> Pules cuidadosamente la formica de las improvisadas coquetas y
> con una hoja húmeda del periódico frotas los espejos que te en-
> tregan de pronto la imagen de la Milagros, sí, de ella misma, ¿es-
> tarás soñando? Pero no, allí está junto a la puerta, mirándote par-
> simoniosamente, sin pestañear, un poco ladeada a causa de una
> maleta que lleva en la mano izquierda . . . Sin volverte la exami-
> nas en el espejo . . . (38).

The scene of Milagros's escape form home is reminiscent of Marina's own escape, through which she had also challenged the expectations of domesticity and motherhood.

Milagros's final physical transformation in the beauty salon represents her ultimate subversion. She expresses her desire for liberation through the materiality of her own body, which she now recognizes as "a site of struggle" (Rose 29). In this final scene, by
reclaiming control of her body, Milagros assumes the power to resist the patriarchal rules reproduced by her mother. Through her
transgressive transformation ("Maquíllame en shocking red, Marina, y córtame como te dé la gana" Lugo Filippi, "Milagros" 38),
Milagros challenges patriarchal norms that construct an image of
submissive femininity that reproduces patriarchal patterns of gender and sexual oppression.

Milagros's transformation would not be possible without Marina's emotional labor, which defines her relationship with Milagros
and reconfigures the space of the beauty salon. While, as critics
have noted, Marina's emotional labor constitutes a "double burden" for the woman who is expected to provide support just by
virtue of being a woman, it is also an instrument for the construction of the sense of female solidarity in the story. Milagros's trust in
Marina allows her to ask for help, and even though at first sight Milagros is the one who benefits from Marina's support, the benefit is
mutual and reciprocal. While Milagros is able to escape the familial
and the urban spaces that punish her transgression of gender and
sexual norms, Marina experiences that liberation vicariously,
through the young woman's resistance. It is Marina's agency,
through her emotional and physical labor, that transforms the space
of the salon into a site of female resistance to patriarchal expectations of honor and respectability. Marina's skills transform Milagros's body, while her emotional labor, along with her ambiguous
desire and identification with Milagros, allow the young girl to use

her body to defy the traditional model of femininity. This relationship of solidarity inscribes the beauty salon in the gendered geographies of patriarchy and resistance that emerge as an alternative to the national model and to the gender norms that it presupposes.

The fact that Milagros's transformation takes place in the beauty salon may seem problematic on several levels. Even though the beauty salon has a number of subversive and liberating aspects, it is also a place where often the body "is molded and worked on in order to achieve a look, and sometimes also a feeling, which is regarded as 'appropriate' in relation to categories of gender, age, sexuality, class and ethnicity" (Black 11). The services offered in the salon, specifically hair-straightening among Afro-Puerto Rican women, serve as a "brega congraciente" (Godreau 113), as a way for women to claim inclusion in the Puerto Rican nation and to navigate a racist society "para abrirse espacio y negociar su posición en la sociedad, sin confrontar, directamente, la lógica racista que determina 'lo negro' del pelo como no deseable, poco atractivo o poco femenino" (113). Milagros's desire for transformation contrasts with these claims for inclusion, which don't necessarily challenge patterns of patriarchal or racial oppression. By asking Marina to cut her hair and to give her a "shocking red' make-up–an allusion to Rosario Ferré's story "Cuando las mujeres quieren a los hombres," in which that color of nail polish connects Isabel la Negra to her "double," Isabel Luberza–Milagros rejects a model of femininity that denies women their agency, and through that, their sexuality, and opts for an alternative that would allow her to construct her own gender and sexual identity that subverts patriarchal norms of femininity.

A subsequent critique of Milagros's transformation is that it occurs through an act of consumption, which here must be analyzed in the context of the relationship between gender, sexuality and citizenship. In the modern city consumption has been associated with national belonging and sexual citizenship, as a society that discriminates on the basis of gender and sexuality is willing to overlook its prejudices if the claim for belonging and citizenship comes through the act of consumption: "S/he who appears to have the capacity to consume can equally take on the appearance of the citizen. The consumer is the citizen-subject of the city par excellence" (Peace 51). Consumption thus enables sexual citizenship, but also acts as a substitute for the rights that societies continue to deny to their citizens based on sexuality: "Could one reason why so many queers enjoy shopping so much (if and when we can afford to do so) is because shopping offers us the opportunity to assert at least some kind of power? Is it an effect of our not having power in other areas, specifically in the realm of social rights? "(Binnie 187). In this analysis of Old Compton Street in London, consumption is an instrument of agency in an environment in which agency, and the rights that come with it, are denied on the basis of sexuality.

Through the transformation of the main characters, "Milagros, calle Mercurio" alludes to this relationship between sexual citizenship, gender and consumption. Both Marina and Milagros resist marginalization based on gender and sexuality: on the one hand, Marina's escape from the oppression of domesticity and marriage, and on the other, Milagros's resistance to the same patriarchal model, reproduced by her mother. Both participate in the process of capitalist exchange, one by providing her services in the beauty salon, the other in the strip club. By offering the services of her beauty salon to other women, Marina participates in Puerto Rican society as a gendered citizen, even though not yet a sexual/queer one, as her desire for Milagros remains silent.

The relationship between gender, sexuality, consumption and citizenship is part of a larger issue, that of the gendered geography of the nation, and of women's participation in it. While modern political theorists like Benedict Anderson have represented the nation as a limited and sovereign imagined community, feminist scholars have critiqued Anderson's thesis of the nation, pointing out that it "assumes an imagined citizen, and this citizen is gendered" (Sharp 99), referencing the (always presumably) male gender and heterosexuality of the fallen soldiers. Lugo Filippi's story both reflects and critiques this masculine and heterosexist image of the national citizen. The story is set in a society that reproduces the masculine, heterosexist model of the national citizen, and denies women participation and agency in the Puerto Rican nation by confining them to the domestic sphere (immediately after her transgression and before she approaches Marina, Milagros is taken back home, her mother becomes the instrument of control and punishment, and the girl is not allowed to leave the house except if she were never to go back). Thus, the story critiques the national imaginary that imposes on women a choice that men don't have to make–whether to conform to the model of the virgin or the prostitute, the only two options that seem available to women as they negotiate the construction of their sexuality. Through the final scene, in which Milagros asks for Marina's help with her transformation and liberation, the story constructs a geography of gender that proposes feminine solidarity and feminist agency as instruments for the construction of alternative communities, not national but built on coalitions around material and symbolic experiences of space and gender.

## FANTASY AS RESISTANCE IN "PILAR, TUS RIZOS"

"Pilar, tus rizos," the second story set in a beauty salon in the *Vírgenes y mártires* collection, uses a different set of techniques to map the gendered geographies of domination and resistance, to critique patriarchal discourse and to suggest the possibility of feminine agency and liberation. In contrast to "Milagros," this story approaches the space and the interactions that develop in the beauty salon from the perspective of the female client. Pilar, who, as the readers discover at the end of the story, is a wife and a mother, is spending the afternoon in Gloria's salon, sitting under a hairdryer, reading a melodramatic romance novel whose characters are Sissy Bite and Piss Ducon, and imagining herself in a similar plot, protagonized by herself and the handsome Mauricio, a character who is a product of her imagination. As the two plot lines (of the romance novel and of Pilar's daydream) evolve, the story constructs the image of a woman who is struggling to negotiate patriarchal structures and traditional norms of gender and sexuality. While Pilar's actions are hardly as daring as Marina's or Milagros's, by setting against each other the spaces of the beauty salon, the home and the romance novel, the short story constructs a powerful critique of the social and the spatial limits that patriarchal society imposes on Puerto Rican women.

Even though the story is set in a beauty salon, much of the plot takes place in the space of the romance novel that Pilar is reading. As the amorous relationship between Sissy and Piss intensifies, so does that of Pilar and Mauricio, the imaginary protagonists of her own romantic daydream. Pilar imagines meeting Mauricio at a dance, he invites her to accompany him for a bolero, and courts her until at the end she proudly rejects his passionate advances. Through these parallel narratives, instead of explicitly critiquing patriarchal discourse, models of gender and structures of power, the story positions the protagonist in the midst of them, as their victim, and uses her situation to expose and condemn gender and sexual oppression.

Pilar's immersion in her own fantasy plot acts as a temporary escape from patriarchy, which in reality reproduces patriarchal structures of oppression. Pilar's depiction in the beauty salon indicates a desire for isolation from the outside world–she sits waiting, unable and unwilling to hear the chatter of the other customers, fully immersed in the romance novel that she is reading. Her attitude is similar to that of one of Quiñones Arocho's interview subjects, who says, "That's why I come here, to fix myself up and forget my troubles in life. If it weren't for these moments . . ." (116). The ellipsis that closes the sentence implies an alternative so undesirable that it is unthinkable. Pilar's voluntary spatial, auditory and visual isolation (when not reading, she only looks at herself in the mirror), intensified by her immersion in a fictional fantasy plot, represents a similar desire to escape a repressive patriarchal reality.

The plot lines of the romance novel that Pilar is reading and of the fictional account that she protagonizes in her mind also act as a space of escape. Through the two fictional narratives the protagonist constructs an identity that attempts to challenge (but in reality reproduces) patriarchal models of gender relations. While Sissy submits to Piss's sexual advances without any resistance, Pilar presents her own character as capable of controlling her relationship with Mauricio. When Sissy appears weak, submissive, and unable to resist Piss's desire, Pilar responds, "Tonta es, tonta la Sissy. No sabe manejar la psicología del hombre" (24). Her response reproduces a patriarchal model of femininity through the suggestion that a woman needs to be a virgin on her wedding day: "No, Mauricio, prometiste que no lo harías hasta llevarme al altar. Quiero ofrendarte mi virginidad" (24). In this scene Pilar is participating in what Quiñones Arocho describes as women "just playing at being other women" in the context of being "denied economic equality or even political power" (Quiñones Arocho 123), inventing an alternate identity that allows her to assume an agency that she does not have in her everyday life. In Pilar's case, however, the alternative is still bound by her internalization of patriarchal discourses and gender expectations.

Parallel to the space of the romance novel is that of the house, the domestic space that imposes restrictions on both social and spatial mobility. Even though its patriarchal logic is present throughout the story and exerts power over the narratives that develop in the beauty salon and in the romance novel, it only becomes part of the plot at the end, when Pilar's husband demands that she go back home so that he can go out for the night.

This final scene has profound implications for the construction of the domestic space and of the space of the beauty salon. Even though up to that moment the salon had been the overall setting, and therefore the privileged space of the plot, Pepe's phone call transforms the relations of power to reveal the beauty salon as a place of otherness, or as an "other in the form of place itself" (Rose 45). Patriarchal discourse becomes the dominant force that orders not only gender relations (Pilar is expected to fulfill her role of a wife and a mother), but also the beauty salon's capacity to function as an alternative place of escape and solidarity. Even though up to that point that possibility had existed, the intervention of the (literal and metaphoric) voice of patriarchy disables it and reinstates the rules that had been suspended during the woman's visit to the beauty salon.

As in the case of "Milagros," and of novels like *The House on the Lagoon* and *Felices días, tío Sergio*, in this story too the home becomes a powerful instrument for the affirmation of patriarchal discourses and practices and for the reproduction of traditional models of gender and sexuality. Feminist critics have long argued that "The limits on women's everyday activities are structured by what society expect women to be and therefore to do. The everyday is the arena through which patriarchy is (re)created–and contested" (Rose 17). In the case of Pilar, the everyday, exemplified by home and family, has a spatial dimension that patriarchy orders and delimits, another "attempt to confine women to the domestic sphere [that is] both a specifically spatial control, and, through that, a social control of identity" (Massey 179). Pilar's spatial mobility and her physical presence in a place are determined by gender roles dependent on patriarchal models of femininity, which construct female identity through space. While Pilar is expected to go home to care for her children, her husband is free to go out and enjoy an evening with friends during his "viernes social"–a situation that quite literally positions the "outside" as the realm of freedom and masculinity, and the home, or the "inside" as that of femininity, gender and sexual oppression.

The hierarchies that emerge between and within the spaces of the beauty salon and the home suggest that the city represented in the story is a dynamic and negotiated construction of multiple axes of power, reaffirming the claim that,

> The identities of place are always unfixed, contested and multiple. And the particularity of any place is, in these terms, constructed not by placing boundaries around it and defining its identity through conterposition to the other which lies beyond, but [. . .] through the specificity of the mix of links and interconnections to that 'beyond.' Places viewed this way are open and porous (Massey 5).

In Pilar's case, an act as simple and everyday as a phone call, which connects the social realms and the physical spaces of the home and the beauty salon, transforms the identity of both spaces and re-arranges relations of solidarity and power, through which the story ultimately exposes and critiques patriarchal models of gender and sexuality. Both the home and the beauty salon, then, become examples of the malleability of urban space, of its constructed nature and the need to think of it as a site of struggle, contradiction and constant negotiation.

The space of the romance novel and the domestic space intersect in the beauty salon, which functions as a temporary escape from the oppression of marriage and motherhood, of domestic work and obligations, and ultimately becomes a space that provides little opportunity to actively question or resist Pilar's subordinated position. This argument is best illustrated in the story's final scene, when Pilar's husband calls to scold her for not being home with the kids when it's his time to leave for the viernes social. The stylist, Gloria, transmits Pepe's angry message without resistance, and accepts that Pilar will do what her husband expects her to: "Acaba de llamar Pepe. ¡Parecía rabioso! Que has tardado mucho y que dejó los nenes con la vecina porque es su viernes. A ese no lo esperes hasta tarde, si llega" (24). In contrast to Marina, Gloria projects traditional norms of femininity, by acting out one of the "multiple ways in which women discipline themselves in order to conform to [. . .] particular expectations of feminine behavior" (McDowell 79). The patriarchal model of "feminine behavior" that Gloria projects and that Pilar reproduces, is that of the housewife and mother who puts her own physical and emotional needs last, prioritizing those of her husband and her children.

Through the interaction between the spaces of the romance novel and of the beauty salon, the story problematizes the question of emotional labor and solidarity, which is a prominent aspect of the relationship between Marina and Milagros in "Milagros, calle Mercurio." Aside from the conversations between the characters in Pilar's fictional narratives, there is hardly any dialogue until the very end of the story, and consequently little possibility for building alliances and for encountering solutions to shared problems. Gloria relates the phone call and provides and observation, but offers no emotional support or advice. While the story illustrates the argument that few women "associate their visits [to the salon] with beauty" (Black 45) and instead enter that space to escape from other everyday problems, it challenges the idea that what develops in the salon is a relationship of solidarity (Godreau 121). Gloria's powerlessness equals Pilar's, she is subject to the same patriarchal norms and she appears to lack the resources to defy them. In this sense, the story presents the beauty salon as a place of temporary escape that fails to act as a challenge to patriarchal structures of oppression, or to construct a valid alternative to them.

Even though at first glance the story places the protagonist in a subordinate position, it does so critically, in order to expose and condemn the violence that lies behind patriarchal models of gender and sexuality, and "con la intención de apelar al cambio y a un progreso social" (Gabiola 40). The story voices this critique through a meticulous development of a relationship of identification between the main character and the reader, made possible by the narrator's point of view, and by the popular and conversational aspects of the story's language.

The identification between protagonist and reader, which allows the story to expose and condemn patriarchal structures of oppression, results from the narrative perspective of the female character who also acts as narrator. The multiple facets of Pilar's identity that the story reveals from the very beginning, from her trivial insecurities ("Quizás ya debería usar gafas," Lugo Filippi, "Pilar" 19) to the memories of her past and her dreams for a perfect partner, reveal different layers of the character's personality and facilitate the readers' identification with her. That identification with Pilar's narrative voice (one of several in the story) is what allows the readers to comprehend and to respond to the violence of the final scene. The narrative perspective, then, is an important factor in the creation of solidarity that makes it possible to condemn patriarchal models of femininity.

The other instrument that the story uses to facilitate the identification, and resulting solidarity, between protagonist and readers is the language, specifically its popular, conversational and oral aspects. It is the language of many of the writers of the 1970s generation, "un lenguaje que [. . .] trasciende el tradicional calco lingüístico de la 'manera de hablar' de los personajes y se convierte en el instrumento versátil, metamórfico y paródico del narrador (Acosta-Belén "En torno" 222). In "Pilar, tus rizos," instead of consistently confident and authoritarian, the narrative is fragmented, filled with interruptions, questions, exclamations, changes of topic, jumps from the present to the past and from reality to fantasy. The informality of such approach allows the reader to relate to the character's concerns and to construct a relationship of solidarity with Pilar's everyday struggles and oppression. It is through the solidarity that the story constructs between reader and protagonist, as opposed to the solidarity that others have argued develops between stylists and clients in the beauty salon, that the story exposes and critiques patriarchal discourses, models of femininity and oppressive practices.

## "Hebra rota": Domestic Violence and Gender Solidarity

While Lugo Filippi and other writers from the Generación del 70 focused on the relationship between space and issues like patriarchy, female independence and mobility, in the 1980s feminist authors traced new geographies of gender around a wider variety of themes, such as domestic violence and a newly-elaborated solidarity along racial lines. Mayra Santos Febres's short story "Hebra rota" and Sonia Fritz's eponymous short film, one of three that she based on stories by Santos Febres, examine some of these issues through the relationship that develops between the two female protagonists, ten-year old Yetsaida and Doña Kety, who straightens the girl's hair in her beauty salon. As the two women share a reality of abuse, in each other they encounter a level of solidarity that surpasses the protection that the family can offer, and thus transforms the space of the beauty salon into a site of shelter and alliance. Even though, like in Pilar's case, the beauty salon is unable to provide strategies for the subversion of patriarchal violence, it offers a space for the development of solidarity that allows women to cope (*bregar*, Díaz Quiñones *El arte* 19-26) with oppression by temporarily escaping the role of the victim, and by constructing their identities in different terms, through race, gender and sexuality.

Like Carmen Lugo Filippi's stories, "Hebra rota" takes place in two spaces, the beauty salon and the family home. The descriptions of the two settings contrast in ways that suggest the protagonists' different associations with each space–while the house is presented as claustrophobic, devoid of communication and support, the beauty salon's location and the relationships that develop in it allow for alternative relations of power and for solidarity along gender and racial lines.

The story's representation of the domestic space contrasts with traditional images of the family house and of *la gran familia puertorriqueña*. The house's physical depiction in Sonia Fritz's faithful cinematic adaptation is hardly reminiscent of the houses in *Dios los cría* or "Ligia Elena" in that, instead of projecting a sense of high class, comfort and luxury, it is small and dark, suggesting claustrophobia and a need to escape (Fritz). More importantly, instead of a unified Puerto Rican family, the story and the film reveal a home characterized by lack of unity and by the violence inflicted on the female characters. The plot begins with an image of aggression against the ten-year old protagonist ["Una niña y un padre y una memoria rota como una nariz a los diez años con aliento a alcohol encima" (Santos Febres, "Hebra" 65)], and soon thereafter the readers discover that Doña Kety, just like many other women in her Trastalleres neighborhood, is the victim of similar violence (66). *Felices días, tío Sergio*'s cultural nationalist image of the family is absent from Santos Febres's story, in which the female protagonists' domestic setting is structured not by consensus but by patriarchy. This depiction of the home "discredit[s] myths created by the nation-building novel" (Henao 96), myths of perfect marriages and of idyllic homes, exposes their characteristic violence, and argues that spaces like the beauty salon offer different possibilities for female solidarity, liberation and inclusion.

As in the case of "Milagros, calle Mercurio," in "Hebra rota" the beauty salon is adjacent to the woman's living space. Located in the neighborhood of Trastalleres, a working-class, Afro-Puerto Rican part of Santurce in which car repair shops and gas stations are common places of employment, the beauty salon "queda alto, alto en el cielo como un pájaro de cemento que transporta hacia la belleza" (Santos Febres, "Hebra" 66). On the one hand, this description alludes to the characters' perception of that space as a site of beauty, but also of escape and the desire to forget: "Este olvido que busca la niña en el alisado se nutre de la esperanza de belleza que encarna Doña Kety y de la práctica seductora del ritual en su beauty casero" (Godreau 121). On the other, the description is also tinged with a sense of irony. The beauty salon in the story and in the film is a simple cement construction, very different from the luxurious salons where Yetsaida dreams of working. Its ordinary quality, combined with the hope with which the girl invests it, serve to emphasize the social marginalization of the characters and their need to find an escape, however temporary and tentative, from the violence of their everyday experience.

Yetsaida's desire to escape is caused in part by the racial violence that she suffers at home, and by the possibility for liberation that she encounters in the salon. In her home her blackness is something to be ashamed of: "El padre ni le toca las pasas del asco, sí, del asco. Ella se lo ha visto en la cara, en los chistes de la mano enredada, en el fastidio de Mami peinándola entre gritos con la peinilla mellá" (67). Yetsaida's parents subscribe to an ideology of colorism that allocates "privilege and disadvantage according to the lightness or darkness of one's skin" (Burke 17). As Linda Burton, Eduardo Bonilla-Silva and others have noted, "Colorism beliefs and practices operate both within and across racial and ethnic groups" (Burton 441)–suggesting that the idea can be perpetuated not only by white but also by Afro-descendant communities. In Puerto Rico, as in many other "Latin American societies [that] have developed rules of racial recognition and elaborate color caste systems that sanction differential opportunity and social status based on skin tone gradations and phenotypic characteristics" (Burton 445), darkness often continues to be seen as a flaw to be ashamed of and to be corrected thorugh beauty rituals. In that sense, it is quite telling that in the film the scene in which the mother brushes Yetsaida's hair is set in the bathroom, a space both claustrophobic and associated with the need for privacy, the desire to avoid the gaze of others, and the danger of embarrassment.

In the Caribbean context, beauty culture and hair straightening have been interpreted in multiple ways–from Isar Godreau's strategic *brega congraciente*, to an element of a patriarchal system in which, "if, on the one hand, the woman who plays the beauty game is condemned for her superficiality, on the other, the woman who refuses to play the game is ascribing herself to a genderless, zero category" (Castillo 148). The beauty ritual that Yetsaida's mother performs on the girl acquires a new meaning as part of the ideology of colorism and pigmentocracy. In "Hebra rota" beauty is once again a product of violence, as, for Yetsaida's parents, it is synonymous with specific configurations of race. Yetsaida's skin is outside of the privileged spectrum of whiteness, and, in the family house, her hair is "corrected" through violence, in order to conform to norms of appearance suitable for inclusion in the racial discourse of the national imaginary.

In contrast, in Doña Kety's salon Yetsaida encounters empathy, solidarity, and the possibility to gain access through certain codes of "acceptable" appearance understood to belong in the national imaginary. One of these codes is straight hair seen as an aspect of the "becoming corporeality" (Peace 51) of race, in a society regulated by racialized norms of appearance and behavior. This corporeality exemplifies "la tensión entre la experiencia corporal femenina y la formación y percepción de sí mismas como sujetos, y la construcción del deseo femenino como el deseo de ser deseadas" (Celis 92). In Yetsaida's case, the reason behind this desire to be desired is the exclusion of Afro-Puerto Rican women from the ideal image of the national family.

The principal code of access that Doña Kety gives Yetsaida in the beauty salon is that of *el alisado*, or hair straightening. More than a symptom of *blanqueamiento*, or a desire to look white, Yetsaida's use of the *alisado* in the beauty salon is a "brega congraciente" which she utilizes to "abrirse espacio y negociar su posición en la sociedad, sin confrontar, directamente, la lógica racista que determina lo 'negro' del pelo como no deseable, poco atractivo o poco femenino" (Godreau 113). Yetsaida's way to deal by looking for an image and for an inclusion into the Puerto Rican national imaginary responds to marginalization and violence parallel to those that Milagros suffers, and which, in Yetsaida's case, are problematized further by the young protagonist's race. In contrast to Milagros (or Petra in *The House on the Lagoon*), however, neither Yetsaida nor Doña Kety has a proper voice, and neither can actively "denounce the racial as well as the gender discrimination they face" (Gosser Esquilín 51).

Instead, these characters' situation alludes to that of Pilar, as it is through the point of view and thus through the readers' identification with the protagonists that the story exposes and critiques the gendered experiences of patriarchy, racism and violence.

The film also overtly criticizes racial hierarchies and colorist ideologies of beauty through the casting of several Afro-Puerto Rican actresses. In the 1970s and the 1980s Carmen Belén Richardson, who plays the role of Doña Kety, was one of the most prominent black Puerto Rican artists, known for her work in theater, film and television (Feliciano Díaz). In the film, her presence, as well as that of Jessica Gaspar, can be seen as an effort to offset the invisibility of black female actresses, and, by doing that, to questions Puerto Rican cinema's "practices of colorism [that] tend to favor lighter skin over darker skin as indicated by a person's appearance as proximal to a White phenotype" (Burton 440). By casting black Puerto Rican actresses in the leading roles, the film becomes a space for identification and solidarity not only for the characters, but also for audiences whose experiences of the intersection of race, gender, beauty and violence are reminiscent of those of Doña Kety and Yetsaida.

The issues of race and the construction of space in "Hebra rota" intersect with the question of violence, specifically physical violence in relation to the female body. The two protagonists are not alone in suffering domestic abuse, evidence of which are the multiple references to the women's broken noses and the "mapamundi," the scarring and coloration on Doña Kety's arm, which may be a result as much of handling the hair-straightening iron, as it could be of the domestic violence to which she is subjected early in the film. Quite literally, the female body becomes "a politicized site of struggle and contestation" (Bell, Binnie, Holliday vii) and "[a map] of the relation between power and identity" (Rose 32), as physical violence acts as an instrument for the construction of a hierarchy of gender, of a subjugated femininity and a dominant masculinity. In this sense, the women's ability to change their appearance according to their own desire is a rare instance in which "The principle of self-transformation, derived from the predominant male-defined gaze, is [. . .] retransformed and restructured as a particularly feminine product, gaze, or discourse" (Castillo 143). The transformative work that Doña Kety does is not only manual and professional, but also emotional—it provides relief and consolation, and gives Yetsaida strength. The operative gaze here is the female gaze, and the solidarity that develops between Doña Kety and Yetsaida rejects patriarchy and colorism to offer strategic support and a necessary escape.

Violence participates in mapping the gendered experience of space, as, by definition, domestic violence has a spatial dimension, normally identified with the family home. Even though, as discussed in Chapter III, the home is frequently seen as a female space, it "has also traditionally been subject to the patriarchal authority of the husband and father" (Duncan 131), who maintains its patriarchal order. By the end of the story Yetsaida's dream of attending a beauty school in Miami parallels another, unspoken dream–leaving behind the patriarchal logic of the family home. After having suffered the violence of patriarchal order in the domestic space, the girl dreams not of a different home, but of a public and female space, which would offer her the possibility to escape patriarchal domination, and to construct an identity based on solidarity, agency and self-realization.

As in the case of Milagros and Pilar, emotional labor is central to the construction of gendered spaces in "Hebra rota." For Yetsaida and Doña Kety, the beauty salon becomes a space of empathy and support, while practices like *el alisado* offer a pretext for the creation of alliances between women who look for ways to resist racial discrimination and violence. Doña Kety's touch steps away from "Western paradigms of subjectivity that are relentlessly fixated on the visual, and she offers other bodily senses, like the tactile and the kinetic" (Chiclana y González 164), and in so doing, offers not only beauty services, but also the affection that Yetsaida lacks at home. For Doña Kety, like for Marina, that emotional labor, unpaid yet expected, represents the "double burden" of women's work. However, it also benefits both her and Yetsaida by transforming their relationship, and, subsequently, the functions of the space of the beauty salon. Instead of simply a space of service, the beauty salon becomes a site of empowerment. For Yetsaida that empowerment is the hope that she attains for a life outside patriarchal and racist violence, and for Doña Kety it is the satisfaction that she receives from the act of comforting the young girl and helping her avoid a future similar to her own. In the story, emotional labor transforms the gendered geographies of violence and offers the protagonists strategies for resistance and for the construction of a community through female agency and alliance.

The questions that remain, upon analyzing the solidarity between Doña Kety and Yetsaida alongside that between Marina and Milagros, is, to what extent does the alliance that develops between the women offer an opportunity for resistance and subversion of the social processes under critique? How do gender and labor, especially emotional labor, intersect to produce feminine solidarities, and how does the experience of solidarity differ for the beauty stylist and for her young client? What literary strategies does Santos Febres use to expose and condemn the patriarchal order of the gendered experience of space, and how do these strategies differ from those used by Lugo Filippi in terms of their ideological effects?

"Hebra rota" and "Milagros, calle Mercurio" use different strategies to critique the unequal participation of women in the Puerto Rican nation, but both demonstrate a "commitment to the possibility of transformative social change" (Hennessy 35). While Milagros's decision to leave her home suggests the need to actively resist patriarchal domination, Yetsaida's relationship of solidarity with Doña Kety and her dreams of going away are more of a way to deal with a situation of violence that she is unable to escape. Doña Kety's labor is not only a service; rather, in her "mano experta y sin violencia" (Santos Febres, "Hebra" 69) and in her "dedos que no quieren romperle nada, que quieren dejarla bella y radiante para que el céfiro juegue con su cabello" (69) Yetsaida finds pleasure and comfort that allow her to dream of an alternative identity–that of a professional woman free of the violence of her family and society. Simultaneously, the relationship gives Doña Kety the opportunity to exercise "the labor of the body and the creation of a sense of self for both the therapist and the client" (Black 101), as she too finds an outlet for her pain in helping alleviate Yetsaida's. In spite of this relationship of identification and solidarity, however, escape for both women is only temporary. Doña Kety is never able to leave, and Yetsaida would have to wait years before she can attempt to escape or to subvert the order that subjects her to violence. By positioning the female protagonists in a situation that borders on imprisonment, and that reveals their lack of protection or liberation, the story takes a stand against sexism and racism. It is through this inability to escape the violence of the family home, and through the gendered experiences of solidarity in spaces like the beauty salon, that the text critiques women's marginalization in patriarchal national imaginaries.

CONCLUSION

In the work of authors like Carmen Lugo Filippi, Mayra Santos Febres and Sonia Fritz, the space of the beauty salon is much more than a site for the reproduction of the beauty industry. It becomes a space characterized by tensions along axes of racial, class and sexual identity, by struggles and negotiations of patriarchal models and gender norms, and by female agency and strategies of resistance. In these texts, emotional labor, intimacy and desire redraw the gendered geographies of domination to propose alternatives to the patriarchal logic, to its national imaginary, and to the models of gender and sexuality that it upholds. Departing from the material and the symbolic space of the beauty salon, the female protagonists of these texts map alternative geographies of female agency, resolve and coalitions. Through their relationships, the beauty salon emerges as a space of solidarity between women who are marginalized and oppressed by intersecting social forces. By setting their stories in the exclusively "feminine" space of the beauty salon, the authors also propose ways to rethink the traditional cultural nationalist idea of the Puerto Rican nation by critiquing the contradictions of a discourse that claims unity and cohesion, but which continues to oppress and marginalize women's voices, labor, spatial and social mobility.

Chapter V

## LOCATING POWER ON THE MARGINS: GENDER AND SEXUALITY IN THE BROTHEL

### Prostitution and State Regulation

T HE geographies of gendered labor and female sexuality mapped out in the spaces of the factory, the house and the beauty salon are redrawn yet again in the brothel, a political, material and symbolic space that is still largely absent from historical, anthropological and cultural analysis. It is only recently that scholars have started to inquire, "¿Cómo eran los prostíbulos en su interior? ¿Cómo se distribuía el espacio y cómo funcionaban?" (Vázquez Lazo 213). This chapter addresses such questions by analyzing the space of the brothel and the female body in two short stories (Rosario Ferré's "Cuando las mujeres quieren a los hombres" and Manuel Ramos Otero's "La última plena que bailó Luberza"), in Efraín López Neris's film *Life of Sin* and in Mayra Santos-Febres's novel *Nuestra Señora de la Noche*. In these texts, the space of the brothel emerges as an alternative to the trope of the family house of *la gran familia puertorriqueña*, mapping new geographies of sexual and racial domination, resistance and agency.

The brothel becomes a matrix for the construction of gendered geographies in Puerto Rican, and more broadly, in Latin American literature, partly because historically it has been a space of transgression and a frequent target of state control. In the brothel, as in other material and symbolic spaces, the state has intervened in defining notions of honor in order to construct "acceptable" models of race, class and gender. In Brazil, these interventions were justified with the claim that, "only by conserving the stabilizing force of 'natural' social hierarchies epitomized by patriarchal honor [. . .] could Brazil's leaders promote progress and civilization" (Caulfield *In Defense* 11). Similarly, in modern Argentina, the historical relationship between prostitution, national discourse and state control has been "shaped by and in turn shaped social organization, culture, and politics" (Caulfield "Women" 170). The regulation of prostitution in Argentina from the mid-19th to the mid-20th century, when "physicians replaced the police as the enforcers of enclosed prostitution" (Gilfoyle 123), relates to gender, sexuality, class and family ideals, as "prostitution became a metaphor for upper- and middle-class fears about the lower class and the future of the Argentine nation" (Guy 44). Similar practices in Guatemala reformulated the relationship between prostitution, class and gender, arguing that, "attempts to regulate prostitution must be understood as part of a liberal drive to mobilize and control society as a whole in the interest of a class-defined vision of national development" (McCreery 334). The discursive and the physical regulation of the brothel became a metaphor for repressive practices and for the construction of particular visions of the ideal Latin American nation.

Even though the state is a main agent of control, the space of the brothel is often the object of different types of informal regulation. In one example from the "sex tourist town" of Sosúa in the Dominican Republic (Brennan 709), the women themselves regulate the sex trade through gossip and through the direct condemnation of other women, constructing a discourse that allows them to self-identify as martyrs, as mothers who sacrifice for the sake of their children. The protagonists of some of the texts that I analyze in this chapter (like Isabel Luberza in Ferré's story) employ similar strategies to distinguish themselves from the patriarchal image of the prostitute and to claim inclusion in a national imaginary that situates the brothel outside its limits.

In addition to being a space subjected to the gaze and the violence of the state, the brothel is also a space in which women and men work, interact with and relate to each other, and form alliances that, albeit problematic, challenge dominant discourses and practices of patriarchal nation-building. As a space of work and a space of pleasure, sex workers (in this case transvestite sex workers in Brazil) identify the brothel with work, "much like any other job—except that their work on the street makes them their own boss, and it provides them with access to more money than they could ever dream of earning through salaried employment" (Kulick 136). This approach to prostitution emphasizes the element of choice and personal empowerment, even when much of the work in the brothel is unpaid, emotional labor, revealing "patterns of sexual commerce in Cuba and the Dominican Republic [that] are opportunistic, fluid and ambiguous" (Cabezas 997) and that redefine the relationship between space, sex and labor.

Although this chapter focuses on fictional representations of the brothel, it is important to remember that brothels are real, material spaces in which empowerment and solidarity often intersect with violence and with concerns about health, family and social inclusion.[1] The voices of the fictional characters that I study often reiterate the preoccupations of actual sex workers, who debate issues like labor, choice, marginality and recognition, who share an interest in the defense of rights like respect, protection from violence, education, and the creation of, in their own words, "espacios que nos posibiliten mejorar la calidad de vida y que nos permitan salir de las stuaciones en las que nos encontramos" (Berkins 24). Women try to accomplish this through initiatives like the workshop *Prostitución/trabajo sexual: las protagonistas hablan*, an encounter initiated by the International Commission of Human Rights, and through international groups like RedTraSex, which encompasses 13 countries of Latin and Central America and the Caribbean, and which is composed of sex workers who organize to actively promote recognition and respect, so that "en América Latina se respeten los derechos humanos de las mujeres trabajadoras sexuales" (Amorín 21). RedTraSex's most important projects to date have been two workshops in 2006 in Costa Rica, that produced the manual *Un movimiento de tacones altos: Mujeres, trabajadoras sexuales y activistas*. Written by sex workers for sex workers, the manual's goal is to ensure that sex

---

[1] It is also important to recognize that the brothel is not the only space of prostitution: "la prostitución en la isla de Cuba, ya por esa época [the late1930s] conocida como el Burdel de América, no se practicaba exclusivamente en las casas de tolerancia, burdeles y prostíbulos de los barrios marginales o pobres de las ciudades y pueblos, sino que, sobre todo en el caso de La Habana y de algunas otras ciudades importantes, también tenía lugar en los más importantes hoteles (Valle 154). In the texts that I study, the brothel is often positioned against other spaces, like the family house and the street, which serve as counterpoints and enrich the understanding of the negotiations of power in the brothel.

workers be "preparadas para incidir en las políticas públicas de nuestros países, para de una vez por todas sentirnos orgullosas de las mujeres que somos y para que nadie más hable en nombre nuestro" (Reynaga y Amorín 9). The criticism explicit in the statement is also a challenge to sex workers, urging them to develop political consciousness and to express their own voice, instead of delegating it to scholars, journalists, social workers and activists.

## THE BROTHEL IN PUERTO RICAN HISTORY AND CRITICISM

Most of the fictional texts in this chapter respond to a set of political, medical and legal discourses on the female prostitute, her body, her agency and her participation in the everyday. Since the late 19th century, these discourses have tended to associate the prostitute and the space of the brothel with delinquency and immorality, making them the targets of regulation, marginalization and exclusion.

The brothel entered the realm of legal, medical and media discourses in the 19th century,[2] when urban growth spurred an increase in prostitution, due to the "migration of many unmarried male laborers, the city's growing importance as a naval port, and the migration of many impoverished and young women, presumably seeking domestic or sex work" (Briggs 58). Collectively, official government policies, press publications, liberal ideology and even early elite feminists constructed a set of "discourses about respectability [that] shaped sexual practices, racial meanings, and sexual regulatory strategies" (Suárez Findlay 6) which responded to a fear of the loss of patriarchy and to the desire to construct a white, patriarchal Puer-

---

[2] The first documented reference to a brothel in Puerto Rico dates back to the year 1526, when the Spanish monarch Carlos I gave his "concesión para instaurar el primer prostíbulo de Puerto Rico" (Vázquez Lazo 40), even though there is no evidence that the brothel was ever opened. The first references to individual prostitutes appear three decades later, in 1555, when Isabel Ortiz is mentioned as the "regente de un burdel que era visitado con asiduidad por algunos de los conquistadores" (42), and when a note regarding a woman called Brígida, "esclava de padre" (42), explicitly references race and colonialism in relation to the history of the brothel. Even though prostitution continued to flourish during the 17th and 18th centuries, there is limited evidence of the existence of brothels in Puerto Rico during that time. Occasional references appear in documents that banned clerics and soldiers from participating in any "encuentro en casas de unas mujeres sospechosas a horas incompetentes de la noche" (Vázquez Lazo 45).

to Rican nation. New medical regulations intended to "reglamentar la prostitución desde un punto de vista sanitario" (Vázquez Lazo 51) were created and, from that moment on, "la medicina y la ley lograron imbricarse en un estrecho diálogo que duraría todo el siglo y desplazaría paulatinamente la figura del sacerdote teólogo, encargado hasta el momento de condenar la prostitución" (Vázquez Lazo 51). This shift, which started in Europe and reached Puerto Rico in the final decades of the 19th century, justified the intervention of government and police in the practice of prostitution.

The regulation of the brothel in Puerto Rico was part of the colonial policy (Briggs 58-60), which the Spanish metropolis "strongly endorsed [. . .] as essential to a 'modern' nation, enjoining a sharp geographic separation between gente decente and prostitutes" (Briggs 59). It was also an institutional process that marginalized women through space, constraining brothels to specific locations in the city. It mapped a network of spaces–hospitals, prisons, so-called zones of tolerance–associated with the brothel, and intended to assist officials in the regulation of prostitution.

This control of urban space and of the spaces of prostitution was conditioned by a set of prejudices that informed the effort to categorize racial, class and sexual traits as undesirable in the Puerto Rican national discourse. As was the case with the ideology of the beneficencia, which stood at the intersection of charity work and social control, "[o]fficial preoccupation with prostitution occurred not because of the existence of a class of women who provided sexual favors for men outside of marriage and the family but because in so doing they mingled indiscriminately with people of a better class: upper- and middle-class women and men" (Martínez-Vergne 32). Thus, the characteristics of race and class with which prostitution was identified in the popular imagination, and its strategic association with disease and delinquency in the final decades of the 19th century[3] turned women into "mujeres doble, triple y hasta cuatro veces marginadas" (Vázquez Lazo 13), providing Puerto Rican nationalism with a convenient "other" that still lives in literary and cinematic representations of the prostitute.

Following measures already in existence in Europe, Puerto Rican officials employed "médicos higienistas" (Vázquez Lazo 55) to work

---

[3] El Reglamento de Higiene Pública, the document that regulated prostitution in Puerto Rico, dates back to the year 1890.

in newly created hospitals that served prostitutes. During the mandatory hospital visits, women had to sign a register that assured their inclusion in the lists of "elementos divergentes" (105), and had to subject themselves to vaginal exams twice a week. The practice of inscription assured the construction of a gendered national ideal through the documentation of undesirable behaviors (76) that did not conform to the traditional model of the nation. The hospitals in which mandatory medical exams were performed and in which women were interned if they were deemed to suffer from a contagious disease often subjected women to dismal conditions (Vázquez Lazo 192-193) and to coercion reminiscent of imprisonment, as the prostitutes were usually interned there against their will. Because poverty, often stemming from the legacy of slavery, and the lack of alternative options for women to support themselves and their children, were common factors for prostitution in 19th century Puerto Rico, black women, former slaves and poor working women practiced prostitution–or at least were denounced and documented as doing so–more often than white women of a higher social class. In medical discourse, these same black, working-class women were seen as aberrations in the ideal Puerto Rican nation, examples of what a wife and a mother was expected not to look like or to act.

Space was the main axis along which women's bodies were regulated. The starkest examples of this control may be found in the 1890 Reglamento de Higiene Pública, which divided prostitutes in three main categories: "Primera. Las internas que viven en casas de efecto matriculadas como tales. Segunda. Las externas o sueltas que acuden a las casas de recibir, hallándose registrados sus nombres en libro especial de la casa [. . .]. Tercera. Las que ejercen sus tratos en su casa o morada" (Reglamento, cited in Vázquez Lazo 113). Women were categorized according to the type of house in which they practiced prostitution–whether they were residents of an officially registered house, temporarily visited one or accepted their clients into their own house. The Reglamento's use of the word "casa" instead of "burdel" or "prostíbulo" reproduces the domestic sphere of femininity, even if the social discourse on prostitution of that period condemned prostitutes as "mujeres públicas." This fact suggests that space, and the domestic sphere in particular, were closely linked both to the practice of prostitution, and to the discourse on gender and sexuality–and, at the same time, indicates how problematic their use was in the context of women who did not conform to traditional gender roles.

Prostitution was also spatially regulated through the social controls of the urban mobility of prostitutes in cities like San Juan and Ponce. The Reglamento ordered that prostitutes could not "circular por las calles ni paseos céntricos de la población antes de las once de la noche ni aun en los días de fiesta nacional, función de teatro o cualquier otro espectáculo público hasta que terminen estos, aunque sea en hora avanzada" (Vázquez Lazo 114). They were expected to keep the houses' doors and windows shut and not to lean outside the windows, so as not to be seen, and so as not to attract clients from the street. In Ponce prostitutes could not go out in the streets before 10:30pm any day of the week (Vázquez Lazo 154). Such rules limited women's spatial mobility, excluding them from most social activities and from everyday life in the cities.

In practice, these rules ensured the implementation of "definitions of 'honor,' 'respectability,' 'race,' and 'proper sexual practices' [to ascertain] who will be included or excluded in the national community being imagined" (Suárez Findlay 12). This community was the creation of 19th century Liberal autonomists who "posited a benevolent but hierarchical paternalism as the glue which would hold a society together under Liberal leadership and which would more effectively mold a pliable workforce" (55), with the implicit understanding that women in their roles as mothers were responsible for the successful construction of this national model. By attributing this new responsibility to female sexuality, the regulations effectively "consolidate[d] elite male Liberal power" (Suárez Findlay 78) and distinguished between women fit to be mothers of the Puerto Rican nation, and those who strayed from the ideal white, "respectable" model. What that meant in everyday life was that prostitutes were implicitly denied full citizenship, as they could not legitimately be present in most spaces and partake in most activities to which the "Puerto Rican national family" had access, even if they were still expected to pay a monthly quota for being included in the official register of prostitution.

Any transgression of these rules on the part of the prostitutes meant official censure, fines and possible imprisonment, and carried the risk of violence in everyday life. Vázquez Lazo cites evidence of the stoning of prostitutes who were complying with the Reglamento's rules of visiting a hospital for vaginal exams twice a week. Men intercepted these women and attempted to throw stones at them or to run them over. Not surprisingly, these acts of violence had little legal consequences for the aggressors, even when women were hurt or exposed as being prostitutes. Social and spatial control thus found its ultimate expression at the expense of women who were already marginalized and who often endured sexual violence for lack of other options of employment.

Another instrument of marginalization through urban space were the "zonas de tolerancia" (Vázquez Lazo 114), specific areas of the city to which brothels were restricted. These areas were inspired by fear and by the desire to control both sexuality and race, as in every city, "the institution of the segregated district for prostitutes also immediately followed the abolition of slavery, and was part of an extensive system of limiting the movements of free laborers, black and white. By the 1890s, the majority of the women in San Juan were black or mixed race" (Briggs 58). The case of Ponce is again representative: its Reglamento ponceño delimited the area between "Las calles de Buenos Aires, Virtud al Norte, Jobo partiendo de la Salud al Este, Callejón del Comercio, calle de la Luna extremos Este y Oeste, calle de Vista Alegre, Barrio de Ballajá, Callejón del perro y Punta brava en la Playa" (Reglamento ponceño, cited in Vázquez Lazo 156), and it became illegal for any woman even "alleged to be a prostitute" (Suárez Findlay 89) to access other parts of the city. Similarly, San Juan only allowed brothels to be located between "las calles de Tetuán desde los números 36 y 39, recintos Norte y Sur y calle de Norzagaray" (Vázquez Lazo 114). These instructions locate sexuality and race onto urban maps that clearly define female (often black) sexuality as undesirable and only allowed in spaces regulated by law–en exclusion evident in the fact that the area outlined by the streets described above compiles the outermost part of the city (its margins), which lays closest to the piers and the military forts. These urban maps also allude to the mapping of the island by the early conquistadors, and enhance the association between the masculine gaze, female sexuality and national discourse, implicit in the Reglamento's rules.

Prisons were the spaces that most commonly complemented the "zonas de tolerancia" and the legal control of brothels and prostitution. In contrast to countries like Spain, which had "casas de recogimiento" (Vázquez Lazo 46) that would "make room for illegitimate sexualities" (Foucault 4), in Puerto Rico the women were taken directly to the city prisons, where they were often abused by guards. Stepping outside and disobeying the rules regarding exposure to the external gaze were among the most frequent causes for the imprisonment of prostitutes.

This history of the social control of prostitution in Puerto Rico is the background against which the texts analyzed in subsequent sections map the relationship between gender, sexuality, race and power in the space of the brothel.


## THE HOUSE AND THE BROTHEL IN "CUANDO LAS MUJERES QUIEREN A LOS HOMBRES"


The brothel has a special place in Puerto Rican cultural production. In the space of the brothel, tensions of gender, sexuality, race and class surface to reconfigure traditional national imaginaries. When writers and directors choose to speak from the space of the brothel, they often do so in order to confront patriarchal national discourses from feminist standpoints. The brothel focalizes power relations of gender and sexuality and offers multiple possibilities to subvert patriarchal hierarchies and traditional views of gender and sexuality in the discursive construction of the Puerto Rican nation.

Several representations of the brothel precede the texts on which I will focus in this chapter. In Luis Rafael Sánchez's story "Tiene la noche una raíz," the traditional patriarchal space of the house is revealed as a brothel through the gazes and the gossip of local women. The story's protagonist, the prostitute Gurdelia Grifitos, lives condemned by these women and exploited by their husbands, until one night she opens the door to a ten-year old boy who wants to find out why men come to Gurdelia's house. At first confused by the boy's request, the woman offers him maternal love that leaves him convinced that he has experienced something divine, in an allusion to the mother/whore paradigm. By juxtaposing two figures—that of the prostitute and that of the mother—the story uses the space of the house as a brothel and as a home, as a male-dominated site of exploitation and a maternal, nurturing space. In this way it inspires empathy, critiques the abuse of female sexuality and proposes a more complex representation of it, one that goes beyond marginalization and condemnation. It is a gesture through which the popular voice (in this case female) "se ha encargado de darle sentido y perdurabilidad, desde su otra historia, a la narración nacional" (Díaz 188). Luis Molina Casanova's film *La guagua aérea* adapts Sánchez's short story but makes Gurdelia Grifitos part of the migratory experience, representing the incident as a flashback while the woman is on a plane to New York, identifying her memory of the incident as a motive for her migration. In the story, as well as the film, the house/brothel is a space that reproduces traditional models of femininity and only allows the construction of temporary solidarity or of an alternative community through an escape from the life of prostitution.

While Gurdelia Grifitos is a fictional character, much of the Puerto Rican cultural production set in the space of the brothel maps the gendered geographies of power and resistance around the central figure of the legendary historical character of Isabel la Negra. Born in Ponce in 1901, Isabel Luberza Oppenheimer was a brothel owner whose entrepreneurship inspired writers to revisit the story of her life. Two of these early narratives–Rosario Ferré's "Cuando las mujeres quieren a los hombres" and Manuel Ramos Otero's "La última plena que bailó Luberza"–first appeared in the magazine *Zona carga y descarga* in 1975, shortly after Isabel's murder, and depicted her life, relationships and agency in profoundly different ways.

Ferré's story is an account of the encounter of Isabel Luberza, *dama de sociedad*, and Isabel la Negra, the prostitute who had been the lover of Luberza's late husband Ambrosio. Isabel la Negra visits Luberza to claim her half of Ambrosio's house, with the intention of converting it into a brothel. During the encounter, the two women transform into one another. Luberza destroys Isabel la Negra physically, yet suggests "a fusion of both women into one indivisible entity" (Aparicio 4), becoming her, absorbing her consciousness, and initiating "una alianza silenciosa entre ambas" (Gelpí 159). Through the representation of the house and the brothel, on the one hand, and of the two female bodies, on the other, the story condemns the women's oppression during their respective relationships with Ambrosio, and becomes a forceful indictment of the patriarchal norms of Puerto Rican society. The story also critiques Puerto Rican cultural nationalism and traditional models of the nation by uncovering the complex ways in which national consensus is built on racial and gender oppression. Ultimately, it proposes a technology of resistance that not simply allows for the inclusion of women, Afro-Puerto Ricans and other marginalized groups in the national imaginary, but envisions a new national model based on gender solidarity and the subversion of patriarchy.

In the story, the gendered and racial hierarchies that permeate the space of the brothel are inevitably tied to the space of the house, and to its complex hierarchies and negotiations of power. The interconnected spaces of the brothel and the house become sites for the critique of traditional configurations of gender and sexuality, and specifically of the virgin/prostitute binary. The house, occupied by Isabel Luberza and desired by Isabel la Negra, emerges as a site of the construction of traditional patriarchal models of respectable femininity, but also problematizes them by exposing the structures of oppression that participate in the reaffirmation and in the reproduction of these models.

The house becomes a site for the construction of traditional models of femininity through the interactions between Isabel Luberza and her husband Ambrosio, and through the woman's internalization of the patriarchal structures of oppression that condition her behavior and self-image as a woman. Traditionally gendered feminine, the house has also historically been a subject of patriarchal authority (Duncan 131), and Isabel Luberza's house is no different. Even though in the story it emerges as the property of women (intended to be shared by the two Isabels after Ambrosio's death), multiple flashbacks reveal it as a site of domination and oppression. It is in the house where Isabel Luberza discovered Ambrosio's relationship with Isabel la Negra, and it is also in the house where she reproduces a gender model in an attempt to get her husband back. When she realizes that Ambrosio is not about to abandon her rival, Isabel Luberza employs other methods to win him back, "por medio de esa sabiduría antiquísima que había heredado de mi madre y mi madre de su madre. Comencé a colocar diariamente la servilleta dentro del aro de plata junto a tu plato [. . .] Colocaba sobre tu cama las sábanas todavía tibias de sol bebido, blancas y suaves bajo la palma de la mano" (Ferré, "Cuando" 75). In the process, she affirms traditional models of domesticity, family and femininity, through practices inherited from other women in her family. These practices make Isabel Luberza an example of the ways in which women themselves can internalize, reproduce and perpetrate patriarchal structures of oppression (Henao 13).

The specific model that Isabel Luberza reproduces in the story is that of the virgin, in a traditional opposition to the prostitute. She is the faithful, devoted wife and housewife who follows the established social norms, exemplifying the model of *marianismo*, conditioned by religion, patriarchal society and culture (Ruíz Meléndez 13). She is also the model of motherhood and domesticity that was constructed in order to uphold the national model, and in order to blame in the instances in which it failed (Suárez Findlay; Briggs). As such, Luberza becomes both a convenient mythical figure, exemplifying acceptable gender roles and behaviors (Palmer López, "Revisión" 254), and a matrix for a possible critique of cultural nationalist models of the Puerto Rican nation, and of the gender and sexual axes of identity that it includes or excludes.

Gender and sexuality in the story become more fluid when the space of the brothel is unveiled as a site of a parallel construction of femininity and masculinity. Isabel la Negra corresponds to the traditional image of the prostitute, both as an archetype and as a sexualized model of femininity, exoticized yet set in the story's specific historical and cultural context: "Isabel la Perla Negra del Sur, La Reina de Saba, the Queen of Chiva, la Chivas Rigal, la Tongolele, la Salomé, girando su vientre de giroscopio en círculos de bengala dentro de los ojos de los hombres" (Ferré, "Cuando" 67). She rejects the "institutionalization of the figure of the feminine as a natural, primordial, but containable and manageable element"(Castillo 23). She is Luberza's antipode, exemplifying everything that is undesirable in the Puerto Rican nation, from blackness to overt sexuality and seductive power.

In spite of these fairly traditional representations of femininity in the house and the brothel, when it comes to the construction of masculinity in the story, the roles of the two spaces seem inverted. The brothel becomes the site of reaffirmation of a specific form of masculinity–white, privileged and heterosexual. In Isabel la Negra's words, fathers took to the brothel their sons,

> para que sus papás pudieran por fin dormir tranquilos porque los hijos que ellos hubieran parido no les habían salido mariconcitos, no les habían salido santoletitos con el culo astillado de porcelana, porque los hijos que ellos habían parido eran hijos de San Jierro y de Santa Daga pero solo podían traerlos a dónde mí para poder comprobarlo (Ferré, "Cuando" 72).

While masculine control and patriarchal power are exercised in the home, it is in the brothel where they are constructed and validated. In this sense, the brothel also becomes a site for the reproduction of the Puerto Rican national patriarchs, whose capacity to rule is often closely associated with masculinity and virility.

Gender and nation, brothel and house also intersect through the relationship between desire, pleasure and the male gaze that polices the space of the brothel and that constructs masculinity in opposition to a desired, but undesirable femininity. Reminiscing of the later years of her relationship with Ambrosio, Isabel la Negra says,

> Cuando te empezaste a poner viejo, Ambrosio, la suerte se me viró a favor. Sólo podías sentir placer al mirarme acostada con aquellos muchachos que me traías todo el tiempo y empezaste a temer que me vieran a escondidas de ti, que me pagaran más de lo que tú me pagabas, que un día te abandonara definitivamente (Ferré, "Cuando" 73).

These lines reference the complex web of power relations that permeate the construction of gender, sexuality and Puerto Rican national imaginaries in the brothel. On the one hand, the configurations of cities and the spaces within cities are often made for male consumption and pleasure, composing a "city of men" (Massey 234). In the case of the story, even in his impotence, Ambrosio subjects Isabel to his gaze and experiences pleasure through her sexuality. On the other hand, his desire and his pleasure weaken him and allow the woman to assume a position of power, as Ambrosio's fear of losing her distances him from the model of the patriarch who can have what he desires, certainly in the domestic sphere. This weakness represents Ferré's inversion of gender roles and positions of power to critique hierarchies of gender and sexuality in the Puerto Rican nation and to propose ways in which they can be subverted and transformed.

Similarly, in the space of the house, Isabel la Negra's gaze and her experience of pleasure redefine the Puerto Rican national model from the standpoint of race, class and gender. Her desire to turn the house into a brothel represents "una redistribución 'escandalosa' de ese espacio doméstico de clase alta" (Gelpí 159). Her visit to the house reaffirms her desire for "the luxury of sitting on the balcony, sharing in the mandated leisure of rich women" (Castillo

162) and evokes "aquella visión que había tenido de niña, siempre que pasaba, descalza y en harapos, frente a aquella casa, la visión de un hombre vestido de hilo blanco, de pie en aquel balcón, junto a una mujer rubia, increíblemente bella, vestida con un traje de lamé plateado" (Ferré, "Cuando" 70). Her memories uncover the racial and class hierarchies that organize the relationship between Ambrosio and the women, and suggest that her desire for the house is part of a complex web of social, economic and racial structures of domination. The contrasting images–of the girl's poverty vs. the couple's wealth, and of the girl's implicit blackness, revealed in her name and in other sections of the story, vs. the couple's whiteness, suggested through the references to the white suit and the blond hair–suggest that Isabel's desire for the house evokes that childhood image, establishing the house as a subversive symbol of pleasure in response to Isabel's subordination by elite white privilege. Because the "performance of gender identity varies according to space" (Black 183), in Isabel Luberza's house Isabel la Negra encounters the opportunity for a different performance of femininity. The possibility of owning the house gives her the chance to imagine herself as a different woman, in a different space: "Sentada en el balcón de mi nuevo prostíbulo sin que nadie sospeche, los balaústres de largas anáforas plateadas pintadas ahora de shocking pink alineados frente a mí" (Ferré 68). These words "[propose] new modes of writing and reading a national Puerto Rican cultural identity in more complex, and, hopefully, more democratic ways" (Aparicio 7). The story uses class and race to redraw the gendered geographies of the Puerto Rican nation through a figure that has previously been excluded from that imaginary–that of the lower-class Afro-Puerto Rican woman.

The spaces of the house and the brothel, together with the bodies of the two women that inhabit them, become metaphoric sites for the construction of a new Puerto Rican national imaginary. Isabel Luberza exemplifies the traditional, acceptable, desired nation, in which Ambrosio, in her words, "depositó en mi vientre la semilla sagrada que llevará tu nombre como debe ser siempre entre un señor y una señora" (Ferré, "Cuando" 76). Thus conceived, literally and metaphorically, the Puerto Rican nation is problematic, as the patriarchal structure of the relationship is rooted not in a "Latin American national romance" (Sommer), but in gender oppression and infidelity. It is a model haunted by the exploitation of women as national mothers, who are simultaneously denied any agency in the construction of the Puerto Rican nation.

The fact that this new Puerto Rican national imaginary is effectuated through the bodies of two women, one black and one white, racializes the discourse of the nation and emphasizes the intersection between gender and race. At the end of their encounter, Isabel Luberza and Isabel la Negra "terminan entrelazadas en un contrapunto racial como fundamento cultural del caribe" (Barraza 89), in an image that symbolically rejects whiteness as the ideal model for Puerto Rican (or Caribbean) society. The fact that Isabel la Negra's body takes over Luberza's house, representative of Ambroio's patriarchal domination, implies "el ascenso de la población negra, la infiltración de las clases bajas en las clases altas y la intromisión de la mujer en el control tradicionalmente masculino de la sexualidad" (Balseiro 8). In that sense, the final fusion subverts cultural nationalism's image of a white, middle-class nation and proposes a different familial structure, defined by female alliance and racial mixing.

The space of the brothel becomes, quite literally, the site of the construction of a Puerto Rican national imaginary through Isabel la Negra's body, and amid the struggle, confrontation and negotiations of *la puertorriqueñidad* of the island Puerto Ricans vs. *la puertorriqueñidad* of the Puerto Ricans in the diaspora. The Puerto Rican diaspora in the US is present in several ways, most notably through Isabel la Negra's language. More than once in the text she uses words in English which, the readers are led to believe, are not only a consequence of her trips to Europe, but also of the fact that among her clients are Puerto Ricans who live in the US and who return to the island periodically. The Puerto Rican national imaginary is thus constructed not only through the character's gender, sexuality, class and racial axes of identity, but also through the language that she uses and that marks both her and the people that surround her.

The Puerto Rican national imaginary also emerges through Isabel la Negra's bodyspace (Duncan), or through her body as a gendered space. She says that "ella era la prueba en cuerpo y sangre de que no existía diferencia entre los de Puerto Rico y los de Nueva York puesto que en su carne todos se habían unido" (Ferré, "Cuando" 66). Isabel's body becomes a matrix for the construction of a Puerto Rican national imaginary beyond the schism of island and diaspora, of authenticity and foreignness. The body, intersected by axes of desire, domination and subjection (terms also relevant when discussing national models), becomes the space in which the "divided borders" of the nation that "struggle[s] over language" (Flores, *Divided Borders* 201) come together. That this happens in the body of a woman is problematic, because it evokes traditional associations of nationhood and motherhood, but that this happens in the body of an Afro-Puerto Rican prostitute is significant because it proposes a different kind of origin, based not on whiteness and class elitism, but, in a sense, on José Luis González's foundational first floor of the four-storied Puerto Rican house, that of blackness and the legacy of slavery.

## RETHINKING POWER IN "LA ÚLTIMA PLENA QUE BAILÓ LUBERZA"

Manuel Ramos Otero's story "La última plena que bailó Luberza," published alongside "Cuando las mujeres quieren a los hombres," depicts a different transformation of the symbolic space of the Puerto Rican nation. The story is set during the final day of Isabel la Negra's life, and follows her from the church to her limousine, to a fortuneteller's house, and back to her Dancing Hall. All the spaces that she inhabits she invests with her power, manipulating priests, calling judges for favors, and dismissing all threats, from malicious gazes to court orders against her. Her brothel endows her with power that she uses to subvert patriarchy. It is murder that puts an end to her life, and even in that final scene she seems in control, following every bullet as it enters her body, tracing its route, as the assassins remain nameless and inconsequential.

At first sight, the organizing element of Ramos Otero's story is time, more than space. The plot begins with a time stamp of 6:13 A.M., and six more indications of time appear throughout the story, in a sequence that spans just over 24 hours. The time stamps create a sense of urgency and an expectation of a climax. This expectation is immediately subverted, however, by a stream-of-consciousness narrative that results in vertiginous changes of perspectives and in a discourse that resists the linearity of time. The visual aspect of the time stamps that precede every episode in the story transgresses the conventions of the short story genre, as though indicating the beginning of a new scene of a film or of a television episode. This fragmentation of the narrative also functions as a fragmentation of the space of the text, literally divided into seven sections. In this way, in contrast with Ferré's story of fusion and possibility, and keeping with the "negación de una historia monumental" (Sotomayor, *Femina Faber*, 292), Ramos Otero questions the possibility of a cohesive national subject in the figure of Isabel, or of any other character in the story.

The fragmentation of the national subject constitutes one of several contrasts between Ramos Otero's and Ferré's stories. Another striking difference between them is the absence of the space of the house, which figures prominently in Ferré's story (and traditionally in her literary work). While there are also references to houses in Santos-Febres's and in López Neris's work, Ramos Otero practically erases the house from the narrative, and from his vision of a Puerto Rican national community. The only reference to a house sounds like a fragment of a memory that appears in parentheses that Isabel quickly closes: "[el] caserón de los Oppenheimer donde Mamá María le espantaba las moscas a la señora por el día y por la noche le espantaba el marido a la señora y se acostaba con el señor como su madre se había acostado con el señor de entonces y había espantado moscas con inmensos abanicos de paja" (Ramos Otero 197). This house is controlled not by a patriarch in the image of Ambrosio (or Quintín Mendizábal, or even the dead father in García Ramis's *Felices días, tío Sergio*), but by the servant, Mamá María, who exercises her sexual power over the master as easily as she scares away the flies. This image inverts the gender relations of power of the traditional nation, and depicts, albeit briefly, the dysfunction in the family house (a triangle that involves a subordinated, yet subordinating servant, as opposed to a traditional patriarchal marriage).

The church and the limousine are two spaces that similarly subvert the traditional Puerto Rican cultural national imaginary. In contrast to official discourse, in which the church reproduces traditional gender roles, Ramos Otero introduces the space of the church in order to expose the contradictions embedded in the relationship between gender, Catholicism and religious norms. Much like in *Negocio redondo*, the second part of Morales's *Dios los cría*, in which a semi-legal transaction takes place in a church, and in which a priest desires one of the nuns, the church in Ramos Otero's story is hardly a model institution. Instead, it is a space marked by hypocrisy that renders impossible the cultural nationalist model of the citizen, and that constructs an alternative figure, whose relationship to different institutions is governed by mutual exploitation.

The first glimpse of the church evokes no piety or traditional Catholic values. It is a secret meeting between Isabel and the Monsignor, in which she makes a generous offer to buy an indulgence: "Vengo a comprar el reino de los cielos para cuando me muera" (Ramos Otero 195). Not only is she in a position to offer a significant amount of money for the controversial practice of the indulgence, but, more importantly, she is in a position to dictate the terms of the transaction, to exploit the priest's interest, and to withdraw the offer: "el Monseñor sabe que ésta será mi última oferta para comprar el reino de los cielos" (Ramos Otero 195). In this way, the story inverts gender and social roles on two levels–first, a woman that is seemingly marginalized (twice, as a woman and as a prostitute) manipulates and dictates the conditions of a significant financial transaction with a powerful institution (the Catholic Church). Second, this episode also blurs the boundaries between corruption and Christian ethics, as the priest accepts money for an absolution that he does not believe should be granted:

> ¡Tú maldita pecadora Luberza a ti no hay padrenuestro que te salve del mangle asqueroso de tu vida! de: ¡Tú Luberza de los mil demonios del fango ni tu dinero ni tus gangarrias de dama elegante pueda tapar la peste de tu sudor de azufre negra bandolera puta arrabalera a ti no te toca ni el pedazo de cielo polvoriento sobre San Antón! (Ramos Otero 195-196).

In addition to constructing a caricaturesque image of the church, exaggerated in its sense of privilege and entitlement, Monsignor's words also exemplify the futility of the racial construction of Puerto Rican national identity, as the notion of the three cultures (an egalitarian combination of the Hispanic, African and Taíno cultures[4]) falls apart in the priest's racist uttering. His racism defies the official discourse on race in Puerto Rico by reinforcing the marginalization of Afro-Puerto Ricans on the island.

The story also critiques the church's hypocrisy regarding celibacy and the condemnation of prostitution. In a surprising turn, the conversation between Isabel and the Monsignor ends with a clarifi-

---

[4] The image propagated by cultural institutions like the Institute of Puerto Rican Culture (El Instituto de Cultura Puertorriqueña), whose logo is an image of an African, a Spanish and a Taíno man, each of them holding an object stereotypically identifiable with their ethnicity and occupation.

cation–the mayor has already reserved the girl that the Monsignor usually requests, but Isabel would be happy to have the fifteen-year old Providencia visit him that night instead. The girl's name is an ironic allusion to divine guidance that contrasts with the Monsignor's abuse of power and transgression of religious norms. The fact that she is a young Dominican girl smuggled into Puerto Rico makes her situation even more tragic, as she cannot rely on the legal authorities for protection. The priest's use of the services of the brothel then complicates the gendered relations of power in the story–on the one hand, Isabel holds the economic and sexual power to control the Monsignor, while on the other hand, one of the instruments that enable her power is the exploitation of other women. In this sense, Isabel subverts gender roles only to extract a personal benefit, which does not result in any large-scale social transformation of gender norms and expectations. In this way, Ramos Otero represents the failure to construct an ethically redeemable subject, whether feminine or masculine, whether associated with the center or with the margins of the national discourse, and consequently expresses a profound, however implicit, critique of cultural nationalism's inability to fulfill its ideological claims.

The second space in which Ramos Otero positions Isabel is her limousine, evocative of luxury and power. Ironically, Isabel's limousine is reminiscent of a hearse: "Las ventanillas de cristal ahumado de la limosina de Frau Luberza no permiten que los que caminan por la calle vean que Frau Luberza, recostada contra los interiores blanco perla de piel y moaré, parece la Viuda Negra de los arácnidos" (Ramos Otero 197). The car's darkness, the position of the woman's body and the reference to the black widow foreshadow Isabel's impending death, and evoke solemnity, solitude and invisibility.

The urban landscape that the limousine traverses references the modernity desired by Puerto Rican cultural nationalism. However, this is a failed modernity, in which "there is here both the invocation of a national identity and its short-cutting" (Cruz-Malavé, "Towards an Art of Transvestism," 159). In it the living only exist to remind Isabel of the dead: "ese parado frente al Parque de Bombas se parece al difunto Meñón; ese otro sentado en el banco de la plaza se parece al difunto Gastón; ese otro recostado sobre la puerta del Comité Pipiolo se parece al difunto Franciscolo; ese guardia de palito se parece al difunto Víctor Virgilio" (Ramos Otero 197). Isabel evokes a feminine version of Benjamin's flâneur, but she is an anachronism, she does not belong. Her marginalization results in part from her gender and occupation, and in part from her power to control, instead of to participate on equal terms in the national community.

The brothel, which dominates the second half of the story, similarly critiques the Puerto Rican cultural nationalist model through the configuration of the space and through the ways in which people inhabit it. Significantly, it lacks a traditional national patriarch, and is instead dominated by Isabel's feminine, yet ghostly figure. The men that enter are rather an afterthought in Isabel's mind, even as she walks down the hallways of the brothel and listens in on every room. She is the omnipresent and omnipotent figure, claiming that "ningún macho es más macho que Frau Luberza" (Ramos Otero 204) and investing the space of the brothel with her presence: "Pasa por las paredes sus ojos Frau Luberza. Se apresura Frau Luberza. Posa el oído sobre la puerta de la Providencia Frau Luberza. Todo lo sabe Frau Luberza" (Ramos Otero 207). She balances her power (and the continuous operation of the brothel) on a blurry line between favors and blackmail, and confronts every governmental or institutional threat with a phone call:

> ¡otra orden de la Corte Suprema del carajo Viejo acusando a Frau Luberza [. . .] de ser la propietaria de un antro de perdición o casa de lenocinio! [. . .] Me busco el directorio de teléfonos influyentes y llamo al juez que se las buscaba con la Meche o llamo al juez que se las arregla con la Polilla todos los jueves [. . .] y otra orden de la Corte Suprema que se va por el inodoro! (Ramos Otero 201).

Corruption allows Isabel to evade the law in order to establish an alternative social order, which she executes not from a governmental office but from the brothel. In this sense, the story presents a matriarchal and subversive figure of leadership that proposes an alternative to the traditional spatial tropes associated with the national imaginary (the house and state institutions). It suggests the brothel as a different space of "government" that denotes the (in)efficiency and the (im)possibility of the national model as conceptualized by Puerto Rican cultural nationalist ideology.

The physical configuration of the space of the brothel enhances the notion of the impossibility of the cultural nationalist model. Instead of a large family house (as in Ferré's *The House on the Lagoon* or García Ramis's *Felices días, tío Sergio*) the brothel is divided into

"20 cuartitos" (Ramos Otero 206), each inhabited by a girl and by her clients. The only one that can move from room to room is Isabel, but even she remains outside, in the hallway, listening and observing without entering. If Isabel had been assigned maternal traits, she would be the figurative "mother" in the brothel, but her presence there is instrumental, it is ghostly, yet pivotal to the space, and the traditional maternal functions lay outside its intents. The *gran familia* is absent from that narrative, and to the extent to which any sort of society exists, it is fragmented, deplete of cohesion or solidarity, and self-sufficient for the benefit of its own reproduction and existence. The racial and class unity of the Puerto Rican nation is an illusion as the brothel emerges as a fragmented space of sexual and economic transactions. In contrast to the space of the beauty salon, in which consumption can be understood to function as a form of agency, in the brothel the consumers are men who enjoy economic and in most cases racial privilege. The women that Isabel employs don't benefit from the transaction, as Isabel continuously reiterates that they are "material" (Ramos Otero 200) and that she is doing them a favor that they now have to repay her.

Ramos Otero's critique of the Puerto Rican national model is most poignant in the story's final episode, which depicts Isabel's assassination by "cuatro machos de humo" (Ramos Otero 208), reminiscent of the four horsemen of the Apocalypse who bring war, disease and imminent death. As Ramos Otero traces the trajectory of every bullet, he turns the readers' attention to Isabel's body, "a dislocated body of difference [that] is violently relocated, a fractured body" (Ríos Ávila "Caribbean Dislocations" 112), and a female body of which Isabel is still in control even at the moment of her death. This Isabel is not Isabel Monfort, the subversive, yet still fairly traditional lady of *The House on the Lagoon*. Isabel la Negra's labor is practical, it has a purpose that is more narrow than that of the emotional labor associated with the maternal figures of Isabel Monfort, Marina, or Doña Kety. In "La última plena," "Ramos Otero se distancia [. . .] de lo que sentía como una opresiva domesticidad colonial, una 'familia de todos nosotros' algo provinciana e hipócrita" (Ríos Ávila *La raza cómica* 223), and puts Isabel in a position that is marginal to the ideal family house, or to *la gran familia puertorriqueña*. In the process, he is less interested in constructing alternatives guided by similar unifying logic than in exposing violence and hypocrisy by employing "una escritura que sólo puede entenderse como un performance de su situación periférica" (Ríos Ávila *La raza cómica* 228)–both of the author and of his protagonist.

In the story, the figure of Isabel la Negra and the way in which she dies can be interpreted as what Jossianna Arroyo has called "la máscara travesti," "un espacio alegórico de codificación ligüístico-cultural desde donde se problematizan [los] códigos de representación" (Arroyo "Exilio y tránsitos" 37). Isabel's character becomes a mask, and from behind that mask the story problematizes the national discourse on gender and belonging, questioning its claims to cohesion through the violent death of the powerful, yet indesirable "mother."

The space of the brothel becomes the site of Isabel's violent death, no longer her fortress, no longer able to protect her. Her assassination is yet another act of subversion of national ideology that "no sólo marca [. . .] una ruptura con el yo patriarcal, autoritario de la generación del 50, sino que rompe también, en términos más generales, con un discurso de formación nacional que convierte la patria en mujer para poseerla y contenerla, para hablar en su nombre o escribir sobre ella" (Cruz-Malavé, "Para virar al macho," 263). Isabel's vulnerability in the space that she used to control yet again subverts the patriarchal model of *la gran familia puertorriqueña*–she is not deposed through legal means, but at the hands of hired assassins, obeying the orders of a nameless master. In the story, hers is a society marked by such disarray and dysfunction that the instruments of control spiral deeper into the underworld, as powerful men find it necessary to employ means more violent and less legal than Isabel's blackmail and favoritism. In a symbolic final scene, the four assassins disappear in the fog after kissing, in a homoerotic gesture that questions whether Isabel's death signifies the beginning of a social order no longer organized around the axis of patriarchy and heterosexuality (that the very Isabel reproduced throughout her life, in the space of the brothel), or whether the violence of Isabel's murder forfeits its chances. In either case, this final act of violence followed by homoeroticism serves as a double critique of the Puerto Rican cultural nationalist imaginary, of its premise of a utopian unity and of heterosexual patriarchy.

Transgression and Punishment in *Life of Sin*

Several years after Ferré's and Ramos Otero's stories, Efraín López Neris released the film *Life of Sin* (1979), a fictional biography that depicts Isabel's life as a tragedy, and imposes a patriarchal pattern of gender and sexual conformism, transgression and punishment, seen as necessary and just in its cultural, religious and national context.

The film opens in a cemetery, immediately following Isabel's funeral. A journalist (Henry Darrow) working on a report on Isabel's death attempts to interview the last people to leave her grave–her cousin Rita,[5] her adopted son Manolín, and another friend–but is denied that request. The rest of the film is set up as a series of flashbacks that create the expectation of the eventual revelation of the causes behind Isabel's death, in a manner reminiscent of Gabriel García Márquez's *Crónica de una muerte anunciada*. The film's condemnation of its protagonist is evident from the title, which suggests that abandonment and betrayal are the inevitable payback for daring to challenge the gender and sexual models of Puerto Rican religious and national discourses. The space of the cemetery thus answers the film's central question before it is even posed: Isabel's life of sin is the implied reason for her death. It is a life that she chose and consequently a death that she brought upon herself, by behaving in a way that is neither "virtuous" nor "honorable," as understood by religious and national discourses.

Notwithstanding the manner of dying, death can be thought of as a collective experience that unites a family in mourning, or in which the cemetery becomes a material and a symbolic space for the construction of a collective national imaginary. The cemetery becomes a site in which "tombs of heroes and great men would be venerated by the state" (Aries 73) and by those who want to ascertain their belonging to it by reproducing it in time. While often those who rest in the cemetery are representative of a particular national project, that

---

[5] Neither "Rita" nor any of the actresses playing the prostitutes in Isabel's brothel are explicitly credited in the film. Their names appear in a list under the collective title "Isabel's Girls": Lottie Cordero, Awilda Lugo, Doris Berminquel, Sandy Sommers and Betzaida Falcón. This fact is notable in that it reproduces the invisibility of female Afro-Puerto Rican actresses in Puerto Rican cinema.

space enables the construction of the nation in yet another way, as "the nation exists precisely because the dead do not speak, or because those in power believe that conversation with the dead is 'undesirable'" (Holland 28), silencing any oppositional or subversive voices that could challenge the national unity and cohesion.

Puerto Rican cultural production has long attributed to the cemetery a similar nation-building function. In Edgardo Rodríguez Juliá's chronicle of the death of Rafael Cortijo in *El entierro de Cortijo* people from different races and classes come together to bid farewell to one of the country's most prominent artists. In contrast to Rodríguez Juliá's depiction, and to the depiction of Isabel's death in other recent works of fiction,[6] the representation of her funeral in *Life of Sin* hardly enables the creation of a national community. Even though her figure appears as important on and beyond the island (a sailor tells Isabel that her fame has spread as far as Hong Kong), her funeral is a private event whose impact does not reach beyond her immediate family. Her cousin, her adopted son and her close friend are the only ones at her grave, suggesting that the punishment for living a life of sin is loneliness and forgetting. The mise-èn-scene in that scene positions the mourners in the center, their black clothes against the whiteness of the gravestones, as if to emphasize their isolation and their silence. The two reporters that frame the shot stand for a sensationalism that sharply contrasts with the mourners' solitude. Even though few mourn Isabel, many are curious about her life and death. Consequently, in López Neris's film the cemetery does not function as a matrix for the construction of a national community in the context of the death of a prominent figure symbolic of that nation, but as a place both of solitude and of exploitative curiosity, as the only outcome of the resistance to acceptable norms of gender and sexuality.[7]

---

[6] Most notably, Mayra Santos-Febres's novel *Nuestra Señora de la Noche*, which opens the possibility for a national imaginary centered not around the figure of the patriarch, but around that of the black prostitute, whose offspring constitutes the foundation of a new family bond, a metaphoric "national family" built around racial and class reconciliation.

[7] In contrast, in Ramos Otero's story "Loca la de la locura" the protagonist's visit to the cemetery becomes a subversion of the national family and of its patriarchal, cohesive, and communitarian characteristics, but without blaming and punishing a character that transgresses its model. After the transvestite Loca la de la locura kills her lover Nene Lindo when he attacks her, she goes to his grave, feels no remorse, and then visits her mother's grave: "Después a la tumba de mamá. Arrodillada

Much like Rosario Ferré's story, the film sets the space of the brothel against the space of the house, like the one that Mr. Ted, one of Isabel's lovers, sets up for her in Ponce, and like Isabel's own house in the city's outskirts.

The opulent house that Mr. Ted gives Isabel is a space "tied up with, both directly and indirectly, particular social constructions of gender relations" (Massey 2). It represents the social tensions of gender, sexuality, class and race. Isabel has a servant and consequently is identifiable as "the lady of the house," a position that carries a specific racial (white) and upper-middle class association. Given that she is of a lower class Afro-Puerto Rican background, the film makes it clear that the house is the American man's gift to her. This gift comes with obligations that impose patriarchal norms and behaviors "suitable" to Isabel's new social identification. Mr. Ted ridicules her taste for pigs' feet and refuses to understand why she continues to eat them when he provides her with the best food on the market. He extinguishes the candles that she lights to Catholic and to Orisha deities, once again distinguishing between a "cultured" lifestyle and Isabel's customs. When Isabel decides to visit her own home in the outskirts of Ponce, he tries to stop her, and when she leaves him, he responds with anger against her and against the island of Puerto Rico: "The hell with you! The hell with this country!" (*Life*). Through the space of the house, the prostitute's body becomes "a site of struggle" (Rose 29), "[a map] of the relation between power and identity" (Rose 32)–of patriarchal power and of feminine, Afro-Puerto Rican identity. Mr. Ted represents American patriarchal power in controlling Puerto Rican society and culture, and at the same time suggests the U.S.'s profound disdain for them. The film also implies the performativity of gender, class and racial identities–if Mr. Ted can't make Isabel act according to the norms of the upper-class white society, he would rather not be associated with her (or with an island that centers its identity on lower-class and Afro-Puerto Rican culture).

---

con un bouquet de miramelindas y pringamosa. Vencida pero jamás acorralada. [. . .] Con un puñal de huesos para unirme a la revolución" (Ramos Otero 240). The "family" in the story consists of people who don't belong in the traditional *gran familia puertorriqueña*–a transvestite, a dead hustler and a dead old woman. Ramos Otero proposes an alternative national model, or none at all, if the final reference to a revolution were to be taken to signify an opposition to the established, dominant (national? legal?) order.

In contrast, Isabel's house in the outskirts of Ponce is guided by different rules and expectations, associated with gender and sexuality that challenge those represented by Mr. Ted and by the Catholic church. This second house is also the place in which home and brothel blend to propose an alternative imaginary, constructed around the figure not of a patriarch, but of an Afro-Puerto Rican woman who uses gender and sexuality as instruments of power and self-realization.

Early in the film, Isabel's house is a type of asylum that shelters women abandoned by men and by their families. Her figure is represented as more maternal, and associated with emotional labor, as she is a rare source of support for these young women. At first, she only envisions the space as an alternative to the violence of the patriarchal order that governs the houses to which they are not allowed to return. It is marginalization, solidarity and a shared reality of violence that inspires that community of women. In this sense, the house's transformation represents a "feminist standpoint [...] as a critical practice" (Hennessy xvii), through which women build solidarity in order to "[reformulate] political alliances and (collective) intervention" (Hennessy 32), resulting in a higher capacity for resistance and political agency.

Upon Isabel's return from Mr. Ted's, she finds the house full of men, even if at that point it is not yet a brothel in the traditional sense. Instead of returning the house to its original function, Isabel orders the women to begin charging the men: "Having fun is not enough. [. . .] From now on we charge. We charge for everything" (*Life*). Her reason for prostitution contrasts with traditional causes like financial need or coercion (Campbell 4). Isabel abandons the aspects of her character associated with emotional labor, nurture and protection, and makes a deliberate choice based on a set of realities that already exist (the men know the house and are used to visiting it). In a sense, she subverts the patriarchal "control over the way that space is produced [which] is fundamental to the heterosexuals' ability to reproduce their hegemony" (Valentine 154). Even though Isabel's actions reproduce heteronormativity, she takes control of the sexual exploitation of the women and assumes the power to begin regulating it.

Curiously, the film does not make Isabel fully responsible for the house's transformation into a brothel, but seems to assign that responsibility to all women, suggesting that it is neither the necessity, nor the entrepreneurial spirit of one, but the moral corruption of many that inspired that transformation. The fact that none of the women object to the new rules can be interpreted in two ways–either that they fear expulsion from yet another home, or that they readily agree to the new order in the house.

From then on, the space of the house is consistently identified as a brothel. Isabel's room (the owner's living quarters) is the only one in which sex is not exchanged for money. Isabel is the driving force behind the brothel's success: she organizes a mock society ball and turns a fight into a deliberate performance that ends when she decides to stop it. She chooses whom to let in and whom to keep out. She hosts dinners for the mayor, intended to earn her the ability to be a phone call away from his protection when the need arises. Isabel's centrality in the brothel challenges Mr. Ted's (or the bishop's, for that matter). She derives power not from colonial relations or traditional religious norms, but from her use of gender and sexuality to legitimize her position in society–not in the society to which the bishop, Mr. Ted, or even the journalist belong, but in the underground society, in which these same people operate according to a different set of rules, to which they won't admit openly (the bishop accepts a generous donation from Isabel but publicly condemns her, while the U.S. Navy offers Isabel an exclusive contract for their sailors that would ban Puerto Rican men from entering the brothel).

In contrast to Ferré's and Ramos Otero's stories, the brothel in López Neris's film is an unsustainable institution, despite its apparent success. Even though the brothel is famous as far away as Hong Kong, Isabel is unable to enforce her own rules. She confronts Shirley, one of the girls, for bringing inside a pimp despite Isabel's warning, and hits Paolo (Raul Juliá), who cuts her, is arrested, and eventually dies in jail. These events suggest that the presumed "sins" of the film's title are too much for one woman to handle. She has power, but is not omnipotent like Ramos Otero's protagonist. In the film, her power fails her as her enterprise becomes bigger, as she amasses enemies and as she continues to practice what society deems reprehensible.

While this representation might appear to contradict Isabel's earlier depiction as a powerful woman (early in the film she is seen walking down a city street, in an image that suggests independence), in reality it is hardly surprising. Cinematic representations of prostitution have traditionally swayed between two extremes:

> Because of the contradictory emotions [that the prostitute] gen-
> erates, she has come to occupy an equivocal position in the male
> imagination, both valued and vilified. A symbol of eroticism in a
> sexually repressive society, or of endurance in the face of intense
> humiliation and suffering, she attains a positive coloring; but as a
> symbol of flesh against the spirit, of the commercial against the
> freely offered, or of the depth of social life against its heights, she
> is negative. (Campbell 5)

Isabel's death outside the brothel and the film's ending–the words of the bishop (José Ferrer) appearing as a voiceover, reaffirming the church's condemnation of fornicators, thieves, adulterers and sodomites–suggest that the subversive central figure that the film initially appeared to depict belongs to a frustrated imaginary doomed to failure and literal demise. The film's ending explains the images in its opening credits–a large building, abandoned and dilapidated, that the audience can now identify as the former brothel. Isabel dies, and the brothel, her space, withers in time to become only a distant memory of a woman and of a place that didn't conform and that were punished for it.

The patriarchal tone of the film's ending can only be understood in the context of the Puerto Rican film industry's conflictive relationship to gender. Puerto Rican cinema's identification as a male craft began long ago, with film pioneers like Rafael Coronado and Juan Emilio Viguié Cajas in the early decades of the 20th Century, continued with the artists working in DIVEDCO (directors like Ángel F. Rivera, Amílcar Tirado, Jack Delano; screenwriters like Ricardo Alegría, René Marqués, Pedro Juan Soto, Emilio Díaz Valcárcel; editors like Adrián Luna, Alfonso Borrell, Ramón Usera, Joseph Lido; and cameramen like Gabriel Tirado, Jesús Figueroa and Luis Antonio Maisonet, among others), and extended to Jacobo Morales and Efraín López Néris, the only two Puerto Rican directors briefly mentioned in John King's classic text *Magical Reels: A History of Cinema in Latin America.* It is only since the 1980s that female directors like Poli Marichal, Ana María García, Sonia Fritz and Frances Negrón-Muntaner have gained visibility and reached critical and commercial success. Their work continues to "problematize dominant ideology and constructions of Puerto Rican history and identity as well as the relationship between anticolonial and gender politics" (Negrón-Muntaner "Of Lonesome").

The scarcity of women in the Puerto Rican film industry might help explain the paternalist representation of Isabel and of the space of the brothel, a representation that can be read as the film's—and the industry's—critical and violent response to the feminist discourse that emerged with the writers of the Generation of the 1970s. As in most films produced in Puerto Rico in the 1970s, very few women were involved in the decision-making aspects of the film's production,[8] and "this male domination led to a confusing double standard; i.e. what made a woman immoral or scandalous would not always be represented in the same manner if applied to a man" (Parish xv).

The depiction of the brothel in *Life of Sin* is also a result of the expectations of the island's cinema. While *Life of Sin* is a Puerto Rican film (in terms of its cast, crew and funding), it is a made-for-Hollywood Puerto Rican film. Its video distributor is Columbia Tristar Home Video, and its production company and theatrical distributor was the 21st Century Film Corporation, which operated from the 1970s to 1996. It casts some of Puerto Rico's most prominent actors, familiar to US audiences through Hollywood film and television productions and through Broadway roles: Raul Juliá, whose career in the US began in 1969, had already acted alongside Faye Dunaway and Tommy Lee Jones; José Ferrer had received an Academy Award and a Golden Globe for his performance as Cyrano de Bergerac in 1950; Miriam Colón had acted since the 1950s; and Henry Darrow was well known for his role as Manolito Montoya in the series *The High Chaparral* (1967-1971). More importantly, the film is in English, intended for an international market. In this sense, the representation of Isabel la Negra can be understood in a context in which, in the case of Hollywood films,

> many moviemakers have gravitated to the daring subject of harlotry because of its exploitative value. Film producers were quick to realize that many moviegoers would be titillated by pictures dealing with the controversial topic and that it would mean size-

---

[8] Aside from the film's leading star Miriam Colón, two women stand out for their role in the production process. Vicky Hernández was one of the producers and Gloria Piñeyro was the editor (which, curiously enough, has been the most common "female" occupation in the Hollywood film industry, much more so than those of director, screenwriter, or producer). The credits indicate a predominantly male presence: Efraín López Neris directed, Emilio Díaz Valcárcel wrote the script, J. Armando Arica produced the film, and Alex Phillips was the cinematographer.

able box-office profits. By presenting such stories, moviemakers allowed filmgoers to enter vicariously the "immoral" world of the streetwalker, thus providing many viewers in the audience their first or only acquaintance with the risqué–and to some forbidden" world of sex-for-pay (Parish xiii).

In this sense, Isabel is both a sexual subject rejected by Puerto Rican nationalist discourse, and a sexualized woman in a twice-exoticized space: the brothel and the island of Puerto Rico as a Caribbean location, from the perspective of Hollywood.

## From the Brothel to the National Family in *Nuestra Señora de la Noche*

The most recent literary representation of Isabel la Negra's life is Mayra Santos Febres' novel *Nuestra Señora de la Noche*. Its plot takes place between several spaces–the brothel, the house in the city of Ponce where one of Isabel's clients lives, the *arrabal* where Isabel's son with Fernando is being raised by another woman, and the Puerto Rican diaspora in the US where Fernando's "legitimate" son Luis Arsenio goes to school. These characters and the spaces that they inhabit all come together at Isabel's funeral. Through that final scene, the novel suggests the formation of a new family, reunited in spite of decades of hatred, exclusion, abandonment and betrayal. In this way, Santos-Febres not only retells the story of the famous prostitute, but also assigns her a key role in reinventing the Puerto Rican national imaginary on the island and in the diaspora.

In the novel, like in Ferré's story, the brothel is set against the space of the house, through which the author critiques traditional models of gender in the national imaginary. The first house that appears in the novel is that of Fernando Fornarís, a lawyer and the father of Isabel's son Roberto. He abandons Isabel to marry Cristina Rangel, who comes from Ponce's high society and conforms to the traditional expectations of femininity. Even when she realizes her husband's involvement in the life of Isabel's child (whom Isabel abandons at birth), she keeps her silence. On the surface, her large house is the perfect family home, inhabited by a successful patriarch and by his obedient wife. Underneath, however, it is frayed with contradictions. Cristina's pain, attributed to Fernando's betrayal, turns her into an alcoholic, leads to her madness and to her death. Her husband's frequent absences make him an unlikely patriarch–he dominates the home without actually being present, in a situation reminiscent of *Felices días, tío Sergio*. Even though Fernando is alive, his frequent and increasingly long absences construct a particular kind of masculinity, so powerful that it need not be present to be obeyed. Although Fernando Fornarís appears as the epitome of the patriarch, his family is in fact fragmented and incomplete–his son with Isabel has no access to the family house, and he only gets to meet his brother at the end of the novel, alluding to the fragmentations that problematize the idea of national unity.

The house associated with the traditional masculinity absent from Luis Arsenio's home is that of his friend Esteban Ferráns. Esteban's house resembles the Fornarís's: "chaflán mallorquín en la entrada, aldaba de bronce, una casa tan idéntica a la suya" (Santos-Febres, *Nuestra* 79). In contrast to Luis Arsenio's house, however, Esteban's is dominated by men: "En el salón biblioteca estaban todos los hombres de la familia. Esteban padre había convocado a sus hermanos, que llegaron de la finca del Tibes y del negocio de la capital tan pronto oyeron la noticia de que se aproximaba el tío Jaume" (80). In contrast to *Felices días*, where the uncle's arrival signifies the beginning of the redefinition of gender and sexuality in relation to the Puerto Rican nation, in the case of the Ferráns the uncle's return from Spain serves as an opportunity to reproduce the patriarchal notions associated with *la gran familia puertorriqueña*. As Luis Arsenio observes, "Esta era claramente una conversación entre hombres, una escuela en proceso que iniciaba a su amigo en los trámites y costumbres de los machos de su estirpe" (Santos-Febres, *Nuestra* 81). The subordination of women in the Ferráns house makes it an exaggerated, almost grotesque depiction of *la gran familia puertorriqueña*, in which women are quite literally invisible.

The third house that composes the novel's gendered map is the hut in the outskirts of Ponce in which Doña Montse raises Roberto Fornarís. Paid by Fernando to care for the boy since his birth, Doña Montse is the epitome of motherhood, so much so that Roberto believes that she is his real mother:

–"Madrina, ¿tú eres mi mamá? [. . .]
–Madre es la que cría, Nene." (Santos-Febres, *Nuestra* 19)

In many ways, Doña Montse approximates the traditional model of motherhood; she cares for the child, and in many ways her labor is also emotional, providing support, love and guidance without compensation. However, the hut in which she raises Roberto contrasts with the symbolic house of the national family. On the one hand, instead of a middle-class urban home, equipped and maintained to support a nuclear family, it is a poor shack in which, in Robertito's words, "Madrina y yo dormimos entre unos sacos." (Santos-Febres, *Nuestra* 68). This house questions the class aspect of the national family, and calls the readers' attention to the poverty that deprives some members of that family from the opportunities that others acquire by birth.

This house also lacks a patriarchal figure. Fernando Fornarís's absence is the cause of the boy's frequent questions, "¿Cuándo viene mi papá? [. . .] ¿Por qué no vive con nosotros? ¿Por qué viene en un carro grande, grande y con el mismo carro se va?" (Santos-Febres, *Nuestra* 18). Doña Montse forces herself to find explanations and to invent excuses, reproducing the image of the patriarch from the standpoint of economic and racial marginalization. Through her subordinated position in Puerto Rican society, and through the incongruities evident in the space of the house, the novel critiques the cultural nationalist model and the social conditions out of which it emerged.

The novel begins to construct an alternative to the traditional national model through Elizabeth's Dancing Place, the brothel that most of the characters at one time or another access. Through the transformation of the space, and through the construction of gender and the idea of the family, the brothel becomes a space that offers an alternative, however fleeting, to traditional national imaginaries and gender roles.

The brothel is the most striking alternative to the family house commonly associated with *la gran familia puertorriqueña*. In contrast to the house in novels like *Felices días* or in films like *Dios los cría*, the brothel in Santos-Febres's book is a dynamic space that transforms with the modernization of Puerto Rican society and with Isabel's increasing social empowerment. While at first it is a well-maintained, yet modest place ("Las mesas estaban vestidas con manteles y velitas acodadas contra la sombra. Una tarima lo suficientemente grande para darle cabida a una banda de charangas se iluminaba con luces de piso." Santos-Febres, *Nuestra* 32-33), towards the end, "le había hecho una ampliación de cuartos en la parte trasera. Un pavimento de brea cubría la carretera de entrada hasta bien metido el monte. Ya no dependía de un generador de manigueta. [. . .] El piso entero era de cemento. Se veía que Isabel había prosperado" (Santos-Febres, *Nuestra* 242). The brothel prospers thanks to the favors that politicians do for Isabel, in exchange for women or for her silence. Her San Antón neighborhood is the only one with electricity: "cerca del río, en ese puterío alejado y montaraz, había generador con poste de luz de los que pone el Gobierno" (Santos-Febres, *Nuestra* 127). These words are a subtle critique of corruption (male government officials order the installation of electricity in that particular place), and at the same time foreground Isabel's power, albeit based on favoritism and in many cases on covert blackmail. By taking advantage of the corruption and the hypocrisy embedded in the patriarchal structure, Isabel also exposes that same traditional, patriarchal, national model.

By decentering the figure of the patriarch and by substituting it with that of Isabel la Negra, the brothel brings forth models of femininity and masculinity that depart from those constitutive of *la gran familia puertorriqueña*. However, even though the brothel in Santos-Febres's novel lays the foundation for an inclusive community, it continues to reproduce a gender structure that doesn't allow for the equitable inclusion of women.

Isabel's figure imbues the brothel's space with power. She is literally at the center of the brothel ("En medio de aquel salón una mujer prominente fumaba sentada en un trono de paja" Santos-Febres, *Nuestra* 34), sitting in a throne, which draws associations with monarchies and queens. She is in complete control of the space that surrounds her: "Paseaba su vista como si estuviera evaluando un espectáculo de variedades y a la vez como si sopesara estrategias de defensa en un territorio minado. Todo lo abarcaban sus ojos. Su piel era azul, azul pantera, azul sombra de ojo hambriento" (Santos-Febres, *Nuestra* 34). On the one hand, in emphasizing Isabel's control over the space, this description inverts the relationship between race and power by situating an Afro-Puerto Rican woman at the center and on the "throne" of the metaphoric space of the nation. On the other hand, the description's allusion to a panther, a dangerous, exotic animal, draws parallels between black female sexuality, exoticism and animal imagery. In this sense, the centrality of Isabel's figure serves as a base for a national model that does not marginalize race, gender and sexuality, but includes them in problematic ways.

In contrast to the image of femininity, in the brothel masculinity is traditional and patriarchal in both its racial and class characteristics. Even though Isabel stands at the center, the women that work for her occupy a subordinate position that serves the needs of the male clients: "Esas mujeres eran las responsables de romper la tirantez de los machos" (Santos-Febres, *Nuestra* 34). Boys like Luis Arsenio go to Elizabeth's Dancing Place to "become men": "Aquella noche, si el plan se daba según lo estipulado, Luis Arsenio, Esteban, Pedrito y Alejandro Villanúa se convertirían en hombres de verdad, según la usanza de los machos de su estirpe" (26). Even when Luis Arsenio finds himself infatuated with Minerva, he knows that her class and race preclude the possibility of a relationship: "Después encontraría la manera de arrancársela de los sueños y de los apetitos. Se echaría una novia quizás, una chica a propiedad a quien besar castamente y presentarle a la familia" (78). Masculinity is enabled by Minerva's gender and sexuality, but also constructed in opposition to her race and class, foregrounding the image of a future patriarch conscious of the social divisions that set him apart from members of *la gran familia* like Minerva.

At first sight, the nation that emerges in the space of the brothel appears diverse and democratic. An early description of the clients points out that "Al Elizabeth's Dancing Place entraba todo el mundo. No había miramientos de edad, color, procedencia o pecas en la piel" (Santos-Febres, *Nuestra* 25). This seemingly inclusive space, however, benefits men in high political and social positions, in return for favors or for information that might be used as blackmail in the future. The "family," consisting of Isabel and the women that work for her, is also far from democratic. Isabel has complete control over decisions like who is allowed to work in the brothel, who gets certain clients, etc. The female solidarity so productive in the construction of the alternative gendered space of the beauty salon is absent from the brothel. Instead, the brothel intensifies structures of oppression, even those (like Isabel's power) that at first glance seem to subvert traditional gender hierarchies associated with the cultural nationalist model.

Aside from the brothel, there are other spaces that problematize gender in relation to patriarchy and national identity. Even though the novel is set in Ponce, a significant portion of it takes place in

Philadelphia, on the campus of the University of Pennsylvania, where Luis Arsenio enrolls as a college student. His experience in Philadelphia constructs a particular image of the Puerto Rican diaspora, which challenges ideas of renewed connections to the island and of the contributions of the Puerto Rican community to US culture. In contrast, the novel constructs a foreign space that is inhospitable, and that makes impossible the construction of a diasporic or a (trans)national community.

Santos-Febres's decision to set a portion of the novel on the mainland alludes both to the history of Puerto Rican migration, and to the problematic relationship between the island, Puerto Rican communities in the United States, and the notion of national identity.[9] In the post-World War II era U.S. government agencies approached the newly-emerging Latino communities through the paradigms of the "culture of poverty" and the "underclass," "racial ideologies that point to particular groups of people, emphasize their 'problems' and hold them culpable for their own poverty" (Whalen 241). This attitude was reflected in the ways in which government and police reproduced stereotypes of Puerto Ricans as violent and criminal, most notably in the events leading up to the Philadelphia riots of 1953. In July of 1953 a Puerto Rican man was accused of stabbing an American in a bar, which caused a group of white men to invade several homes of Puerto Rican families. The fighting that followed involved up to a thousand people (Whalen 183). These riots,

> reflected white residents' fears of racial change, racism against Puerto Ricans, and perceived competition for housing and jobs. White residents moved out and sometimes reacted with violence. Puerto Rican migrants, in turn, faced the racial hostility that came with racial change in northern urban areas in the postwar era. As they responded to the incident, policy makers and social service workers transformed the riots from a racial incident against Puerto Ricans into an indication of the 'Puerto Rican problem' (Whalen 184).

---

[9] Jorge Duany's *The Puerto Rican Nation on the Move* and Yolanda Martínez-San Miguel's *Caribe Two Ways* focus precisely on these tensions and negotiations of island and diasporic identities.

Even though the novel takes place before these events, the section set in Philadelphia relies on the historical memory of the racial and ethnic conflicts between the city's Puerto Rican and white residents. The setting enhances the book's critical approach to the possibility of a transnational Puerto Rican and Latino community. Luis Arsenio arrives in Philadelphia with great hopes for the symbolic value of his trip: "Emigraba. Ampliaba los horizontes de su clan" (Santos-Febres, *Nuestra* 164), but quickly realizes that in the US he is not the person that he is accustomed to being in Puerto Rico. In Philadelphia he is not quite white, his island origins are confusing, and lead to his exclusion from the upper-middle class sectors of US society to which his family belongs in Puerto Rico. His girlfriend, Maggie Carlisle, explains her betrayal with the impossibility of the racial and class integration of Puerto Ricans in US society: "¿cómo iba yo a presentarte a mi familia? Hola, éste es Louie Forneress from some island. No sé si tiene medios para sostenerme. Nos queremos casar y vivir en la selva, en un árbol junto a los monos. [. . .] 'Me, Jane; tú, Tarzán'" (Santos-Febres, *Nuestra* 247). Because of his race and national origins, Luis Arsenio is emasculated, as the possibility of creating a traditional family is denied to him by a white, upper-class woman. In this way, the novel questions Duany's ideas of the viability of a transnational community, as well as Negrón-Muntaner's notion of the "latinization of American culture." Instead, it remains rooted in a traditional notion of national community, reminiscent of the cultural nationalist idea of *la puertorriqueñidad* in that it excludes the possibility of establishing lasting connections with Puerto Ricans in the US or between the US and Latino community, for the benefit of the redefinition of the notion of *la puertorriqueñidad*.[10]

--------

[10] In contrast to Mayra Santos's novel, films like *AIDS in the Barrio* and *Brincando el charco* assume a different perspective regarding the relationship between gender, sexuality, diasporic space and community. Frances Negrón-Muntaner (co-director of the first and writer/director of the second film, both set in Philadelphia) acknowledges the difficulties in building a diasporic Latino community in the context of colonial and economic domination. *AIDS in the Barrio* explores the intersections between economic and social marginalization, patriarchal attitudes toward masculinity and homosexuality, and the problem of AIDS in the Latino community, exposing and indicting the social factors that derail the prevention of AIDS among Latino men (and some women). Similarly, *Brincando el charco* critiques the notion of the "melting pot," and the "myth of racial democracy" (*Brincando el charco*), and looks at the complex relationship between Latinos, U.S. society, gender, sexuality and race. By revealing the factors that derail the recognition of the contributions of

The novel does culminate in a national reunification, but one that takes place in an unlikely space, and whose nature is problematic in many respects. The national unity that Santos-Febres proposes is represented by the reunification of the two brothers (Luis Arsenio and Roberto) through their coincidental encounter on the SS Seaborn during World War II, and through their first direct interaction in Manila, during the investigation of the murder of a Philippine man committed by Roberto. By staging the brothers' reunification in the Philippines, the book appears to challenge the indispensability of territory and space in the construction of the nation. The brothers could have met anywhere, but the historical circumstances set their encounter in the Philippines, which shares Puerto Rico's colonial legacy in relation to both Spain and the U.S. In this way, the novel argues that this non-traditional model of the nation, represented by the two brothers, can be (re)constructed independently of place.

However, the brothers' reunification in Manila is fleeting, and neither is sure whether the other one recognized him as a brother. That recognition only comes when both return to the island, to the material space of the Puerto Rican nation, at Isabel's funeral (an act that symbolically associates the family with the space of the island, as Isabel is buried on the island, in a gesture that alludes to "diversas genealogías: de la familia, de la nación, del cuento mismo [Sotomayor, *Femina Faber* 279]). On the one hand, the scene is reminiscent of that of Rodríguez Juliá's description of the multitude at Cortijo's funeral: "Eran personas de todos los caminos de la vida. Putas niñas y matronas, antiguos clientes que se quedaron debiéndole a Isabel algún favor, representantes de todos los partidos políticos, ancianos y lavanderas, cantantes de poca monta y artistas de renombre internacional" (Santos-Febres, *Nuestra* 356). On the other, these family bonds and family history evoke "an epistemological crisis of both family and nation from which the characters emerge and to which the characters return" (del Río Gabiola 84). The author subversively associates the social impact of one of Puerto Rico's most prominent artists with that of Isabel la Negra, an in

Latinos to U.S. society, and by suggesting solutions to some of the problems related to AIDS, to stereotypes and to the reproduction of patriarchal attitudes towards sexuality, the films become instruments for the construction of a Puerto Rican and Latino community in the U.S. that *Nuestra Señora* appears to deny.

this way proposes a different center around which to construct a national model–that of an Afro-Puerto Rican woman who rose to power by using her sexuality.

What remains problematic is the image of the national family in the aftermath of Isabel's death. On the one hand, it is based on the cultural nationalist model of racial reconciliation–the black and the white Fornarís, together with Manolo, are greeted by the people as Isabel's sons: "La multitud se dispersaba, la gente se iba despidiendo. Hasta hubo quien le presentara condolencias a Manolo, a su hermano y a él" (Santos-Febres, *Nuestra* 359). The image of the brothers standing at Isabel's grave includes Afro-Puerto Ricans in the national imaginary and places them at its center. On the other hand, it is reminiscent of the notion of racial consensus on which the idea of cultural nationalism is based. Instead of exposing problems like racism and marginalization, the final scene suggests a reconciliation that is still difficult to conceive of in contemporary Puerto Rico. The family is also an entirely masculine brotherhood, depicting the three symbolic founders of the nation becomes a soldier, a lawyer, and an overseer in the brothel. In this sense, the novel constructs a national imaginary in which women occupy a subordinate position, and from which they are absent, except in the figure of the now deceased Isabel.

The image of Isabel la Negra in the texts discussed in this chapter is part of the larger discussion of the status of the state and the law in Puerto Rican society. In recent years, historians and cultural critics have brought to the forefront the ways in which, "Although the state in Puerto Rico at one time or another has performed most of the duties it has been entitled to carry out, it has been, for many extended periods of time, absent from the everyday life of the communities and the individuals of most portions of the island" (Picó, F. "The Absent State" 21). As an example, Picó explains that in the second half of the 19th century, when Cuba and Puerto Rico were the last remaining colonies of Spain in the Americas, the Spanish state increased its control over municipal affairs–however, efforts at regulating private life were mostly met with "apathy and resistance" (22). Similarly, in the early 20th century, "mistrust and sabotage" met the U.S. government's "directives and policies on health, labor, welfare, urban order, and social relations" (25). Subsequently, Picó emphasizes the ways in which Puerto Ricans have questioned the sovereignty of the state and its power to control everything, from political, social and cultural relations, to the bodies that inhabit them. As a consequence, Picó and critics like Carlos Pabón have argued that, "the nation-state, as an isomorphic configuration of the territory, ethnos, and state apparatus finds itself in a serious and profound crisis" (Pabón "The Political Status" 66).

The texts studied in this chapter depict Isabel la Negra in ways that may appear contradictory in relation to the state and the law. On the one hand, her gender and her race define her as a second-class citizen in the context of the white, patriarchal national discourse of the second half of the 20th century. On the other hand, in the absence of a sovereign state, of a state willing and able to fulfill its obligations to the people, Isabel becomes a sovereign in her own right, and it is her law that is to be obeyed as she administers the brothel in Ramos Otero's story, or as she takes advantage of the politicians' corruption and sets her rules of male conduct in the brothel in Santos Febres's novel. In this sense, it is her law, and not the law of the state, that constructs the ideal white male citizen. This situation is both problematic and empowering–on the one hand, Isabel could be seen as perpetuating the patriarchal structure that oppresses her and the women that work for her. On the other, it is her agency, and her law, that is functional, beyond the limited capacity of a state that has abnegated its responsibilities, or that is no longer able to fulfill them. This interpretation implicitly suggests a criticism of Puerto Rico's colonial relationship to the United States as an order that is unable to organize and to serve the Puerto Rican people, and reinforces the need to look for different communities and strategic solidarities to resist and subvert the patriarchal national discourse of the nation.


## Conclusion

An analysis of the relationship between space, gender and sexuality in Puerto Rican cultural production must include a discussion of the brothel as a site where historical tensions of class, race, gender and sexuality surface and reconfigure traditional national imaginaries. When writers and directors choose to speak from the space of the brothel, they often do so in order to confront patriarchal discourses with respect to female roles and participation in the Puerto Rican nation. The brothel focalizes power relations of gender and sexuality while offering multiple possibilities to subvert patriarchal hierarchies and to reorder traditional views of gender and sexuality in national discourse.

Puerto Rican authors and film directors have used the figure of the prostitute and the space of the brothel as instruments for the critique and the construction of a variety of national imaginaries. From Rosario Ferré's and Mayra Santos-Febres's models based on feminist and racial unity and solidarity, to Efraín López Neris's condemnation of the brothel as a space of "sin," and to Manuel Ramos Otero's denial of the possibility of any alternative, ethically redeemable community, the brothel has been a controversial space in which power hierarchies along axes of race, class and gender have clashed and struggled to negotiate the representation and the construction of the Puerto Rican nation. The literary and cinematic texts analyzed above depict the space of the brothel as a gendered and political space that serves as a matrix for social critique from different standpoints of gender, racial and national debates in Puerto Rico.

CHAPTER VI

CONCLUSION

O VER the course of the 20th century, Puerto Rican authors and film directors have used space as a matrix from which to challenge the dominant discourses on nation, gender and sexuality, to voice critiques and to propose alternatives to the tropes of the official cultural nationalist model and to the hierarchies that organize it. The authors of the novels, the short stories and the films analyzed in the preceding chapters participate in this tradition in creative and innovative ways. As they explore the representation of gender, sexuality and nation in everyday gendered spaces, they pose a number of questions related to the discursive construction of the Puerto Rican nation: What hierarchical aspects of the cultural nationalist discourse need to be exposed and critiqued in order to ensure what Arjun Appadurai and James Holston have called substantive citizenship for all (Holston and Appadurai 4)? What narrative and visual strategies have the potential to best dismantle the patriarchal discourse of gender and nation, and to critique traditional models of *la puertorriqueñidad*? What spaces can serve as productive alternatives to the house of *la gran familia puertorriqueña*, founded on patriarchal expectations of femininity and masculinity, and constructed according to traditional pedagogies of gender? What are the figures that can displace the patriarch and that have the potential to organize the space of the nation in non-hierarchical ways? What configurations of the national model would be more egalitarian? And are there models outside the restrictive model of the nation that allow for the construction of other types of commu-

193

nities, based not on territorial, racial or class characteristics, but on solidarities along multiple axes of identities?

The geographies that emerge from the texts that I study draw elaborate maps of patriarchal domination, gendered resistance and feminine agency. The violence that many of the literary and cinematic texts discussed here foreground inspires their authors to look for ways to dismantle patriarchal discourses on gender and nation by critiquing limited and limiting models of sexuality, of race, of labor, and of the configuration of the trope of the national family.

The Puerto Rican texts that I analyze construct race in unorthodox ways that often contradict official national models. Cultural nationalist discourse strategically defined race in inclusive, yet hierarchical ways. Its claim that Puerto Rican culture was founded on the union of Hispanic, indigenous and African heritage advanced a version of history that ignored the violence of the conquest and the silenced, dehumanizing history of slavery. Over the course of the 20th century, and in an effort to contribute to the construction of the Puerto Rican nation, both politicians and cultural agents embraced the narrative of cohesion and national union to reaffirm the dominant narrative of the nation. It was a narrative that spoke of inclusion but privileged whiteness, as the figures of leadership that emerged (like that of Luis Muñoz Marín in Edgardo Rodríguez Juliá's glorifying account of the governor's funeral in *Las tribulaciones de Jonás*) belonged predominantly to the white middle and upper class.

It was only in the 1970s that Afro-Puerto Rican, female and queer authors began to question the cultural nationalist narrative and to organize their short stories, novels and films around indigenous and Afro-Puerto Rican characters. From José Luis González's *El país de cuatro pisos* to Ana Lydia Vega's "Otra maldad de Pateco," black characters began to occupy the central position in unorthodox versions of the Puerto Rican national narrative. In my discussion of the intersection between race and national discourse, I focus on one specific character, that of Isabel la Negra, and on four of the recent representations of her life. While some of the authors that I study (Ferré and Ramos Otero, and to an extent López Neris) emphasize her feminine agency and the unusual social standing that she achieved thanks to her sexuality, writers like Mayra Santos-Febres underline the question of race and the the issue of how, in spite of consistent exploitation and abuse, a poor, Afro-Puerto Rican woman was able to achieve a level of power and social status that few women–even fewer black women–were able to attain. Santos-Febres's novel positions Isabel la Negra at the center of a new national imaginary set not in the big house of *la gran familia puertorriqueña*, but in the brothel, a space of complex negotiations of race, class, gender, sexuality and belonging.

The literary and cinematic geographies that I uncover in this study also take a critical standpoint regarding the traditional cultural nationalist approach to sexuality. The cultural nationalist discourse of *la gran familia puertorriqueña* is heterosexual, leaving little space for what it conceives of as non-normative sexualities. In literature and in films produced by DIVEDCO, for example, men fulfill traditionally masculine roles, and find their masculinity threatened when they fail to act as the faithful husband and father. Women, on the other hand, are frequently depicted as mothers, housewives and workers, building the modern nation alongside their husbands, reproached and condemned if they dared stray from this prescribed role, as in the case of Maruja, who repays her transgression with her life. Homoeroticism and homosexual desire is nonexistent in this discourse that seeks to reproduce heterosexuality as the default, normative and acceptable sexual identification of the nation.

As in the case of the construction of race, in the second half of the 20th century authors and artists began to question the exclusion of non-normative sexualities from national discourses, and started to consider alternative identities and communities, organized around gender and sexual differences. They tended to do that from specific spaces–locations associated with the space of the nation, as well as symbolic spaces that resisted patriarchal discourses and practices to propose alternative communities.

Authors of the Generation of the 70s began using the house as a privileged setting for new, transgressive models of sexuality, previously excluded from the national discourse. Their female protagonists were either heterosexual women who transgressed the expectations of what a "good" wife and mother should be, or female characters that desired other women, disregarding the social condemnation of such desire. Rosario Ferré's novel *The House on the Lagoon* belongs to the first group and foregrounds a character that transgresses gender expectations of obedience and subordination. In the process, she goes as far as to question the foundational narrative of her husband's family, and, by association, of the symbolic "national" family that he, as a patriarch, represents. In this way, Ferré's Isabel refashions the house from a space of patriarchal control to a fragile, fragmented space of alternative histories of gender oppression, resistance and agency.

In contrast to the family house, a space traditionally associated with national discourse and subverted by feminist authors, the beauty salon's relationship to the patriarchal national imaginary has been more complex and problematic. As a space of gathering, of discursive and of physical interactions, the beauty salon allows for the transgression of gender and sexual roles. As a space that has historically been associated with a strict gender binary (female, in the case of the beauty salon, and male, in the case of the barbershop), it is also a space in which feminine solidarities have the potential freedom to emerge, shielded, albeit temporarily, from patriarchal discourse and practices. These are the conditions that enable the gender solidarities and the subtle attractions between the female characters in Carmen Lugo Filippi's and in Mayra Santos-Febres's short stories.

For Marina and Milagros, the salon is not only a space of the exchange of beauty services–it is a space of solidarity, of alliance, and ultimately of agency. It is in the salon where Marina's attraction for Milagros begins, and it is also in the salon where Milagros looks for Marina, looking for help with her physical transformation, which accompanies her rebellion and her escape from the violence of the family home. Similarly, in "Hebra rota" Doña Kety's salon is a space of escape for the young Yetsaida, who sees it as an alternative to the violence inflicted by her father in the family home. Although the salon does not have the ability to subvert the patriarchy that defines its context, it allows the women to form a bond across generations and around the need to give (Doña Kety) and to receive (Yetsaida) kindness, support and the knowledge that they are not alone in their struggle against violence. The fact that in each story the beauty salon is set against the background of multiple family houses is a reminder of the patriarchy that surrounds the salon, and, at the same time, of its function as a space of escape and of potential strategies for liberation. The fact that the results of these strategies are only temporary does not discredit the salon as a potential space of resistane and liberation, but speaks to the power of the oppressive forces to which the women that frequent the salon have to stand up.

In addition to race and sexuality, the gendered geographies that emerge from the texts that I analyze subvert traditional cultural nationalist models of labor. Since its inception, for cultural nationalism the purpose of labor has been to modernize and to ensure the progress of the developing Puerto Rican nation. Labor, whether agricultural, industrial or intellectual, was to contribute to the construction of a society based on cultural cohesion, which tended to intentionally ignore differences and social schisms, to reaffirm gender, racial and class hierarchies, and to silence dissident voices. While it recognized both productive and reproductive labor, it insisted on controlling women's reproductive labor in the space of the house, the school and even the workplace, as Ana María García has shown in her documentary *La operación*.

The authors and the film directors that I study reconsider the relationship between labor and national discourse through a variety of spaces, from the factory traditionally associated with the construction of the modern nation, to the brothel, a space officially excluded from the "acceptable" models of labor and social belonging. While many of the protagonists of the texts that I analyze do contribute to the construction of the Puerto Rican nation through their factory work, documentaries like *La operación* and *Luchando por la vida* also expose the inequalities and the state violence that women had to endure in the factories, from harrowing working conditions to population control through forced sterilizations. These films also position the factory at the intersection of gender and labor, recognizing its potential both for oppression and for feminist liberation.

In contrast to the labor performed in the factory, the labor associated with the brothel has not traditionally been part of the ideal national model constructed in political and cultural discourse. Instead, it has been excluded, and has been deemed unacceptable for its potential to clash with a variety of discourses, like that of the Catholic Church. In the texts that I study, the brothel is a threat–however, the threat that it poses is not of undermining the ethical principles of the nation, but instead of exposing the hypocrisy of those who condemn what they simultaneously and surreptitiously practice. The cases that stand out are those of Isabel la Negra in López Neris's film *Life of Sin* and in Ramos Otero's short story "La última plena que bailó Luberza." In both texts, the owner of the brothel is feared and punished for having acquired too much powerin the eyes of her powerful male clients, too much power for an Afro-Puerto Rican woman who is not entitled by birth to the wealth that she has amassed, and too much power for someone who is not afraid to use it in exchange for favors, for bribing the church and for blackmailing politicians. While the texts interpret her assassination in profoundly different ways–the film as a well-deserved punishment, the story as a testimony of her strength–what becomes clear is that, for both authors, the brothel is the space that enabled Isabel's agency and her ability to confront social, political and religious structures of oppression.

Finally, the gendered geographies that emerge from the texts analyzed here employ a variety of spatial tropes to rethink and to propose alternatives to the family house of *la gran familia puertorriqueña*. While some do so from within the discourse of the nation, others go beyond the national model and consider other communities of female solidarity, sexual agency and transformative possibility of social change.

Many of the authors that I study speak from within the discourse of the nation, yet find themselves dissatisfied with the limited possibilities that the trope of the house, as proposed by cultural nationalism, offers women, queer subjects and other historically marginzlied groups. These writers and filmmakers see the family house as a patriarchal space that denies women the freedom to exercise their agency, to explore their sexuality and to include their voice in the national master narrative. In response to these structural limitations, authors like Carmen Lugo Filippi and Mayra Santos-Febres, among others, have considered how spaces like the factory, the beauty salon and the brothel may become matrices for the construction of alternative communities, whether national or based on other types of connections.

In the process of searching for alternatives to the family house, Santos-Febres's *Nuestra Señora de la Noche* reproduces a version of the Puerto Rican national imaginary, but dissolves several of its principal hierarchies. It displaces the nation from the house to the brothel and rejects its association with a cohesive family. Instead, it depicts families frayed with violence, infidelity, corruption and abandonment, in a gesture determined to uncover the inequalities and the injustices that traditional national discourse had silenced. It makes the figure of Isabel la Negra–a poor, Afro-Puerto Rican woman–the foundation of the new Puerto Rican nation, challenging unifying narratives of race, class and gender. At the same time, it exposes the hypocrisy that permeates the seemingly traditional houses in the novel, and depicts the shack in which Doña Montse brings up Robertito as one of the few nurturing, productive spaces in the text.

Other authors have chosen to look for alternatives to the discourse of the nation, again reconsidering the viability of the tropes of the house and of the national family. Albeit a precursor to the discourse of cultural nationalism, Luisa Capetillo's work enters a dialogue with the concerns of the authors that I discuss in this book. Capetillo's rejection of marriage and of the traditional family leads her to consider education and sexuality as possible strategies for female liberation and agency. Similarly, stories like "Hebra rota" and "Milagros, calle Mercurio" rely not on the traditional family model, but on alternative models of female solidarity and lesbian desire to construct networks of alliance and support. For authors like Lugo Filippi and Santos-Febres, the space of the beauty salon opens possibilities for different kinds of communities, based not on gender, sexual, racial and class hierarchies, but on the shared memory of violence and on the shared desire for liberation.

One of the main goals of this study has been to interrogate the liberating possibilities of the relationship between the fields of feminist geography, Caribbean and Puerto Rican Studies, and to engage them in a productive conversation. Until recent years, the discussion of space in Puerto Rico had focused primarily on the space of the island and on its relationship to the United States, whether regarding the debate on the Puerto Rico's political status, the economic and cultural interactions between the island and the mainland, or the politics of language and identity. While many of these debates have existed since the Spanish colonial period and the development of the independence movement, they intensified during the 20th century. My hope is that this book makes a contribution to these debates, and that it allows for a broader discussion of the intersections and the negotiations between space, gender, sexuality and national discourses.

What this book intended to show through the analysis of the factory, the house, the beauty salon and the brothel has been the complex ways gender and sexuality are constructed, limited and enabled by the configuration of the everyday spaces in which they exist, and by the negotiations between individual spaces and axes of power and creativity. Such coexistence is only possible if, as feminist geographers have argued, spaces are understood not as static, but as flexible, malleable, and always in transformation. The agency that the female characters of the novels, short stories and films claim enables the analysis of space in these terms, and consequently, the understanding of identities and different communities not as cohesive and immutable, but as dynamic, creative and imbued with possibility.

# WORKS CITED

Abadía-Rexach, Bárbara. "(Re) pensando la negritud: La racialización en la música popular." ILASSA Annual Conference. University of Texas at Austin, Feb. 5-7, 2009.

Acosta-Belén, Edna. "En torno a la nueva cuentística puertorriqueña." *Latin American Research Review* 21.2 (1986): 220-227.

Acosta-Belén, Edna., ed. *La mujer en la sociedad puertorriqueña*. Río Piedras: Ediciones Huracán, 1980.

Acosta Cruz, María. "Historia y escritura femenina en Olga Nolla, Magali García Ramis, Rosario Ferré y Ana Lydia Vega." *Revista Iberoamericana. Número especial dedicado a la literatura puertorriqueña*. LIX.162-162 (enero-julio 1993): 265-277.

Adjarian, M. M. *Allegories of Desire: Body, Nation, and Empire in Modern Caribbean Literature by Women*. Westport, CT: Praeger, 2004.

*AIDS in the Barrio: Eso no me pasa a mí*. Dir. Peter Biella and Frances Negrón. 1990. Film.

Alexander, Bryan Keith. "Fading, Twisting and Weaving: An Interpretive Ethnography of the Black Barbershop As Cultural Space. *Qualitative Inquiry* 9.1 (February 2003): 105-128.

Alexander, M. Jacqui. *Pedagogies of Crossing: Meditations on Feminism, Sexual Politics, Memory, and the Sacred*. Durham: Duke University Press, 2005.

Álvarez Curbelo, Silvia. "La conflictividad en el discurso político de Luis Muñoz Marín: 1926-1936." *Del Nacionalismo al populismo: Cultura y política en Puerto Rico*. Eds. Silvia Álvarez Curbelo, María Elena Rodríguez Castro. Río Piedras: Ediciones Huracán, 1993. 13-35.

———. "Pasión de cine." *Idilio Tropical: la aventura del cine puertorriqueño*. San Juan: Banco Popular, 1994: 1-8.

———. "Vidas prestadas: el cine y la puertorriqueñidad." *Revista de Critica Literaria Latinoamericana* 23.45 (1997): 395-410.

Amorín, Eva. *La experiencia de la organización de la Red de Trabajadoras Sexuales de Latioamérica y el Caribe*. Buenos Aires: RedTraSex, 2007.

Aparicio, Frances. *Listening to Salsa: Gender, Latin Popular Music, and Puerto Rican Cultures*. Hanover: Wesleyan University Press, 1998.

Aponte Alcina, Marta. *Fúgate*. Cayey: Sopa de Letras, 2005.

Arcelay Santiago, Carmen L. *Aló, ¿quién llama? María Luisa Arcelay. Pionera de la Legislatura olvidada en el tiempo*. Puerto Rico: First Book Publishing of Puerto Rico, 2004.

Aries, Philippe. *Western Attitudes Towards Death: from the Middle Ages to the Present.* Trans. Patricia M. Ranum. Baltimore: The Johns Hopkins University Press, 1974.

Arroyo, Jossianna. "Exilio y tránsitos entre la Norzagaray y Christopher Street: Acercamientos a una poética del deseo homosexual en Manuel Ramos Otero." *Revista Iberoamericana* LXVII.194-195 (enero-junio 2001): 31-54.

———. *Travestismos culturales: Literatura y etnografía en Cuba y Brasil.* Pittsburgh: Instituto Internacional de Literatura Iberoamericana, 2003.

Asencio, Marysol. "Migrant Puerto Rican Lesbians: Negotiating Gender, Sexuality and Ethnonationality." *NWSA Journal* 21.3 (Fall 2009): 1-23.

Azize Vargas, Yamila. "Mujeres en la lucha: orígenes y evolución del movimiento femininsta." *La mujer en Puerto Rico: Ensayos de investigación.* Ed. Yamila Azize Vargas. Río Piedras: Ediciones Huracán, 1987. 9-25.

Baerga, María del Carmen, ed. *Género y trabajo: La industria de la aguja en Puerto Rico y el Caribe Hispano.* San Juan: Editorial Universidad de Puerto Rico, 1993.

———. "El género y la construcción social de la marginalidad del trabajo femenino en la industria de la confección de ropa." *Género y trabajo: La industria de la aguja en Puerto Rico y el Caribe Hispánico.* Ed. María del Carmen Baerga. San Juan: Editorial de la Universidad de Puerto Rico: 1993. 3-55.

———. "Las jerarquías sociales y las expresiones de resistencia: género, clase y edad en la industria de la aguja en Puerto Rico." *Género y trabajo: La industria de la aguja en Puerto Rico y el Caribe Hispánico.* Ed. María del Carmen Baerga. San Juan: Editorial de la Universidad de Puerto Rico: 1993. 103-137.

Baldrich, Juan José. "From Handcrafted Tobacco Rolls to Machine-Made Cigarettes: The Transformation and Americanization of Puerto Rican Tobacco, 1847-1903." *CENTRO Journal of the Center for Puerto Rican Studies.* XVII.2 (Fall 2005): 144-169.

———. "Gender and the Decomposition of the Cigar-Making Craft in Puerto Rico, 1899-1934." *Puerto Rican Women's History: New Perspectives.* Ed. Félix Matos Rodríguez. Armonk: M. E. Sharpe, 1998. 105-125.

Balseiro, Isabel. "Through the Looking Glass, Darkly: Rosario Ferré's Cuando las mujeres quieren a los hombres." *Afro-Hispanic Review* 16.2 (1997): 3-9.

Barak, Julie. "Navigating the Swamp: Fact and Fiction in Rosario Ferré's 'The House on the Lagoon'." *The Journal of the Midwest Modern Languages Association* 31.2 (Winter 1998): 31-38.

Barceló-Miller, María de Fátima. "Halfharted Solidarity: Women Workers and the Women's Suffrage Movement in Puerto Rico During the 1920s." *Puerto Rican Women's History: New Perspectives.* Ed. Félix Matos Rodríguez. Armonk: M. E. Sharpe, 1998. 126-142.

Barraza, Vania. *(In)Subordinadas: Raza, clase y filiación en la narrative de mujeres latinoamericanas.* Santiago de Chile: RiL Editores, 2010.

Barreneche, Gabriel Ignacio, Jane Lombardi and Héctor Ramos-Flores. "A New Destination for "The Flying Bus"? The Implications of Orlando-Rican Migration for Luis Rafael Sánchez's "La guagua aérea." *Hispania* 95.1 (2012): 14-23.

Bejel, Emilio. *Gay Cuban Nation.* Chicago: The University of Chicago Press, 2001.

Benamou, Catherine. "La gran fiesta." *Cineaste* 16.4 (1988): 47-50.

Berkins, Lohana and Claudia Korol, eds. *Diálogo: Prostitución/trabajo sexual: Las protagonistas hablan.* Buenos Aires: Feminaria Editora, 2007.

Binnie, Jon. "Trading Places: Consumption, Sexuality and the Production of Queer Space." *Mapping Desire: Geographies of Sexuality.* Ed. David Bell and Gill Valentine. London and New York: Routledge, 1995. 182-199.

Binnie, Jon, Robyn Longhurst and Robin Peace. "Upstairs/Downstairs–Place Matters, Bodies Matter." *Pleasure Zones: Bodies, Cities, Spaces.* Eds. David Bell, Jon

Binnie, Ruth Holliday, Robyn Longhurst and Robin Peace. Syracuse: University of Syracuse Press, 2001: vii-xiv.

Black, Paula. *The Beauty Industry: Gender, Culture, Pleasure.* New York: Routledge, 2004.

*Boletín del Archivo nacional de teatro y cine del Ateneo Puertorriqueño.* No. 1 (enero-julio 2004).

Boris, Eileen. "Needlewomen Under the New Deal in Puerto Rico, 1920-1945." *Puerto Rican Women and Work: Bridges in Transnational Labor.* Ed. Altagracia Ortíz. Philadelphia: Temple University Press, 1996. 33-54.

Bost, Suzanne. "Transgressing Borders: Puerto Rican and Latina Mestizaje" *MELUS* 25.2 (Summer 2000): 187-211.

Bourasseau Alvarez, Ana Isabel. "Aplasta el último zumbido del patriarcado." *Hispania* 84.4 (Dec. 2001): 785-793.

Brennan, Denise. "Women Work, Men Sponge, and Everyone Gossips: Macho Men and Stigmatized/ing Women in a Sex Tourist Town." *Anthropological Quarterly.* 77.4 (Fall 2004): 705-733.

Briggs, Laura. "Familiar Territory: Prostitution, Empires, and the Question of U.S. Imperialism in Puerto Rico, 1849-1916." *Families of a New World: Gender, Politics, and State Development in a Global Context.* Eds. Lynne Haney and Lisa Pollard. New York: Routledge, 2003: 40-63.

*Brincando el charco: Portrait of a Puerto Rican.* Dir. Frances Negrón-Muntaner. 1994. Film.

Burke, M. "Colorism." *International Encyclopedia of the Social Sciences.* Vol. 2. Ed. W. Darity Jr. Detroit: Thomson Gale, 2008: 17-18.

Burton, Linda, Eduardo Bonilla-Silva, Victor Ray, Rose Buckelew, and Elizabeth Hordge Freeman. "Critical Race Theories, Colorism, and the Decade's Research on Families of Color." *Journal of Marriage and Family* 72 (June 2010): 440-459).

Butler, Judith. *Gender Trouble: Feminism and the Subversion of Identity.* New York: Routledge, 1990.

Cabezas, Amalia. "Between Love and Money: Sex, Tourism, and Citizenship in Cuba and the Dominican Republic." *Signs* 29.4 (Summer 2004): 987-1015.

Cabrera Collazo, Rafael. "La DIVEDCO y el cine en el Puerto Rico de los cincuenta." *Cuadernos Americanos: Nueva Época* 2.116 (2006): 71-87.

Campbell, Russell. *Marked Women: Prostitutes and Prostitution in Cinema.* Madison: University of Wisconsin Press, 2006.

Candelario, Ginetta. *Black Behind the Ears: Dominican Racial Identity from Museums to Beauty Shops.* Durham: Duke University Press, 2007.

Capetillo, Luisa. *A Nation of Women: An Early Feminist Speaks Out. Mi opinión sobre las libertades, derechos y deberes de la mujer.* Ed. Félix Matos Rodríguez. Houston: Arte Público Press, 2004.

————. *Ensayos libertarios. Dedicado a los trabajadores de ambos sexos.* Arecibo: Tipografía Real Hermanos, 1907.

————. *Influencias de las ideas modernas. Notas y apuntes. Escenas de la vida.* San Juan: Tipografía Negrón Flores, 1916.

————. *La humanidad en el futuro.* San Juan: Tipografía Real Hermanos, 1910.

Carrión, Juan Manuel. "The National Question in Puerto Rico." *Colonial Dilemma: Critical Perspectives on Contemporary Puerto Rico.* Ed. Edwin Meléndez. South End Press, 1993.

Castillo, Debra A. *Talking Back: Toward a Latin American Feminist Literary Criticism.* Ithaca: Cornell University Press, 1992.

Caulfield, Sueann. *In Defense of Honor: Sexual Morality, Modernity, and Nation in Early-Twentieth-Century Brazil.* Durham: Duke University Press, 2000.

Caulfield, Sueann. "Women of Vice, Virtue, and Rebellion: New Studies of Representation of the Female in Latin America." *Latin American Research Review* 28.2 (1993): 163-174.

Celís, Nadia. "La traición de la belleza: Cuerpos, deseo y subjetividad femenina en Fanny Buitrago y Mayra Santos-Febres." *Chasqui* 37.2 (Nov. 2008): 88-105.

Chiclana y González, Arleen. "The Body of Evidence: Body-Writing, the Text and Mayra Santos Febres' Illicit Bodies." *Unveiling the Body in Hispanic Women's Literature: From Nineteenth-Century Spain to Twenty-First-Century United States.* Ed. René Scott and Arleen Chiclana y González. Lewiston: The Edwin Mellen Press, 2006: 161-186.

*Cimarrón, El.* Dir. Iván Daniel Ortíz. 2006. Film.

Colón Warren, Alice. "The Feminization of Poverty among Women in Puerto Rico and Puerto Rican Women in the Middle Atlantic Region of the United States." *Brown Journal of World Affairs* 5.2 (1998): 262-282.

Colón Warren, Alice and Elsa Planell Larrinaga. "Silencios, presencias y debates sobre el aborto en Puerto Rico y el Caribe Hispano." San Juan: Proyecto Atlantea, Intercambio Académico Caribe-Universidad de Puerto Rico, 2001.

Colón Warren, Alice and Idsa Alegría Ortega. "Shattering the Illusion of Development: The Changing Status of Women and Challenges for the Feminist Movement in Puerto Rico." *Feminist Review* 59 (summer 1998): 101-117.

Cruz-Janzen, Marta I. "Latinegras: Desired Women: Undesirable Mothers, Daughters, Sisters, and Wives." *Frontiers: A Journal of Women Studies* 22.3 (2001): 168-183.

Cruz-Malavé, Arnaldo. "Para virar al macho: la autobiografía como subversión en la cuentística de Manuel Ramos Otero." *Revista Iberoamericana* 59.162-163 (enero-junio 1993): 239-263.

———. "Toward an Art of Transvestism: Colonialism and Homosexuality in Puerto Rican Literature." *¿Entiendes? Queer Readings, Hispanic Writings.* Eds. Emilie Bergmann and Paul Julian Smith. Durham: Duke University Press, 1995: 137-167.

Cubano-Iguina, Astrid. "Political Culture and Male Mass-Party Formation in Late-Nineteenth-Century Puerto Rico." *The Hispanic American Historical Review* 78.4 (1998): 631-62.

Da Cunha, Gloria. *Pensadoras de la nación.* Madrid: Iberoamericana, 2006.

Dávila, Arlene. *Sponsored Identities: Cultural Politics in Puerto Rico.* Philadelphia: Temple University Press, 1997.

Del Río Gabiola, Irune. "A Queer Way of Family Life: Narratives of Time and Space in Mayra Santos-Febres's *Sirena Selena Vestida de Pena.*" *Arizona Journal of Hispanic Cultural Studies* 11 (2007): 77-95.

Delano, Jack. "Mi participación en los comienzos de la División de Educación de la Comunidad. *Idilio Tropical: La Aventura del cine puertorriqueño.* Banco Popular: Sala de Exhibiciones Rafael Carrión Pacheco, 1994: 42-47.

Díaz, Luis Felipe. *La na(rra)ción en la literatura puertorriqueña.* San Juan: Ediciones Huracán, 2008.

Díaz Basteris, María Fernanda. "¿Independentismo o afiliación? *Felices días, tío Sergio* de Magali García Ramis: una batalla literaria contra el olvido." *Ciencia ergo sum* 20.2 (Julio-octubre 2013): 163-169.

Díaz Quiñones, Arcadio. *El arte de bregar.* San Juan: Ediciones Callejón, 2000.

———. *La memoria rota.* San Juan: Ediciones Huracán, 1993.

Dietz, James. *Historia económica de Puerto Rico.* Río Piedras: Ediciones Huracán, 1989.

———. "La reinvención del subdesarrollo: Errores fundamentales del proyecto de industrialización." *Del nacionalismo al populismo: Cultura y política en Puerto*

*Rico.* Ed. Silvia Álvarez-Curbelo and María Elena Rodríguez Castro. Río Piedras: Ediciones Huracán, 1993: 179-204.

Dinzey-Flores, Zaire. Zenit. *Locked In, Locked Out: Gated Communities in a Puerto Rican City.* Philadelphia: University of Pennsylvania Press, 2013.

*Dios los cría.* Dir. Jacobo Morales. 1979. Film.

*Doña Julia.* Dir. Skip Faust. 1959. Film.

Dowdy, Michael. "A mountain / in my pocket": The Affective Spatial Imagination in Post-1952 Puerto Rican Poetry." *MELUS* 35.2 (Summer 2010): 41-67.

Dowler, Lorraine, Josephine Carubia and Bonj Szczygiel. Introduction. *Gender and Landscape: Renegotiating Morality and Space.* London and New York: Routledge, 2005: 1-15.

Duany, Jorge. *The Puerto Rican Nation on the Move: Identities on the Island and in the United States.* Chapel Hill: University of North Carolina Press, 2002.

———. "The Rough Edges of Puerto Rican Identities: Race, Gender, Transnationalism." *Latin American Research Review* 40.3 (October 2005): 177-190.

Duncan, Nancy. "Renegotiating Gender and Sexuality in Public and Private Spaces." *Bodyspace: Destabilizing Geographies of Gender and Sexuality.* Ed. Nancy Duncan. London: Routledge: 1996: 127-145.

Edwards, Sarah. "Remembering and Forgetting: Private and Public Lives in the Imagined Nation." *Writing the Modern City: Literature, Architecture and Modernity.* Ed. Edwards, Sarah and Jonathan Charley. London: Routledge, 2012: 21-31.

*El beso que me diste.* Dir. Sonia Fritz. Vanguard Cinema. 2000. Film.

*El de los cabos blancos.* Dir. Willard Van Dyke. 1955. Film.

Falicov, Tamara. "La operación" Film Review. *Film and History: An Interdisciplinary Journal of Film and Television.* October 2006. http://www.uwosh.edu/filmandhistory/documentary/women/operacion.php 20 May 2009.

Feliciano Díaz, Enrique and Javier Santiago. "Carmen Belén Richardson." Fundación Nacional para la Cultura Popular. 9 agosto 2012. http://www.prpop.org/biografias/c_bios/carmen_belen_richardson.shtml 1 junio 2014.

Fernández Olmos, Margarite. "Luis Rafael Sánchez and Rosario Ferré: Sexual Politics and Contemporary Puerto Rican Narrative." *Hispania* 70.1 (March 1987): 40-46.

Ferré, Rosario. "Cuando las mujeres quieren a los hombres." *Aquí cuentan las mujeres.* Ed. María M. Solá. Río Piedras: Ediciones Huracán, 1990. 65-78.

———. *The House on the Lagoon.* New York: Farrar, Straus and Giroux, 1995.

———. *Papeles de Pandora.* México: Joaquín Mortíz, 1976.

Flores, Juan. *Divided Borders: Essays on Puerto Rican Identity.* Houston: Arte Público Press, 1993.

Foucault, Michel. *The History of Sexuality: Volume I: An Introduction.* New York: Vintage Books, 1990.

Frade León, Ramón. *El pan nuestro.* 1905. Oil.

Franco, Jean. *Plotting Women: Gender and Representation in Mexico.* New York: Columbia University Press, 1989.

Gabiola, Irune del Río. "A Queer Way of Family Life: Narratives of Time and Space in Mayra Santos-Febres's Sirena Selena vestida de Pena." *Arizona Journal of Hispanic Cultural Studies* 11 (2007): 77-95.

———. "La articulación del cuerpo femenino como alegoría de la identidad nacional puertorriqueña en "Milagros, calle Mercurio" de Carmen Lugo Filippi." *Letras Femeninas* 30.1 (Verano 2004): 40-50.

Gandía, Zeno. *La charca.* San Juan: Publicaciones Puertorriqueñas, 1996.

García Calderón, Myrna. *Espacios de la memoria en el Caribe Hispánico insular y sus diásporas.* San Juan: Ediciones Callejón, 2012.

García, Kino. *Cine puertorriqueño: Filmografía, fuentes y referencias*. Cuadernos del Ateneo V.1 (1997).

García Ramis, Magali. *Felices días, tío Sergio*. San Juan: Editorial Antillana, 1986.

Gelpí, Juan. *Literatura y paternalismo en Puerto Rico*. San Juan: Editorial de la Universidad de Puerto Rico, 1993.

Gilfoyle, Timothy. "Prostitutes in History: From Parables of Pornography to Metaphors of Modernity." *The American Historical Review* 104:1. Feb. 1999: 117-141.

Gill, Tiffany. *Beauty Shop Politics: African American Women's Activism in the Beauty Industry*. Urbana-Champaign: University of Illinois Press, 2010.

Godreau, Isar. "Peinando diferencias, bregas de pertenencia: El alisado y el llamado 'pelo malo'." *Caribbean Studies* 30.1 (January-June 2002): 82-134.

Golden, Kristen and Barbara Findlen. *Remarkable Women of the Twentieth Century: 100 Portraits of Achievement*. New York: Friedman/Fairfax Publishers, 1998.

González, José Luis. *El país de cuatro pisos y otros ensayos*. 6th ed. Río Piedras: Ediciones Huracán, 1987.

Gordon, Linda. *The Moral Property of Women: A History of Birth Control Politics in America*. Urbana-Champaign: University of Illinois Press, 2007.

Gosser Esquilín, Mary Ann. "Nanas negras: The Silenced Women in Rosario Ferré and Olga Nolla." *CENTRO Journal of the Center for Puerto Rican Studies*. XIV.2 (Fall 2002): 49-61.

Grosfoguel, Ramón. "Cultural Racism and Colonial Caribbean Migrants in Core Zones of the Capitalist World-Economy." *Ìrìnkèrindò: A Journal of African Migration* 2 (December 2003) http://www.africamigration.com/archive_02/r_grosfoguel.htm June 1 2014.

Guerrero, Elizabeth and Anne Lambright. "Introduction." *Unfolding the City: Women Write the City in Latin America*. Ed. Anne Lambright and Elizabeth Guerrero. Minneapolis: University of Minnesota Press, 2007: xi-xxxii.

Guy, Donna. *Sex and Danger in Buenos Aires: Prostitution, Family and Nation in Argentina*. Lincoln: University of Nebraska Press, 1991.

Haesendonck, Kristian van. "Sirena Selena vestida de pena de Mayra Santos-Febres: ¿Transgresiones de espacio o espacio de transgresiones?" *CENTRO Journal of the Center for Puerto Rican Studies* 15.2 (2003): 79-96.

*Hebra Rota*. Dir. Sonia Fritz. Isla Films, 1999. Film.

Henao, Edna Biviana. "Nation, Culture and Identity: The Colonial Subject's Search for Identity in the Works of Julia Álvarez, Rosario Ferré and Ana Lydia Vega." CUNY. PhD Diss. 2001.

Hennessy, Rosemary. *Materialist Feminism and the Politics of Discourse*. New York: Routledge, 1993.

Hewitt, Nancy A. "Luisa Capetillo: Feminist of the Working Class." *Latina Legacies: Identity, Biography, and Community*. Eds. Vicky Ruiz and Viginia Sánchez Korrol. Oxford: Oxford University Press, 2005. 120-134.

Hill Collins, Patricia. *Black Feminist Thought: Knowledge, Consciousnes and the Politics of Empowerment*. New York: Routledge, 2008.

———. *Black Sexual Politics: African American: Gender, and the new Racism*. New York: Routledge, 2005.

Hintz, Suzanne S. *Rosario Ferré: A Search for Identity*. New York: Peter Lang Publishing, 1995.

Holland, Sharon Patricia. *Raising the Dead: Readings of Death and (Black) Subjectivity*. Durham: Duke University Press, 2000.

Holston, James and Arjun Appadurai. "Introduction: Cities and Citizenship." *Cities and Citizenship*. Ed. James Holston. Durham: Duke University Press, 1999: 1-20.

Irizarry, Guillermo. *José Luis González: El intelectual nómada*. San Juan: Ediciones Callejón, 2006.

Jiménez-Muñoz, Gladys. "Literacy, Class, and Sexuality in the Debate on Women's Suffrage in Puerto Rico During the 1920s." *Puerto Rican Women's History: New Perspectives*. Ed. Félix Matos Rodríguez and Linda Delgado. New York: M. E. Sharpe, 1998.

Kang, Miliann. *The Managed Hand: Race, Gender and the Body in Beauty Service Work*. Berkeley: The University of California Press, 2010.

Kevane, Bridget, and Juanita Heredia. *Latina Self-Portraits: Interviews with Contemporary Women Writers*. Albuquerque: University of New Mexico Press, 2000.

King, John. *Magical Reels: A History of Cinema in Latin America*. New York: Verso, 1990.

King, Rosamond. "More Notes on the Invisibility of Caribbean Lesbians." *Our Caribbean: A Gathering of Lesbian and Gay Writing from the Antilles*. Ed. Thomas Glave. Durham: Duke University Press, 2008: 191-196.

Knopp, Lawrence. "Sexuality and Urban Space: A Framework for Analysis." *Mapping Desire: Geographies of Sexuality*. Ed. David Bell and Gill Valentine. London and New York: Routledge, 1995: 149-161.

Kulick, Don. *Travesti: Sex, Gender, and Culture Among Brazilian Transgender Prostitutes*. Chicago: The University of Chicago Press, 1998.

La Fountain-Stokes, Lawrence. *Queer Ricans: Cultures and Sexualities in the Diaspora*. Minneapolis: University of Minnesota Press, 2009.

La Fountain-Stokes, Lawrence. "Tomboy Tantrums and Queer Infatuations: Reading Lesbianism in Magali García Ramis's *Felices días, tío Sergio*." *Tortilleras: Hispanic and US Latina Lesbian Expression*. Ed. Lourdes Torres and Inmaculada Petrusa-Seva. Philadelphia: Temple University Press, 2003: 47-67.

*La guagua aérea*. Dir. Luis Molina Casanova. 1993. Film.

*La operación*. Dir. Ana María García. 1982. Film.

Lauderdale Graham, Sandra. *House and Street: The Domestic World of Servants and Masters in Nineteenth-Century Rio de Janeiro*. Austin: University of Texas Press, 1988.

*Life of Sin*. Dir. Efraín López Neris. MCMXC 21st Century Productions. 1979. Film.

*Ligia Elena*. Dir. Francisco López. New York: First Run/Icarus Films, 1983. Film.

Lindsay, Claire. *Locating Latin American Women Writers: Cristina Peri Rossi, Rosario Ferré, Albalucía Angel, and Isabel Allende*. New York: Peter Lang Publishing, 2003.

López, Iraida. "Not Many Options for Contraception: Interview with *La operación*'s Ana María García." Transl. Kimberly Safford. *Jump Cut: A Review of Contemporary Media* 29 (February 1984): 38-39.

Lorde, Audre. "I Am Your Sister: Black Women Organizing Across Sexualities." *A Burst of Light: Essays by Audre Lorde*. Ithaca, NY: Firebrand Books, 1988: 19-26.

Lozada, Ángel. *La patografía*. México: Planeta, 1996.

*Luchando por la vida: las despalilladoras de tabaco y su mundo*. Dir. José Artemio Torres. 1984.

Lugo Filippi, Carmen. "Milagros, calle Mercurio." In Vega, Ana Lydia and Carmen Lugo Filippi. *Vírgenes y mártires*. 6th ed. San Juan: Editorial Cultural, 2002.

———. "Pilar, tus rizos." *Vírgenes y mártires*. Ana Lydia Vega y Carmen Lugo Filippi. 6th ed. San Juan: Editorial Cultural, 2002.

*Luisa Capetillo: pasión de justicia*. Dir. Sonia Fritz. Isla Films. 1993.

Marqués, René, ed. *Cuentos puertorriqueños de hoy*. Río Piedras: Editorial Cultural, 1971.

―――. *El puertorriqueño dócil y otros ensayos, 1953-1971*. San Juan: Editorial Antillana, 1977.

―――. *La carreta: drama en tres actos*. 18 ed. Río Piedras: Editorial Cultural, 1983.

―――. *Purificación en la calle Cristo y Los soles truncos*. Río Piedras: Editorial Cultural, 1983.

―――. *Teatro I: Los soles truncos, Un niño azul para esa sombra, La muerte no entrará en palacio*. Puerto Rico: Editorial cultural, 2002.

Martin, Michael T. *New Latin American Cinema*. Detroit: Wayne State University Press, 1997.

Martínez-San Miguel, Yolanda. *Caribe Two Ways: Cultura de la migración en el Caribe insular hispánico*. San Juan: Ediciones Callejón, 2003.

Martínez-Vergne, Teresita. *Shaping the Discourse on Space: Charity and Its Wards in Nineteenth-Century San Juan, Puerto Rico*. Austin: University of Texas Press, 1999.

*Maruja*. Dir. Oscar Orzábal Quintana. Probo Films, Inc. 1959. Film.

Massey, Doreen. *Space, Place and Gender*. Minneapolis: University of Minnesota Press, 1994.

Matos-Rodríguez, Félix and Linda Delgado, eds. *Puerto Rican Women's History: New Perspectives*. Armonk: M. E. Sharpe, 1998.

Mattos Cintrón, Wilfredo. *Desamores*. San Juan: Ediciones La sierra, 2001.

―――. *La puerta de San Juan*. San Juan: Ediciones La sierra, 1997.

Mattos Cintrón, Wilfredo. *Las dos muertes de Catalino Ríos*. San Juan: Ediciones La sierra, 2012.

McCreery, David. "This Life of Misery and Shame: Female Prostitution in Guatemala City, 1880-1920." *Journal of Latin American Studies* 18.2 (1986): 333-353.

McDowell, Linda. "Body Work: Heterosexual Gender Performances in City Workplaces." *Mapping Desire: Geographies of Sexuality*. Eds. David Bell and Gill Valentine. London and New York: Routledge, 1995: 75-95.

Meléndez, Edwin and Edgardo Meléndez, eds. Introduction. *Colonial Dilemma: Critical Pertpectives on Contemporary Puerto Rico*. Boston: South End Press, 1993. 1-16.

Miller, Marilyn Grace. *Rise and Fall of the Cosmic Race: The Cult of Mestizaje in Latin America*. Austin: University of Texas Press, 2004.

*Modesta*. Dir. Benji Doniger. 1955. Film.

Mohanty, Chandra Talpade. "Introduction." *Third World Women and the Politics of Feminism*. Eds. Chandra Talpade Mohanty, Ann Russo and Lourdes Torres. Bloomington: Indiana University Press, 1991: 1-47.

Morales, Jacobo. *Linda Sara: el guión y su historia*. San Juan: Editorial Plaza Mayor, 1998.

Negrón-Muntaner, Frances. "Of Lonesome Stars and Broken Hearts: Trends in Puerto Rican Women's Film/Video Making." *New Latin American Cinema Vol. 2: Studies of National Cinemas*. Ed. Michael T. Martin. Detroit: Wayne State University Press, 1997. 233-257.

―――. *Boricua Pop: Puerto Rican and the Latinization of American Culture*. New York: New York University Press, 2004.

Núñez Negrón, Manolo. *Barrachina*. San Juan: Libros AC, 2012.

Ostolaza Bey, Margarita. *Política sexual en Puerto Rico*. Río Piedras: Ediciones Huracán, 1989.

Pabón, Carlos. *Nación Postmortem: Ensayos sobre los tiempos de insoportable ambigüedad*. San Juan: Ediciones Callejón, 2003.

Pabón, Carlos. "The Political Status of Puerto Rico: A Nonsense Dilemma." *None of the Above: Puerto Ricans in the Global Era*. Ed. Frances Negrón-Muntaner. New York: Palgrave Macmillan, 2007: 65-72.

Palmer-López, Sandra. "Re-visión de la ideología patriarcal y del mito femenino en la narrativa y ensayos de Rosario Ferré." Florida State University. PhD Diss. 1994.

———. "Rosario Ferré y la Generación del 70: Evolución estética y literaria." *Acta Literaria* 27 (2002): 157-169.

Parish, James Robert. *Prostitution in Hollywood films: plots, critiques, casts and credits for 389 theatrical and made-for-television releases*. Jefferson, N.C., and London: McFarland, 1992.

Peace, Robin. "Producing Lesbians: Canonical Proprieties." *Pleasure Zones: Bodies, Cities, Spaces*. David Bell, Jon Binnie, Ruth Holliday, Robyn Longhurst and Robin Peace. Syracuse: University of Syracuse Press, 2001: 29-54.

Pedreira, Antonio S. *Insularismo*. Río Piedras: Editorial Edil, 1992.

Pérez Rodríguez, Marialy. *Desmaterialización del espacio doméstico*. Tesis de Maestría. Escuela de Arquitectura, Universidad de Puerto Rico, Río Piedras, 2005.

Picó, Fernando. *Al filo del poder: Subalternos y dominantes en Puerto Rico, 1739-1910*. Río Piedras: Editorial de la Universidad de Puerto Rico, 1993.

———. "The Absent State." *None of the Above: Puerto Ricans in the Global Era*. Ed. *Frances Negrón-Muntaner*. New York: Palgrave Macmillan, 2007: 21-28.

Picó, Isabel. "Apuntes preliminares para el estudio de la mujer puertorriqueña y su participación en las luchas sociales de principios del siglo XX." *La mujer en la sociedad puertorriqueña*. Ed. Edna Acosta Belén. Río Piedras: Ediciones Huracán, 1980. 23-40.

Pino-Ojeda, Walescka. *Sobre castas y puentes: Conversaciones con Elena Poniatowska, Rosario Ferré y Diamela Eltit*. Santiago: Editorial Cuarto Propio, 2000.

Quiñones Arocho, María Isabel. "Beauty Salons: Consumption and the Production of the Self." *None of the Above: Puerto Ricans in the Global Era*. Ed. Frances Negrón-Muntaner. New York: Palgrave Macmillan, 2007. 109-128.

Quintero-Rivera, Ángel G. "Socialist and Cigarmaker: Artisans' Proletarization in the Making of the Puerto Rican Working Class." *Latin American Perspectives*. 10.2/3 Social Classes in Latin America. Vol. II: Class Formation and Struggle (Spring-Summer 1983): 19-38.

Ramos Otero, Manuel. "La última plena que bailó Luberza." *Cuentos de buena tinta*. San Juan: Instituto de Cultura Puertorriqueña, 1992.

———. "Loca la de la locura." *Cuentos de buena tinta*. San Juan: Instituto de Cultura Puertorriqueña, 1992. 233-240.

Ramos Rosado, Marie. *La mujer negra en la literatura puertorriqueña*. Río Piedras: Editorial de la Universidad de Puerto Rico, 1999.

Ramos, Julio, ed. *Amor y anarquía: los escritos de Luisa Capetillo*. Río Piedras: Ediciones Huracán, 1922. 11-58.

———. "Luisa Capetillo: una escritura entre más de dos." *Revista de Crítica Literaria Latinoamericana*. 17.33 (1991): 235-251.

Ramos-Zayas, Ana Yolanda. *Street Therapists: Race, Affect, and Neoliberal Personhood in Latino Newark*. Chicago: The University of Chicago Press, 2012.

Randall, Margaret. *El pueblo no sólo es testigo: La historia de Dominga*. Río Piedras: Ediciones Huracán, 1979.

Reynaga, Elena and Eva Amorín, Eds. *Un movimiento de tacones altos: Mujeres, trabajadoras sexuales y activistas: Reflexiones y actividades para fortalecer nuestras organizaciones*. Buenos Aires: RedTraSex, 2007.

"Retrospectiva de la DIVEDCO en documental." *Fundación nacional para la cultura popular*. 25 September 2005. http://www.prpop.org/noticias/sept05/diveco_sept23.shtml 4 January 2008.

Ríos Ávila, Rubén. "Caribbean Dislocations: Arenas and Ramos Otero in New York." *Hispanisms and Homosexualities*. Ed. Sylvia Molloy and Robert McKee Irwin. Durham: Duke University Press, 1998: 101-119.

————. *La raza cómica del sujeto en Puerto Rico*. San Juan: Ediciones Callejón, 2002.

Ríos Díaz, Raul and Francisco González. *Dominio de la imagen: hacia una industria de cine en Puerto Rico*. Cuadernos del Ateneo 2, 2000.

Rivera Quintero, Marcia. "Incorporación de las mujeres al mercado de trabajo en el desarrollo del capitalismo (Esbozos para un análisis). *La mujer en la sociedad puertorriqueña*. Ed. Edna Acosta Belén. Río Piedras: Ediciones Huracán, 1980: 41-65.

Rodríguez Castro, María E. "Foro de 1940: Las pasiones y los intereses se dan la mano." *Del Nacionalismo al populismo: Cultura y política en Puerto Rico*. Eds. Silvia Álvarez Curbelo, María Elena Rodríguez Castro. Río Piedras: Ediciones Huracán, 1993. 61-105.

Rodríguez Juliá, Edgardo. *El entierro de Cortijo*. Río Piedras: Ediciones Huracán, 1983.

————. *La piscina*. Buenos Aires: Corregidor, 2012.

————. *Las tribulaciones de Jonás*. Río Piedras: Ediciones Huracán, 1981

Rodríguez, María Cristina. "La aventura de la identidad en el cine puertorriqueño de hoy." *Idilio Tropical: la aventura del cine puertorriqueño*. San Juan: Banco Popular, 1994: 64-79.

Romero-Cesareo, Ivette. "Whose Legacy? Voicing Women's Rights from the 1870s to the 1930s." *Callaloo* 17.3 Puerto Rican Women Writers (Summer 1994): 770-789.

Roncador, Sônia. *A domestica imaginária: literatura, testemunhos e a invençao da empregada doméstica no Brasil (1889-1999)*. Brasília: Editora Universidade de Brasília, 2008.

Rose, Gillian. *Feminism and Geography: The Limits of Geographical Knowledge*. Minneapolis: University of Minnesota Press, 1993.

Rosenstone, Robert. *Visions of the Past*. Cambridge: Harvard University Press, 1995.

Roses, Lorraine Elena. "Las esperanzas de Pandora: prototipos femeninos en la obra de Rosario Ferré." *Revista Iberoamericana. Número especial dedicado a la literatura puertorriqueña*. LIX.162-162 (enero-julio 1993): 279-287.

Ruiz-Meléndez, Mónica. "Mujer o mito: el personaje femenino en los cuentos de Ana Lydia Vega, Rosario Ferré y Magali García Ramis." MA Thesis. Georgia State University. 2000.

Russ, Elizabeth Christine. *The Plantation in the Postslavery Imagination*. Oxford: Oxford University Press, 2009.

Safa, Helen Icken. "Conciencia de clase entre las trabajadoras en Latinoamérica: Un estudio de casos en Puerto Rico." *La mujer en la sociedad puertorriqueña*. Ed. Edna Acosta Belén. Río Piedras: Ediciones Huracán, 1980. 157-182.

————. *The Myth of the Male Breadwinner: Women and Industrialization in the Caribbean*. Boulder: Westview Press, 1995.

Safford, Kimberly. "La operación: Forced Sterilization." *Jump Cut: A Review of Contemporary Media* 29 (February 1984): 37-38.

Sánchez González, Lisa. *Boricua Literature: A Literary History of the Puerto Rican Diaspora*. New York: New York University Press, 2001.

Sánchez, Luis Rafael. *La guagua aérea*. San Juan: Editorial Cultural, 1994.

Sánchez, Luis Rafael. "Tiene la noche una raíz." *En cuerpo de camisa*. 5th ed. San Juan: Editorial Cultural, 1990.

Sancholuz, Carolina. "Puerto y cuerpo: género e identidad en un texto de Rosario Ferré." *Cehelis* 5.6,7,8.3 (1996): 575-582.

Santiago-Valles, Kelvin. *Subject People and Colonial Discourses: Economic Transformation and Social Disorder in Puerto Rico, 1898-1947*. Albany: State University of New York Press, 1994.

Santos-Febres, Mayra. *Cualquier miércoles soy tuya*. Barcelona: Mondadori, 2002.

———. "Hebra rota." *Pez de vidrio*. Río Piedras: Ediciones Huracán, 1996.

———. *Nuestra Señora de la Noche*. Madrid: Editorial Espasa, 2006.

———. *Sirena Selena vestida de pena*. Barcelona: Mondadori, 2000.

Scalway, Helen. "The Contemporary Flâneuse." *The Invisible Flâneuse? Gender, Public Space and Visual Culture in Nineteenth-Century Paris*. Eds. Aruna D'Souza and Tom McDonough. Manchester: Manchester University Press, 2006: 164-171.

Scarano, Francisco A. "Liberal Pacts and Hierarchies of Rule: Approaching the Imperial Transition in Cuba and Puerto Rico." *The Hispanic American Historical Review* 78.4 (1998): 583-601.

———. "The Jíbaro Masquerade and the Subaltern Politics of Creole Identity Formation in Puerto Rico, 1745-1823." *The American Historical Review* 101.5 (1996): 1398-431.

Sharp, Joanne P. "Gendering Nationhood: A Feminist Engagement with National Identity." *Bodyspace: Destabilizing Geographies of Gender and Sexuality*. Ed. Nancy Duncan. London: Routledge: 1996: 97-108.

Shaw, Deborah. *Contemporary Latin American Cinema: Breaking into the Global Market*. Lanham: Rowman and Littlefield, 2007.

Sheller, Mimi. *Citizenship from Below: Erotic Agency and Caribbean Freedom*. Durham: Duke University Press, 2012.

Silva, Elizabeth. "Gender, Class, Emotional Capital and Consumption in Family Life." *Gender and Consumption: Domestic Cultures and the Commercialization of Everyday Life*. Ed. Emma Casey and Lydia Martens. England: Ashgate Publishing, 2007: 141-159.

Solá, María M. "Angel, arpía, animal fiero y tierno: mujer, sociedad y literatura en Puerto Rico." *La mujer en Puerto Rico: Ensayos de investigación*. Ed. Yamila Azize Vargas. Río Piedras: Ediciones Huracán, 1987. 193-227.

———. "Para que lean el sexo, para que sientan el texto, escribimos también con el cuerpo." *Aquí cuentan las mujeres: muestra y estudio de cinco narradoras puertorriqueñas.* Río Piedras: Ediciones Huracán, 1990.

Sommer, Doris. *Foundational Fictions: The National Romances of Latin America*. Berkeley: University of California Press, 1991.

Soto, Pedro Juan. "La cautiva." *Spiks* Mexico: Los presentes, 1956.

Sotomayor, Áurea María. *Femina Faber: Letras, música, ley*. San Juan: Ediciones Callejón, 2004.

———. *Hilo de aracne: Literatura puertorriqueña hoy*. San Juan: Editorial de la Universidad de Puerto Rico, 1995.

———. "Si un nombre convoca un mundo: *Felices días, tío Sergio* en la literatura puertorriqueña contemporánea." *Revista Iberoamericana. Número especial dedicado a la literatura puertorriqueña*. LIX.162-162 (enero-julio 1993): 317-328.

Stoner, Lynn K. "Directions in Latin American Women's History, 1977-1985." *Latin American Research Review* 22.2 (1987): 101-134.

Suárez Findlay, Eileen. *Imposing Decency: The Politics of Sexuality and Race in Puerto Rico, 1870-1920*. Durham: Duke University Press, 1999.

*Tejedoras de vida: Puerto Rico, España y Nueva York*. Dir. Sonia Fritz. Isla Films. 2005. Film.

Thompson, Becky. "Multiracial Feminism: Recasting the Chronology of Second Wave Feminism." *Feminist Studies* 28.2 (Summer 2002): 336-360.

Tinsley, Omise'eke Natasha. *Thiefing Sugar: Eroticism Between Women in Caribbean Literature*. Durham: Duke University Press, 2010.

Torres, Lourdes. "The Construction of the Self in U.S. Latina Autobiographies." *Third World Women and the Politics of Feminism*. Eds. Chandra Talpade Mohanty, Ann Russo and Lourdes Torres. Bloomington: Indiana University Press, 1991: 271-287.

Torres Ortíz, Víctor. "Los esfuerzos por recuperar y preservar el cine puertorriqueño." *Boletín del archivo nacional de teatro y cine del Ateneo Puertorriqueño* No.3 (enero-junio 2005): 96-99.

Trelles Plazaola, Luis. *Ante el lente extranjero: Puerto Rico visto por los cineastas de afuera*. San Juan: Editorial de la Universidad de Puerto Rico, 2000.

———. *Imágenes cambiantes: Descubrimiento, conquista y colonización de la América Hispana vista por el cine de ficción y largometraje*. San Juan: Editorial de la Universidad de Puerto Rico, 1996.

Umpierre, Luz María. "Incitaciones lesbianas en 'Milagros, calle Mercurio' de Carmen Lugo Filippi." *Revista Iberoamericana* vol. LIX (enero-junio 1993): 162-163. Número especial dedicado a la literatura puertorriqueña: 309-316.

Valentine, Gill. "(Re)Negotiating the Heterosexual Street: Lesbian Productions of Space." *Bodyspace: Destabilizing Geographies of Gender and Sexuality*. Ed. Nancy Duncan. London: Routledge: 1996: 146-155.

Valle, Amir. *Jineteras*. Bogotá: Editorial Planeta, 2006.

Valle Ferrer, Norma. *Luisa Capetillo: Historia de una mujer proscrita*. Puerto Rico: Editorial Cultural, 1990.

Vázquez Lazo, María de los Ángeles. *Meretrices: La prostitución en Puerto Rico de 1876 a 1917*. Hato Rey: Publicaciones Puertorriqueñas, 2008.

Walker, Lynne. "Home Making: An Architectural Perspective." *Signs* 27.3 (Spring 2002): 823-835.

Whalen, Carmen Teresa. *From Puerto Rico to Philadelphia: Puerto Rican Workers and Postwar Economies*. Philadelphia: Temple University Press, 2001.

Wigley, Mark. "Untitled: The Housing of Gender." *Sexuality and Space*. Ed. Beatriz Columnia. New York: Princeton Architectural Press, 1992.

Wright, Melissa M. *Disposable Women and Other Myths of Global Capitalism*. New York: Routledge, 2006.

# INDEX

# NORTH CAROLINA STUDIES IN THE ROMANCE LANGUAGES AND LITERATURES

## Recent Titles

SUBJECT TO CHANGE: THE LESSONS OF LATIN AMERICAN WOMEN'S *TESTIMONIO* FOR TRUTH, FICTION, AND THEORY, by Joanna R. Bartow. 2005. (No. 280). *978-0-8078-9284-X.*

QUESTIONING RACINIAN TRAGEDY, by John Campbell. 2005. (No. 281). *978-0-8078-9285-8.*

THE POLITICS OF FARCE IN CONTEMPORARY SPANISH AMERICAN THEATRE, by Priscilla Meléndez. 2006. (No. 282). *978-0-8078-9286-6.*

MODERATING MASCULINITY IN EARLY MODERN CULTURE, by Todd W. Reeser. 2006. (No. 283). *978-0-8078-9287-4.*

*PORNOBOSCODIDASCALUS LATINUS* (1624). KASPAR BARTH'S NEO-LATIN TRANSLATION OF *CELESTINA*, by Enrique Fernández. 2006. (No. 284). *978-0-8078-9288-2.*

JACQUES ROUBAUD AND THE INVENTION OF MEMORY, by Jean-Jacques F. Poucel. 2006. (No. 285). *978-0-8078-9289-0.*

THE "I" OF HISTORY. SELF-FASHIONING AND NATIONAL CONSCIOUSNESS IN JULES MICHELET, by Vivian Kogan. 2006. (No. 286). *978-0-8078-9290-4.*

BUCOLIC METAPHORS: HISTORY, SUBJECTIVITY, AND GENDER IN THE EARLY MODERN SPANISH PASTORAL, by Rosilie Hernández-Pecoraro. 2006. (No. 287). *978-0-8078-9291-2.*

UNA ARMONÍA DE CAPRICHOS: EL DISCURSO DE RESPUESTA EN LA PROSA DE RUBÉN DARÍO, por Francisco Solares-Larrare. 2007. (No. 288). *978-0-8078-9292-0.*

READING THE *EXEMPLUM* RIGHT: FIXING THE MEANING OF *EL CONDE LUCANOR*, by Jonathan Burgoyne. 2007. (No. 289). *978-0-8078-9293-9.*

MONSTRUOS QUE HABLAN: EL DISCURSO DE LA MONSTRUOSIDAD EN CERVANTES, por Rogelio Miñana. 2007. (No. 290). *978-0-8078-9294-7.*

BAJO EL CIELO PERUANO: THE DEVOUT WORLD OF PERALTA BARNUEVO, by David F. Slade and Jerry M. Williams. 2008. (No. 291). *978-0-8078-9295-4.*

ESCAPE FROM THE PRISON OF LOVE: CALORIC IDENTITIES AND WRITING SUBJECTS IN FIFTEENTH-CENTURY SPAIN, by Robert Folger. 2009. (No. 292). *978-0-8078-9296-1.*

LOS *TRIONFI* DE PETRARCA COMENTADOS EN CATALÁN: UNA EDICIÓN DE LOS MANUSCRITOS 534 DE LA BIBLIOTECA NACIONAL DE PARÍS Y DEL ATENEU DE BARCELONA, por Roxana Recio. 2009. (No. 293). *978-0-8078-9297-8.*

MAPPING THE SOCIAL BODY. URBANISATION, THE GAZE, AND THE NOVELS OF GALDÓS, by Collin McKinney. 2009. (No. 294). *978-0-8078-9298-5.*

ENCOUNTERS WITH BERGSON(ISM) IN SPAIN: RECONCILING PHILOSOPHY, LITERATURE, FILM AND URBAN SPACE, by Benjamin Fraser. 2009. (No. 295). *978-0-8078-9299-2.*

IMPERIAL STAGINGS. EMPIRE AND IDEOLOGY IN TRANSATLANTIC THEATER OF EARLY MODERN SPAIN AND THE NEW WORLD, by Chad M. Gasta. 2013. (No. 296). *978-1-4696-0996-6.*

INSTABLE PUENTE. LA CONSTRUCCIÓN DEL LETRADO CRIOLLO EN LA OBRA DE JUAN DE ESPINOSA MEDRANO, por Juan M. Vitulli. 2013. (No. 297). *978-1-4696-0997-3.*

ILUSIÓN ÁULICA E IMAGINACIÓN CABALLERESCA EN *EL CORTESANO* DE LUIS MILÁN, por Ignacio López Alemany. 2013. (No. 298). *978-1-4696-0998-0.*

THE TRIUMPH OF BRAZILIAN MODERNISM. THE METANARRATIVE OF EMANCIPATION AND COUNTER-NARRATIVES, by Saulo Gouveia. 2013. (No. 299). *978-1-4696-0999-7.*

ETNOGRAFÍA, POLÍTICA Y PODER A FINALES DEL SIGLO XIX. JOSÉ MARTÍ Y LA CUESTIÓN INDÍGENA, por Jorge Camacho. 2013. (No. 300). *978-1-4696-1000-9.*

PUTTING MONET AND REMBRANDT INTO WORDS: PIERRE LOTI'S RECREATION AND THEORIZATION OF CLAUDE MONET'S IMPRESSIONISM AND REMBRANDT'S LANDSCAPES IN LITERATURE, by Richard M. Berrong. 2013. (No. 301). *978-1-4696-1365-9.*

MAPPING THE LANDSCAPE, REMAPPING THE TEXT: SPANISH POETRY FROM ANTONIO MACHADO'S *CAMPOS DE CASTILLA* TO THE FIRST AVANT-GARDE (1909-1925), by Renée M. Silverman. 2013. (No. 302). *978-1-4696-1522-6.*

GENDERED GEOGRAPHIES IN PUERTO RICAN CULTURE. SPACES, SEXUALITIES, SOLIDARITIES, by Radost Rangelova. 2015. (No. 303). *978-1-4696-2616-1.*

---


Send orders to:    University of North Carolina Press
P.O. Box 2288
Chapel Hill, NC 27515-2288
U.S.A.
www.uncpress.unc.edu
FAX: 919 966-3829